Fires of Gold

ATELIER: ETHNOGRAPHIC INQUIRY
IN THE TWENTY-FIRST CENTURY
Kevin Lewis O'Neill, Series Editor

Fires of Gold

Law, Spirit, and Sacrificial Labor in Ghana

————

Lauren Coyle Rosen

UNIVERSITY OF CALIFORNIA PRESS

University of California Press
Oakland, California

© 2020 by Lauren Coyle Rosen

Library of Congress Cataloging-in-Publication Data

Names: Coyle Rosen, Lauren, author.
Title: Fires of gold : law, spirit, and sacrificial labor in Ghana / Lauren
    Coyle Rosen.
Other titles: Atelier (Oakland, Calif.) ; 4.
Description: Oakland, California : University of California Press, [2020] |
    Series: Atelier: ethnographic inquiry in the twenty-first century ; 4 |
    Includes bibliographical references and index.
Identifiers: LCCN 2019044982 (print) | LCCN 2019044983 (ebook) |
    ISBN 9780520343320 (cloth) | ISBN 9780520343337 (paperback) |
    ISBN 9780520974739 (ebook)
Subjects: LCSH: Gold mines and mining—Political aspects—Ghana. |
    Gold mines and mining—Ghana—Religious aspects. | Ethnology—
    Ghana—Religious aspects.
Classification: LCC HD9536.G52 C69 2020 (print) | LCC HD9536.G52 (ebook) |
    DDC 338.2/74109667—dc23
LC record available at https://lccn.loc.gov/2019044982
LC ebook record available at https://lccn.loc.gov/2019044983

Manufactured in the United States of America

28   27   26   25   24   23   22   21   20
10   9   8   7   6   5   4   3   2   1

For Jeffrey Rosen, for the vast truth, grace, and light, emanated at all times

CONTENTS

MAPS

In the firmament lies a place
Where each fallow falls to fortune
In the heart of blazing furnace
All aflame with sinews of tune

So soft and pacifying as rain
On panes of every window
Between worlds that confer again
Blows of the plaintive bellow.

Terror of the unvarnished light
Cut to the quick in the All
Hovering above all tarry and smite
Bricks so laid, as they fall.

Golden masonry in skies
So resplendent with abundance
Escaping all that bespies
Sun's whirl in her secret dance.

—LAUREN COYLE ROSEN

Introduction

At the end of March 2013, bands of enraged miners stormed the streets of Obuasi, a legendary gold-mining town in the Ashanti Region of southern Ghana. As they fired guns into the air, passersby dove for cover, shopkeepers closed their doors, and residents fled the town. State military personnel met the miners in the street, exchanged gunshots, and arrested several of the protestors. In retaliation, the miners smashed and shattered two cars of the local mine management. They also threatened to kidnap the children of mine officials who attended the mine's primary school, forcing the school to close for days.[1]

This particular clash was only one instance in ongoing heated conflicts, merely a fragment within a history of violent confrontations between artisanal miners and the state military, which intermittently reinforces the mine's policing of its property. These small-scale miners are locally called *galamseys*.[2] They operate, often illegally, in the shallow streams and in the depths of the mud within the 100-square-mile concession of transnational mining giant AngloGold Ashanti (AGA), which runs an underground mine in Obuasi, operational since 1897.[3] Obuasi, effectively a company town, holds the third-most-plentiful gold mine in Africa, after two voluminous deposits that lie near Johannesburg, South Africa.[4] The galamseys, who are mostly Ghanaian, mine for gold at the margins of the formal mining operation, using traditional tools and methods, with pick axes, panning techniques, and little machinery. They claim ancestral and national rights to the gold, and they harbor great fury over an extremely profitable corporate mining industry that they feel only further impoverishes, displaces, and disinherits them.

In this clash, the military arrived at the behest of the mine and executed a flashout, a form of policing intended to cleanse the mine's property of the galamseys. Military personnel traveled to Obuasi, popularly called Ghana's Golden City, from the nearby city of Kumasi, capital of the Ashanti Region, to sweep the principal sites of the galamsey operators. They arrested some and destroyed their equipment. The military personnel also used bulldozers to seal some of their underground pits with soil and rock—chillingly, trapping twenty-seven galamseys underground. They were buried alive—"in the belly of the earth," as people said—for two days, before national security forces rescued them. Soldiers pulled their enervated bodies, still alive, to the surface. Locals and media reports also voiced worry that some remained trapped underground, where presumably they perished.[5]

Yet the matter in dispute is not merely about earthly things—soil, mud, gold, and bodies. It is also thoroughly suffused with matters metaphysical and spiritual. Off the official news records, in private conversations, many in town described the forced burials as a kind of improper sacrifice, offered principally to certain spirits in exchange for facilitating or hastening the production or the appearance of gold. Other acts of violence were often interpreted in similar fashion.

In local systems of ritual reckoning, various spirits preside over the gold or otherwise interact with it. Many ethnic groups in southern Ghana, including the Asante, fall within the canopy ethnic group of the Akan and speak various mutually intelligible dialects of Twi.[6] In Akan and other cosmologies that prevail in this ethno-cosmopolitan, spiritually plural mining town, gold carries an energetic frequency that resonates with some spirits, some deities, and with the omniscient creator deity. This predominant belief in the spiritual nature of gold is also true for those from groups originally from the northern regions of Ghana, as many miners are, as well as for those who primarily identify as Christian (common in southern Ghana) or Muslim (common in northern Ghana). In the Akan system of belief and nomenclature, this divine creator is called Nyame (also Onyame), the ultimate generator of all that is, seen and unseen or only partially seen. Nyame is all-knowing, all-seeing, and benevolent. In gendered and more anthropomorphic form, Nyame is conceived as male and as lord of the sky. In this rendering, his consort is Asaase Yaa, the supreme Earth goddess, who also intimately resonates with gold.[7] However, neither is thought to produce gold or to provide access to it for worshippers in response to rituals considered improper or illicit. The supreme deities may provide wealth, usually by working through the intercessory deities, in exchange for unselfish and religiously proper offerings or prayers. Rather, it is lower forms of spirits that may respond with gold to unethical rituals performed by those seeking wealth. Any such gains tend to dissipate in short order, however, as they are derived through injustice and falsehood; that is, the rituals that generate such fruits are not aligned with the highest orders of what is just, pure, and true.

In Akan and other local belief systems, as in many other places throughout time and across cultures, gold is a physical representation of conscious spirit. As such, the metal occupies a material space of high forms of divine consciousness. Spiritual adepts often interpret appearances of gold, in essence, as tangible referents for variations of transcendental fire or light, spirit or soul, which ordinarily remain shrouded in everyday life. Gold's allure commands mysterious and magnetic power for polities, for religious communities, for systems of cultural valuation, and for moral economies—that is, economies based on a sense of rightness or fairness, rather than exclusively on market principles.[8] As some *abosom* (Akan deities, who have emanated as discrete beings out of the creator; sing., *obosom*) explained through some of their Obuasi-area *akomfo* (Akan priests and priestesses; sing., *okomfo*) during my ethnographic research, gold has an energetic frequency of a very pure spiritual constitution, yet it carries no consciousness of its own. Rather, it acts as a substance of empowerment, protection, prestige, value, and amplification of multidirectional connection—like a telephone, or a microphone—between humans and some beings in the spiritual realm.[9]

More broadly, gold is matter of prime importance to this society, lying at the crossroads between the economic and the metaphysical, the mundane and the transcendent. Spirits govern the gold, and, in many ways, the spirits are sovereign. All legal and political forms, all cultures of labor, operate in dynamic tension—and, at times, co-creation—with the numinous and the transcendental realms. Here, gold's sacred dimensions as spirit and body (matter) also bespeak its mystical integrative alchemical capacity to make the spirit a body and the body a spirit, a transmutation that at once marks and collapses the domains of signifier and signified, concept and referent, in fine dialectical fashion.

Fires of Gold lifts the veils of the key social dramas at play and explores the deeper cultural reckonings of violence, labor, spirits, and the rebirth of sovereign power in the gold fields of Ghana. The ethnographic stories stand as prisms for an extended meditation on the powers of gold in these cultural spaces—in the enigmatic shadows of mining conflicts, in the corridors of soul-craft, in the anchoring of law, in the torrents of economic struggle, and in the fashioning of novel politics. The book explores contemporary violence and uncovers the often hidden effects of the mining industry, which is widely lauded, internationally, as an economic success in one of Africa's most celebrated democracies. However, within Ghana, mining is regarded as the poisoned chalice of the contemporary economy—at once the most lucrative sector and the most socially disruptive.

A few central inquiries animate the endeavor: What are the critical legal and political paradoxes, new cultures of labor, and powerful forms of spiritual vitalities that often lie concealed in the shadows of the mining industry? How do these oft-obscured phenomena unsettle and complicate Ghana's wide reputation as a rule-of-law success story for Africa? More broadly, what do these social worlds reveal about theories concerning transformations in forms of power, spirit, and sovereignty in Africa and beyond? At a fundamental level, what are the embodied ethnographic implications for the classical philosophical triad of the city, the soul, and the sacred?

Here, I use *city* in the figurative sense of the public, or the polity, the political sphere—not in the sense of urbanized worlds specifically. The classical philosophical triad is found, among many other places, in ancient philosophy. It has been conceived to demarcate various domains of power, transcendence, politics, selfhood, values, community, and being-in-the-world. The foundational political and ethical questions of how people define and reconcile their struggles over these realms have beset cultures and societies throughout history. My invocation of the triad in this case is to show, ethnographically, how these mining struggles manifest and evince newfound forms of politics, ethics, and authority with respect to the demarcation and reconciliation of these often conflicting domains of the classical triad.[10]

At its most basic, *Fires of Gold* advances two central arguments. First, significant forces and sources of power that lie outside of the formal legal systems have arisen to police, adjudicate, and otherwise govern this theater of struggles. The centrality of these forms, which often are more vital than official bodies of government, reveals a reconstitution of sovereign power. The principal informal authorities at stake in this story include the mining company; the galamsey miners' association; civil society advocacy networks for those adversely affected by mining; and various African, Islamic, and Christian religious figures. I argue that these figures are shadow sovereigns—that is, sovereign-like authorities that function alongside formally instituted legal and political systems.

The abundance and significance of these shadow forms in the nation's sovereign constellation undercut the popular claim that contemporary Ghana is a secular rule-of-law exemplar. It is not that the state's legal regimes are absent or nonfunctional in these spaces, as one might infer. Rather, legal orders surround and, at times, give rise and shape to these shadow sovereigns, which sometimes undermine enshrined legal rights and institutions.[11] Yet these novel forces also can function as a supplement that *enhances* the strength of formal legal regimes and statecraft. Further, shadow sovereign realms increasingly serve as innovative domains of political resistance, spiritual empowerment, and economic livelihood. As such, they furnish new modes for the effective reclamation of imperiled entitlements, such as rights to property, labor, security, and even life itself.

Second, the book argues that the spiritual powers at play are much more significant than one might think at first glance, in that they anchor the powers of shadow sovereigns and of others—and fuel contests and collaborations among those in the gold fields. Vital spiritual forces thoroughly permeate the ranks of shadow sovereigns as well as the broader dynamics among miners, politicians, activists, lawyers, and many others. In a profound sense, spiritual powers suffuse all forms of authority in this theater, whether those forms are enshrined in law or otherwise. Spirits also perpetually threaten to unseat or obscure power and legitimacy. Prominent ritual authorities and their spiritual connections furnish crucial symbolic power for those navigating, among many other things, the novel cultures of casual labor among the galamseys, who often enjoy much de facto collectivized power vis-à-vis the corporate mine. This artisanal mining force starkly contrasts with conventional portrayals of hopelessly diffuse, precarious labor power in deindustrialized or under-industrialized settings around the world. The spiritual realms, often in surprising ways, help to account for this collective power. More generally, spiritual fields serve as critical nexuses for labor politics and for refashioning sovereignty. They help to link forms of economic value and ethical values to deep-seated cultural systems of referential truth and justice. These linkages, in turn, help to create—or co-constitute—the ostensibly secular transformations in law and statecraft, in sovereign power, and in political economy.[12]

In order to establish these two central arguments, the book explores the many dimensions of mining conflicts in Ghana, including the complex spiritual contests and ritual relations that animate them, the clash of property regimes involved in them, the ways in which they often elude the formal court systems, and the shadow sovereigns that figure prominently in these struggles. Recently, Obuasi has been the site of bitter controversies surrounding drastic labor retrenchments, destructive surface-mining practices, violence against the galamseys, and a more general sentiment that the mining company, AGA, is not reciprocating, not enhancing life in the town or the nation.[13] It is currently the site of Ghana's most acute mining conflicts, following the dispossession and destruction of many indigenous farmlands and streams, the declining political and spiritual legitimacy of traditional rulers, the forcing of much mine labor into temporary status (casualization), soaring youth unemployment, and the rise of an increasingly organized and militarized shadow labor force of galamseys. Increasingly, foreigners, especially from southern China, are operating with or alongside the Ghanaian galamseys.[14] Artisanal miners are one key symbol of the new face of global extractive labor. Kindred forms of informal, small-scale mining currently account for an estimated one-third of Ghana's gold production, as well as an estimated 80 percent of the world's gold output.[15] Ghana now ranks as the second-largest gold producer in Africa, and as the tenth-largest in the world. The Obuasi mine has been a key generator of the gold that confers this stature upon the country.

Amid much devastation, one central form of sustenance for people is spiritual life, which is deeply imbricated with the spiritual relations to gold, the economic mainstay of the town. Members of all faith traditions in town relate to the spiritual nature of gold, each in their own religious vernaculars and through their own respective protocols. Each tradition holds significant sway over the mining communities, and an understanding of the spirits behind the gold prevails throughout each of them—but through different codes and symbolic valences.

In this realm, we witness shades of the spiritual economies among mine laborers, natural resources, and lands found in many classic anthropological works, not least among them Michael Taussig's and June Nash's famous works on Bolivian tin miners.[16] Spirits and other numinous dimensions also inhabit much of the more recent anthropological work on mining, which offers a true wellspring of deeply creative, significant studies.[17]

While it might be tempting to view the spiritual matters in this book as sites of subjugation and resistance within local cosmologies and moral economies, this is not simply about miners using mystical powers against oppressive mine lords or against a monolithic, antagonistic state. All parties at play, including corporate mine officials and state authorities, draw upon transcendent sources of empowerment, with varying degrees of temporal duration, economic success, and moral consequence. Here, the spiritual powers that relate to the sacred nature of gold also reflect and intensify more general dreams and nightmares for those in town, concerning labor politics and conflicts over sovereign wealth. Both state and traditional authorities are supposed to hold their respective resources "in trust" for their subjects, governing them to collective benefit.[18] However, these authorities often violate this trust, by many local lights. Spiritual undertones and repercussions abound. What is more, those within the various groups in this study—the mining company, the state, the miners, the union, the activists, the lawyers, the politicians, the religious authorities—utilize the spiritual powers both in contest and in concert. At times, they use the powers to foster solidarity or to underwrite a cooperative endeavor; at other times, they use the powers to compete as individuals or as subgroups within larger collectives or social bodies. The spiritual forces here are multifaceted and multidimensional. Sources of spiritual power stand behind and, variously, stabilize or disrupt forms of rule, whether those forms are shadow sovereigns or officially—that is, legally—constituted.

Notably, this spectrum of visibility applies to the formal legal regimes themselves —not only to spirits or to shadow sovereigns. Legal orders shape the contours of mining contests and of life, even in apparent legal vacuums, in zones where legal signals seem to fade. The mining violence and the shadow forces might *seem* merely to defy a properly functioning legal order. However, the background rules of the legal and economic systems at play actually give rise to—and even perversely incentivize—the forces and violence, the interplays of subjection, displacement, and dispossession. Shadow sovereigns are given life in relation to law. Further, they function in relation to law at all times, even when they are flouting or circumnavigating legal orders, and even in spaces where law appears, to the untrained eye, to be absent. In many ways, the mining violence evinces not a legal system broken down but rather a heavily liberalized legal system that is working all too well.

In the gold fields, power is anchored in forms that are both earthly and transcendental, visible and invisible—or alternately flashing and fading from view, like reflections in water, figures in flames, or silhouettes in a half-lit room. Cultural beliefs and social practices that many are wont to disregard as outmoded—or, at least, as ancillary dimensions of so-called universal political, economic, and legal means—are, in fact, critical sites of labor, subjectivity, and social revitalization. Here, informal mining groups, spiritual jurisdictions and topographies, and other key cultural forms abound in the shadows of the formal legal and political systems. They wield tremendous power and legitimacy that received modernist wisdom would deny them. These forces operate in unobvious and vital ways, generating new forms of value and values that are irretrievably enmeshed in—and yet irreducible to—the cultural repertoires at play.

These shadow authorities operate, ambivalently, as forces of beneficence and terror—at once governmental and exceptional, earthly and otherworldly—and exercise sovereign-like rule over territories and populations. The legal system itself is founded on parallel jurisdictions, on the dual existence of a colonially constructed customary law and a liberal state legal regime. The struggles and collaborations among these shadow authorities are fashioning the economic, cultural, and social lives of the Ghanaians who inhabit their worlds. This is especially so for those who sense that their lands, labor, and sources of livelihood have been sacrificed to a mine and to a state—to conceptions of sovereign wealth—that do not offer them viable sources for future life. Multivalent sacrificial logics fuel reckonings of destruction, deprivation, and dispossession. Further, these logics crucially empower the bold spirit of those who seek to labor for land and gold—themselves imbued with spirits and, at times, governed by them—and to claim forms of entitlement that state and traditional rulers often no longer secure for them.[19]

Here, we witness a boldly charted pursuit of justice on the part of the displaced, the dispossessed, the retrenched, and the superfluous miners, in order to address the perilous labor of their existence. Theirs is a slow insurgency, conducted in a theater of shadows, at once in the goldfields, at the ruler's palace, in the realm of the transcendental, and in the interstices of the sovereign polity by means of simulations of laws—or of laws repurposed and redrawn. This reveals the complex ways in which dispossessed or imperiled persons and casual laborers—outside of formally recognized political structures and often outside of formal employment—are organizing themselves into new structures of potent political action. They are doing so in deep relation to various domains of the spiritual realm that exercise jurisdiction over these territories, substances, persons, and relations. Understanding these dynamics and cultural formations is important for apprehending the workings of contemporary global extractive regimes. And it is essential for making sense of the worlds being partially remade by capitalism and the distinctive forms of law, politics, and sovereign power in the twenty-first century. The figures of this text craft a new cultural politics of labor and of law at the heart of a growing African economy, one that, on pain of their flesh and blood and spirit, levels a forceful claim on the future.

THE GOLDEN CITY, IMPERIAL ECHOES,
AND THE PUBLIC EYE

Obuasi is a town of many faces and symbolic ambivalences. The town is coursing with gold, christened with dust, and fraught with social unrest. The Obuasi mine was pivotal to the economy and the sacred power of the storied Asante Empire in the eighteenth and nineteenth centuries. Later, the mine was central to British incursions and, ultimately, to colonial overrule.[20] Obuasi sits about forty miles southwest of Kumasi, the capital of the Ashanti Region and the site of Manhyia Palace, the ritual and political apex of the Asante Kingdom. Since the onset of industrial mining in 1897, Obuasi effectively has been a company town—run first by Ashanti Goldfields Corporation (AGC), and then by the corporate successor, transnational mining giant AngloGold Ashanti (AGA), which took over in 2004. The Obuasi mine has served as a pillar of the country's neoliberal economy, heavily contributing to Ghana's leading status as a gold producer for Africa and the world.

Although precise census data are elusive, the most recent governmental statistics state that there are around one hundred seventy-five thousand people who live in the Obuasi municipality. The town of Obuasi lies wholly within the concession of AGA, by which the national government confers exclusive rights, recently renewed in a ninety-nine-year lease, to harvest gold within its territory. The makeup of the town is truly ethno-cosmopolitan, as well as religiously and spiritually plural. Obuasi rests in the Ashanti Region, in the sub-region of Adansi.[21]

Over the course of its centuries-long life with an operative mine, the town has drawn laborers from all over the country. This especially has been so during this past century, with the town's operation of an industrial mine. Over its lifespan, mine owners or managers have drawn laborers from elsewhere—particularly from the Northern Region of Ghana, sometimes by force. The Asante Empire's slave-acquisition campaigns and also the British colonial-era practices of forced labor coercion echoed the notorious "South African model" for creating mine laborers through capture and servitude.[22]

In the struggles for independence from Britain, nationalist control of natural resources—principally gold—was a key mobilizing factor and political platform. In the midst of these many complex and devoted statist protectionist efforts, in which newly independent leaders from the first president, Kwame Nkrumah, through long-running head of state, Jerry Rawlings, strove to protect Ghana's gold and other resources from the depredations of neocolonial markets (often populated and dominated by white financial interests), Ghana found itself in the throes of crushing sovereign debt and the aftershocks of a global recession. Consequently, in 1986, Ghana became the first site of structural adjustment reforms in Africa, inaugurating the neoliberal era on the continent. In exchange for favorable debt refinancing, the World Bank and the International Monetary Fund (IMF) negotiated dramatic

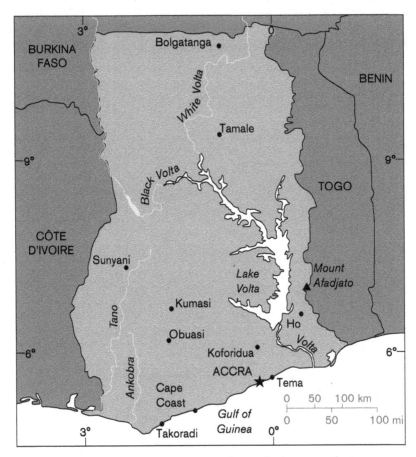

MAP 1. Ghana, showing Obuasi, near Kumasi, along with other principal cities. Source: "Ghana," From *The CIA Factbook*, 2012. U.S. Department of State website. https://www.state.gov/p/af/ci/gh/ (accessed April 18, 2019).

liberalization and denationalization of Ghana's key economic sectors. The gold-mining industry was the first target of denationalization and deindustrialization.[23] The multilateral lending bodies also commanded a gradual move toward a constitutional democracy, a greater level of privatized governmental and economic functions, and the enshrining of putatively impartial rule-of-law mechanisms. All of this, of course, entailed a move away from more state-centered paradigms of government and economy.

A crucial component of the birth of neoliberalism in Ghana was the legalization of surface mining, which has caused untold environmental destruction, human displacement, and social turmoil in Obuasi and elsewhere throughout

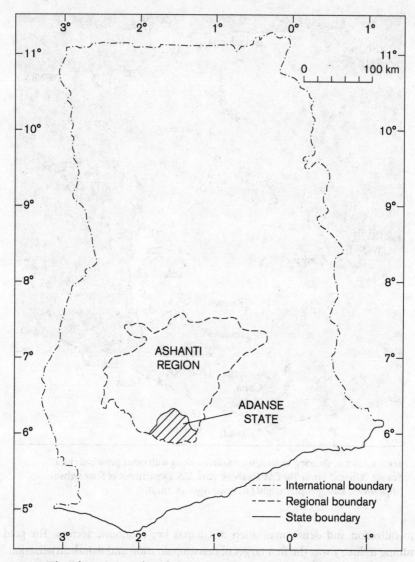

MAP 2. The Adanse State in the Ashanti Region of Ghana. Source: Emmanuel Ababio Ofosu-Mensah, "Traditional Gold Mining in Adanse," *Nordic Journal of African Studies* 19, no. 2 (2010): 127.

Ghana. Obuasi hosted the onset of this open-pit blasting in the nation. Since the 1990s, AGC (later AGA) has inflamed local populations with its turn to this highly lucrative yet deeply destructive form of mining in the town and its environs. The method has wrought tremendous violence upon local lands, spirits, environments, labor, and lives. Further exacerbating the situation, the shift to surface mining

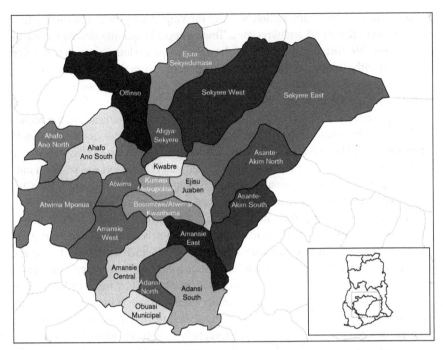

MAP 3. The districts of the Ashanti Region, showing Obuasi Municipal District, within which Obuasi sits as the capital, in the southern part of the region. Source: "Obuasi Municipal District," Wikipedia: https://en.wikipedia.org/wiki/Obuasi_Municipal_District (accessed April 18, 2019).

has obviated much underground labor, entailing significant casualization and retrenchment of AGA's workforce alongside further evisceration of an already rather weak and skeletal Ghana Mineworkers Union (GMU). Many among the galamsey ranks in Obuasi tell me that they have master's degrees in mining-related subjects, such as electrical or mechanical engineering, but now find themselves without work. Many of those rendered jobless or landless—or beset by precarious casual labor contracts with AGA—have drifted into the burgeoning galamsey ranks and, increasingly, have turned to striving for security through accessing the powers of the spiritual realm. They seem to be magnetized by the straightforward attraction of a viable living almost as much as by the lure of the quick riches such work may produce—efficacious labor pragmatics and auspicious spiritual conditions permitting.

Following the flashout in 2013, Ghana's military assembled, for the first time, a permanent base in Obuasi, and began conducting continual surveillance to ensure that the galamseys did not reappear to resume their work. In the ordinary course of events, galamseys always have returned to reassemble their informal sites of production, even in the immediate wake of the violent suppression of their activities, whatever the blood and wreckage. Townspeople frequently describe them as an irrepressible force, with stunning devotion to precarious labor that is often interlaced with ritual pacts and spiritual allegiances. Given the soaring unemployment rate, galamsey mining provides a reprieve, however temporary, from the despair of acute deprivation.

The secretary of the galamseys' unofficial governance organization, the Small-Scale Miners Association (SSMA), reported that their leaders were caught completely unawares. He said that National Security personnel *had* given the SSMA prior notice of the sweep, but security personnel had claimed that the mission was to "flash out" the foreigners who were increasingly involved in these activities, especially the Chinese miners, and that Ghanaians engaged in galamsey would not be disturbed.

The ensuing violent protest may appear, at first glance, to have been merely a spontaneous revolt of social bandits, or a popular uprising—what the local press variously cast as an "armed galamsey insurrection," in which they were "taking the law into their own hands,"[24] and as a "state of anarchy," with galamseys "on a rampage."[25] In fact, this spectacular violence was borne of much more ordered, protracted conflict grounded in long-running contests over gold and concerning, specifically, a significant breach in the terms of an informal social contract that the local leadership of the galamseys had forcefully negotiated with the mine. This bears witness to a complicated network of vying sovereign authorities, each seeking spiritual and practical powers to variously organize, undergird, or upend forms of labor politics and moral economies of mining. The galamseys are a chief shadow sovereign force in this social drama, and their laboring powers, spirits, and significations run through the core of this ethnography. Wealthier galamseys have tended to assume the stature of economic mainstays in communities with compromised chiefs and other imperiled customary authorities. In these, they have come to function as de facto customary authorities, sovereigns in their own rights, moonlighting in the vacant or otherwise compromised offices.

This contract, whose breach occasioned the violence, is grounded in a shadow regime of informal property rights, coded as the "Gentlemen's Agreement." In 2009, four years prior to this particular flash out, the galamsey leadership, now assembled as the SSMA, received informal permission from AGA to operate on certain parts of its concession—especially in its abandoned pits and waste dumps. In exchange, the galamsey leadership promised to ensure that its estimated thirty thousand members in Obuasi—a figure that towered over AGA's more modest figure of about three thousand mine employees at the time—would not continue to invade AGA's underground mines.[26] Before this agreement, the galamseys frequently had wielded collective coercive might, attacking AGA security personnel and mine laborers, killing some and driving others mad through spiritual and physical assaults. They also had destroyed mine equipment, setting it ablaze or

smashing it to rubble. In contrast to much that is written in contemporary literature regarding the nearly absent collectivized power of casual labor, all of this
aggressive action had significant cumulative effects akin to traditional unionized
labor strikes: the galamseys, very fundamentally, had disrupted industrial production and had threatened future investment in the mine.

Despite the Gentleman's Agreement between the galamseys and the mine officials (and some local politicians, chiefs, state police, and private security forces),
violence continues to erupt. The flashout in 2013 crystallizes a host of dynamics
that power the pulse of this book. The clash involving the military, the mine, and
the galamseys exemplifies much broader cultural histories of destruction, dispossession, casualization, spiritual contests, heavy-handed policing, and informal
labor collectivization.

Significantly, these patterns of violence in Obuasi contributed to the January
2011 conferral to AGA of the ignominious "Public Eye Award."[27] The Berne Declara-
tion and Greenpeace annually organize the Public Eye Awards ceremony in Davos,
Switzerland, as a "critical counterpoint to the World Economic Forum."[28] In bestow-
ing this award, global civil society groups crowned AGA the "most socially and
environmentally irresponsible company in the world" for the year 2010. In particular, the award recognized the contested histories of AGA's Obuasi operations. AGA
personnel found the timing particularly ill-starred, as the company had won out
over fellow nominee British Petroleum (BP) in the same year as BP's notorious oil
spill in the Gulf of Mexico, already a clear source of global outrage.

An advocacy organization, Wacam—whose name roughly approximates "you
have disturbed me" in Twi—had spearheaded the advocacy campaign that culminated in the conferral of this award. Wacam is a prominent mining nongovern-
mental organization (NGO) in Ghana—one that generally has styled itself as more
grassroots than most other mining NGOs in the nation. In contrast to many other
prominent NGOs, which often originated in Accra and are based there, Wacam
emerged in mining towns and has carried out most of its activities with leaders
and members drawn from mining-affected communities.[29] As this movement
gained momentum and assumed an active role in the local and national media, the
NGO, though small, was able to secure a strong budget for expansion from transnational donors. After Wacam started up in the other main mining town of Ghana,
Tarkwa (in the Western Region), it expanded to Obuasi. The Wacam officials first
touched base with local advocates in the form of radio station hosts—featured on
recently liberalized radio airwaves, a press freshly freed from governmental and
mining-company control. Wacam also approached local district assembly representatives—that is, local-level state government officials—from communities
acutely affected by surface mining and home to many galamsey operators. It was
through these initial contacts that the Wacam presence in Obuasi eventually
gained momentum in the late 1990s and early 2000s, at which point the Obuasi

organizers—locals themselves—began to hold radio shows to awaken local populations to various wrongs committed by the mine as well as to inform people of relevant constitutional and statutory rights that people scarcely knew they held as citizens. The activists also traveled to affected communities and began to help to organize the galamsey forces into forms of leadership to dialogue with personnel from the mining company.

Wacam's securing of the Public Eye Award for AGA was a landmark victory in the history of the organization. This event had ramifications for the Obuasi mine and for the company's informal rule and relations with various groups in town. It empowered activists and other community members, and it shifted the local balances of power between the mine and the galamseys toward a further emboldening of the artisanal forces. The conferral of the award delivered a hefty blow to AGA's recently lauded global human rights efforts and "corporate social responsibility" endeavors.[30]

The organizers of the Public Eye Awards express their aim as to incite public ire and to create a cascade of reputational consequences. These consequences may include the prompting of socially responsible divestment or other forms of what has come to be known as shareholder activism. These, of course, increasingly operate in tandem with locally driven efforts of NGOs or grassroots social movements. After the award, AGA faced significant threats of divestment from the parent company.

In nominating AGA for this ignoble award, Wacam drew upon vociferous community mobilization, environmental studies, and various advocacy campaigns from over a decade of organizing in Obuasi and other mining towns across Ghana.[31] Although Wacam is a resolutely grassroots advocacy organization, the bulk of its funding—and some of the discursive frameworks for its mining campaigns—come from the large transnational donors Ibis and Oxfam-America.

Wacam, in fact, was how I came to know Obuasi, and a few of its local leaders helped me to call it a home during my fieldwork. I carried out this fieldwork in Obuasi in the summers of 2010 and 2011, and then over the course of the calendar year of 2012, so I was there soon before and soon after AGA received the Public Eye Award. While I have kept in touch with key interlocutors over the course of the years since 2012, I returned to Ghana for follow-up field research in the summer of 2018, while finishing this book.

When living in Obuasi for this research, I stayed in the extended family home of one of the journalists and principal activists in town who was then the main local organizer of Wacam. In this book, I call him Kofi. (All names in this book have been changed, unless expressly noted otherwise, in an effort to preserve anonymity.) Kofi is a brilliant and determined writer, advocate, and scholar. He grew up in Obuasi. In many ways, this book unfolded by virtue of the proverbial door of access that he originally opened for me. For a time, Kofi even lived in the house where I stayed, the house being owned by one of his sisters, Sylvia, on his maternal side; Sylvia is the biological daughter of Kofi's mother's sister, Ann, who also lived in the house. Kofi is Nzema by ethnicity, which is part of the larger Akan group, all matrilineal.

Kofi and other local activists provided my entry points to the subjects about whom I write in this book. Over the course of my time, I developed many friendships and working relationships with a broad range of people in Obuasi—politicians, chiefs and queen mothers, galamseys, pastors, Akan priestesses and priests (*akomfo*), AGA personnel, and many others throughout the town.

I initially entered the town to go deeper into the cultural, spiritual, and social dynamics that propelled many of Wacam's campaigns revolving around the mine's alleged human rights abuses and histories of displacements and environmental destruction. I had first learned about the issues that were besetting mining communities in Ghana in 2007, while I was a law student, working on a summer fellowship in Accra before I started my doctoral program in anthropology. It was my first time in Ghana, and I was immersed in legal research for the Ghanaian chapter of an international environmental justice organization. Among other things, I delved into the mining dramas. Their complexities and mysteries magnetized me—so much so that I returned to focus on the cultures of mining struggles when I returned to Ghana a few years later to begin my long-running ethnographic research.

As this book attests, the study rapidly grew into much more than a focus on law, displacement, environmental justice, and human rights. My ethnographic research extended well beyond those initial confines, which were almost preformulated in my mind by the activist discourses. Throughout, I was aided by the great generosity and auspicious unfolding of many patterns of informal contacts; one conversation or friendship led to another, as the broader picture slowly emerged, took shape, and entered my fields of vision. Whole networks of social dynamics, relations, and phenomena that were at first invisible to me gradually came into view, at times thrown into high relief.

SOVEREIGN SHADOWS AND SPECTRAL LABOR POLITICS

The forms of shadow rule, casual labor politics, and spiritual forces and jurisdictions that I trace in *Fires of Gold* advance versions of law, economy, and sovereign power that run counter to much conventional wisdom about the contemporary world. They reveal deep and reciprocally constitutive interrelations with novel cultures of moral economy, of vital soul-craft, and of political life. This multivalent manifestation of sovereign power, I submit, is neither formal—a privileged, ideal-typical feature of the nation-state, what Max Weber called a "monopoly of the legitimate use of violence within a given territory" within an ever more disenchanted or secular polity—nor is it absolute or indivisible, as in classical political theory.[32] Though always provisional and in a state of becoming, forms of sovereign power are ever present and critical in policing, provisioning, and adjudicating—in both earthly and spiritual dimensions. They also are central to deploying decisional violence with varying shades of legitimacy.

Despite the now prevalent accounts of the "denationalization" and the "deterritorialization" of sovereignty, I argue that forms of national and territorial rule merely have shifted.[33] They have been recalibrated to contemporary circumstances. As Donald Moore insightfully observed, "In Africa as elsewhere, sovereignties have been reterritorialized rather than deterritorialized."[34] I take this into the spiritual realm, demonstrating how numinous jurisdictions and decisional prerogatives also have been redrawn and reterritorialized, in ways at once enigmatic and exacting. It is now more imperative than ever fully to comprehend the ways in which spiritual and cultural forms of sovereignty are severable from formal state rule—and yet continue to exist in dynamic tension and interrelationship with it. Despite Michel Foucault's early declarations about the need to "cut off the king's head" in political theory—that is, to stop focusing on formal sovereign governments as the key source and locus of power in contemporary times and, instead, to study the percolating and capillary networks of power exercised through disciplinary knowledges and performative techniques of society and of selves—his work also had the effect of unlocking new conceptual potential for sovereignty, untethering it from the sole possession of formal state rule.[35]

In my approaches to sovereignty and power in this book, I centrally draw upon suggestions that Hansen and Stepputat have issued for a reorientation of anthropologies of sovereignty.[36] These reconceptualizations allow us to more meaningfully grasp the manifold dimensions of authority, power, moral economy, and rule in the shadow balances of labor, territories, spirits, subjects, and politics in Obuasi. Hansen and Stepputat urge a move away from emphases on those sovereign forms inscribed in or derived from formal legal codes and systems. Instead, they argue for a more capacious approach to sovereignty, as a "tentative and always emergent form of authority, grounded in violence that is performed and designed to generate loyalty, fear, and legitimacy from the neighborhood to the summit of the state."[37] They note that Giorgio Agamben's revisitation of Foucault's biopolitics—via Carl Schmitt's theory of the sovereign as he who decides the "state of exception," allocating life and death along lines drawn with reference to the foundational political distinction of friend or enemy[38]—has revived interest in the body as a privileged site of sovereignty, while revealing that it is not just the divine king or queen who has two bodies, but that modern citizens and subjects do as well.[39] One body is inscribed and managed as "qualified life" within the biopolitical order, and the other is stripped to "bare life" and rendered expendable (though not sacrificial) when the sovereign relegates it to a state of exception—with the modern (labor, death, detention) camp as the paradigmatic example.[40]

In the case of Obuasi—and for Ghana, more broadly—we witness the disaggregation and lateralization of a previously more unified sovereign power, to be sure, in line with much recent research.[41] This process has generated a widespread parceling of sovereignty that has rendered contemporary nation-states a "patchwork of sovereignties."[42] This has begotten new, large zones of social life that are not directly governed, or that do not appear to be governed, but in fact are molded and sustained by background legal regimes that help to fashion patterns of violence even as their presence fades from view. This is to say, even zones of exception, as well as areas appearing to be abandoned or disregarded by the state, have legal underpinnings; it is only that such legal regimes are invisible to the casual observer.[43]

Neoliberal constrictions, or reductions, of legislative, executive, and administrative state oversight (more vertical forms of governing) are deeply entwined with these broader processes of lateralization—that is, making state functions more horizontal and disaggregated (greater parceling out of public into private and semi-public institutions), and less vertical and integrated (diminished public, top-down consolidation in governmental institutions). The rule-of-law development programs that have accelerated this move toward greater privatization of governmental functions and of key industries such as mining, in turn, have led to an overemphasis by governments and multilateral lending organizations—principally, the World Bank and the IMF—on the formal mechanisms of contracts, constitutions, and courts. These programs are grounded in the assumed sanctity and efficiency of private contracts, the integrity of adjudication, and the importance of having the highest sovereign principles enunciated in constitutions, whose enshrined rights are invoked (if not universally realized) with fundamentalist fervor.[44]

Broadly speaking, Ghana's sovereign transformations over the past three decades have echoed those throughout much of the Global South. Its national political economic prerogatives have been rewritten by structural adjustment reforms that have entailed the privatization of, among other things, the mining industry, which previously was heavily nationalized. As is true throughout much of the world, the national government holds all mineral rights in trust for the citizens of the nation. The state then grants concessions, through leases, of the most plentiful ore deposits to transnational mining corporations who employ financial mechanisms that result in the bulk of the profits' leaving the country, escaping state revenue and, consequently, possible benefit to the country.

This relatively recent disaggregation of the mine and the state, especially as it has unfolded in an old mining town such as Obuasi, has rendered the mine the object of popular regard as a shadow sovereign for labor politics, spiritual governance, and much else—or, as many in town say, "a law unto itself." For almost a century, leading up to the neoliberal reforms in 1986, the mining company *was* the most visible, palpable, addressable manifestation of the state government for the local population. In fact, it arguably wielded much more social provisioning and policing power, much more coercive might, and much more sway over adjudicatory bodies and proceedings than any other state organ or functioning parastatal body in town.

Contemporary Obuasi resonates with a wider pattern across Africa and the world. Mining often operates through privileged enclave economies, subject largely to the private sovereign apparatuses of mining companies or warlords who control lands and populations in mineral-rich locales, often through various forms of overt coercion—or, at least, through heavily asymmetrical bargaining agreements under "corporate social responsibility" rubrics.[45] As James Ferguson recently has argued, neoliberal states and their corporate shadow forms do not conform neatly to the expanding optic of increasingly standardized, homogenized, grid-based territorialization.[46] The uneven, spotty infrastructural investment and the internally integrated enclave shadow structure is, arguably, seen more starkly in the extractive sectors than elsewhere in neoliberal Africa and across the Global South.[47]

In Ghana, we witness something other than, simply, a desiccated central state form that has all but vanished, and something other than a widespread renunciation of traditional authority and spiritual power among disaffected younger generations. We see, instead, both the partial unseating and the selective reinscription of "traditional," transcendent forms of sacred authority, as the leaders of these internally hierarchical shadow sovereign forces draw upon spiritual sources—as well as forms of ancestral and political entitlement—to anchor and undeaden forms of authority, power, and legitimacy to which they lay claim.

In part, intensely local processes produce this shift. Yet these emergent social forms and sovereign formations also clearly partake of transformations wrought within the broader dynamics of contemporary capitalism, including the selective retreat of the state and the denationalization of industry; the casualization of labor forces and soaring unemployment; heavy executive policing in the names of the sanctity of rule-of-law, of property concessions, and of corporate purview cast as national interest; and the resurgence of prominent forms of private indirect government, particularly in extractive realms—a phenomenon that courses with the added material weight and affective charge of pronounced colonial echoes.[48]

While the transformations in this book bear witness to the widespread disaggregation of sovereign power into comparatively dispersed social constellations, they also evince a resurgence of vertical authority *within* the arrangements of these shadow sovereigns, which are hierarchical and stratified, and within the moral economies that animate them. Further, potent forms of spiritual power support—and, at times, eviscerate—these cultural forms. Here, rather than a chaotic, spontaneous irruption of an undifferentiated multitude, we see the unfolding and consolidation of hierarchical, vertical forms of shadow rule that, in fact, mimic the scaffolding of the modernist state in many uncanny ways.[49] Likewise, these new constellations do not jettison but rather *draw upon* traditional forms of sociality and claims to spiritual sanction and symbolic power. That is, they breathe novel synthesized forms of life into late liberal meta-narratives of sacrifice and redemption, of present suffering, bleeding, and death that somehow will be redeemed in the future.[50] They aspire to rework the terms of access to the myriad universalisms promised by modernity, promissory notes that merely continue to paper over what Rosalind Morris poignantly calls the "constantly weeping lacerations" of unresolved difference and destruction, sullen figures that haunt the empty forms of what they should have been or become.[51] Moreover, these forces draw strength from fervent, unrelenting demands that are anchored in continuous, deep-seated senses of basic entitlements—to labor, to livelihood, to a viable future, to a just share in sovereign wealth.

It is well worth considering, in the case of Ghana and in a wider analysis, the demands made of and by law and sovereignty in the contemporary world—in particular, with respect to the ways in which arbitrary, impassioned, whimsical exactions of force under the sovereign's exceptional prowess—here, for example, through state military sweeps against Ghanaian galamseys to protect the purported national security interests of transnational corporate mining productivity—might *appear* to define sovereignty as its ultimate expression, but in fact might be found most potently in the shades of sovereign power's fading out. That is, when subtler, more far-reaching and effective modes of instrumentalizing social wealth and managing populations fail—both through biopolitical regimes and through more traditional forms of sovereign coercion—the exceptional aspects of sovereignty perhaps emerge as a figural, violent acting out. The head of a body politic trembling, with fury, at the sight of its own fragility.

Also at stake are the spectral dimensions of power, which echo throughout the pages of this book—though, here, with much greater emphases on the specific metaphysical domains of such power than are ordinarily engaged—in addition to the often discussed, fascinating phenomenon of staged political artifice or otherwise fantastical simulacra of power.[52] Spiritual presences, absences, and traces populate the stories throughout this text—not as mere ciphers, metaphors, or screens for something else, something simply mundane, but as active figures and participants in the earthly dramas at stake. Sovereign maneuvers require consumers and audiences, receptors of authoritative calls. These receivers, in fact, anchor, alter, and sometimes undo sovereign power, which is itself internally incoherent, fragmented, and dispersed—never the univocal, volitional sovereign will of Thomas Hobbes's *Leviathan*, as much powerful anthropological and social theoretical work has established through many other veins.[53] Here, the sovereign audiences *and* the voices of sovereign power are also spectral, in the most literal sense: they are the souls, the spirits, and the deities implicated in all of these struggles over lives, lands, labor, livelihoods—the *materia* of vitality itself.[54]

LINEAMENTS, FIGURES, FIRES

The book moves through the textures of the field, charting figures as though they are walking through fire—in spirit, in word, and in flesh. Chapter 1 opens with the mystery and controversy surrounding the murder of a young galamsey, shot dead in August 2011 by the head of a security company working for the mine. The chapter discusses the spiritual interplays and the shadow balances of power at issue behind the public portrayals in the theater of struggles to place blame and to offer an accounting. Indeed, the shooting may well have been a spiritual sacrifice. The chapter discusses the broader patterns of multivalent violence against galamseys that helped to fuel the vociferous advocacy campaigns against AGA. It also details the rise, structure, and moral economies of the shadow sovereign labor force, the Small-Scale Miners' Association, which claims to rule over all galamseys in Obuasi.

Chapter 2 turns to the forms of indigenous ritual practices and the broader symbolic power of which the galamseys' association and other miners partake. These shadow forces are heavily buttressed by empowerment and claims to rule that are anchored in economic and other administrative capacities, as well as in transcendental, divine realms. Again, sacrifice is a central force. Miners routinely draw upon the powers and forces of spiritual authorities to protect themselves during their labor; to pacify the local deities, ancestors, and other spirits; and, especially, to charm and to beckon the principal earth deity in the area, Bona, and the other spirits governing the gold so that it will appear for the taking.

Chapter 3 turns to recent controversies over the use of traditional rituals by AGA and by its underground miners, alongside the broader shadow sovereign roles played by the voluminous assortment of Christian churches in town, especially those of the predominant Pentecostal and charismatic denominations, which have increasingly taken aim at indigenous practices. One central contention concerns the proper modes and means of sacrifice—and blood sacrifice, in particular. The chapter foregrounds the ritual and political dramas surrounding AGA's own history of annual traditional blood sacrifices at its six principal mine shaft openings. Recently, AGA formally abandoned these annual traditional ceremonies—much to the ire and dismay of local traditional authorities and, according to them, the ancestors and deities. Instead, the mine turned to a Christianized, biannual "Pray for the Mine" ceremony, adding also, the following year, a cognate Islamic ceremony. This chapter also analyzes the more expansive spiritual controversies and ritual contests that have attended these shifts in the mine's transcendental grounding of its claims to wealth and forms of shadow rule in town.

Chapter 4 commences with the effective overthrow of a chief in a prominent village on the outskirts of Obuasi. Inflamed members of the community charged the chief with having sold the community to the mine for private gain—in effect, improperly sacrificing them—resulting in the demolition of homes and farmlands, the destruction of sacred streams, and widespread spiritual and social disruption. Here, powerful galamseys rule, in effect, where the chief no longer can. This is merely one instance of a broader phenomenon of political revolt and shadow rule: a number of chiefs around town have lost legitimacy. They are seen to have betrayed their sacred duties to hold the stool in trust for the ancestors and for subjects living, unborn, and yet to be reborn. This visits violence upon the collective social spirit, including the health and vitality of subjects, ancestors, local deities, and other beings.

Chapter 5 turns to labor agitation, major strikes, and the casualization of AGA's labor force—as well as the casual laborers' surprisingly successful legal challenge to the mine. The chapter also traverses the terrains of the mine's—and, at times, the state's—pragmatic and spiritual sacrifices of mine labor in order to enhance profitability. The casual laborers organized in an unregistered association and sued both AGC (AGA's predecessor) and the Ghana Mineworkers Union. In the suit against the mine, the casual laborers were successful up to the Court of Appeals, right before the Supreme Court of Ghana, at which point they settled with AGC—in an almost unheard-of victory for casual laborers who filed against a transnational mining giant.

The conclusion of the book turns to recent developments in the shadow balances of power, spiritual and earthly, in Obuasi and also at the national level. It explores Ghana's attempts to implement "upward adjustment" reforms, designed to gather enhanced state takings from its mining industry for the enrichment of the nation. Industry officials immediately opposed and thwarted the changes. AGA soon after, in fall 2014, announced plans to close the Obuasi mine for around two years, while it mechanizes underground operations. The mine operations remain suspended. Many have joined the ranks of the ever-burgeoning galamsey forces, which have taken over much of the concession. Many also have turned to even fuller devotion to spiritual authorities—whether Christian, Islamic, or traditional African. Rumors run rampant that mechanization will obviate most underground manual labor. The nightmare of a ghost town looms as a probable prospect for one of the world's leading repositories of gold. Thus, we witness the novel cultures of labor, law, sacrifice, and soul-craft that are forged in the fires of these extractive realms, alternately spirited and spiritless.

1

Artisanal Miners and Sacrificial Laws

In August 2011, private security personnel of AGA shot and killed a twenty-three-year-old man, Kwesi, alleged to have been trespassing on the mine's concession and stealing gold from it. By many accounts, the security guard delivered no less than sixteen shots into the body of the man, as he was fleeing from the drawn weapon. The assailant was the head of Ghanatta, one of the principal security companies that AGA employed at its Obuasi mine. The victim was out with a group of galamseys who regularly ventured onto parts of the concession. Kwesi, for his part, hailed from a nearby village whose lineages lay ancestral claim to the lands where he had been roaming in search of gold.

An enraged group of men, Kwesi's coworkers and family, immediately went in search of the Ghanatta security head, calling for his death. They stormed his office in town and encircled it, chanting war songs and demanding that he come forth. Failing to find him at the Ghanatta headquarters, they set ablaze the office building, burning it to the ground.

Meanwhile, AGA personnel had transported Kwesi to the Obuasi government hospital and then transferred him to a higher-level hospital in nearby Kumasi, where he died a few days later.

Immediately following the death of Kwesi in the Kumasi hospital, the director of Wacam issued a press release, widely circulated in the national media. The release decried the murder as merely the latest in a long legacy of the mine's violent treatment of galamseys, who often hail from areas in which the company had destroyed farmlands and vital streams with little or no compensation.

The Wacam statement denounced the extra-judicial killing and the mine's continued fostering of a "culture of lawlessness." The Wacam director, himself

Ghanaian, contrasted AGA's operations with Ghana's constitutional commitments to the rule of law. The difference was one of instant, unreflective justice versus cool, impartial deliberation. The director said such inflamed policing methods encouraged the same militant activity on behalf of dispossessed communities and the galamsey operators who often hail from them. He declared:

> Wacam is deeply saddened by the death of [Kwesi] at the prime age of 23 because he did not have the opportunity of being tried in a court of competent jurisdiction to be found guilty or set free through our judicial system. It is even more painful to recognise that he did not die a natural death but became the unfortunate victim of corporate lawlessness and irresponsibility. . . . Ghana is a democratic country which upholds the rule of law, and the presumption of innocence is a cardinal principle of our legal system. There are records to show that security agencies acting on behalf of mining companies in Ghana—especially Ashanti Goldfields Company and its successor AngloGold Ashanti—had shot galamsey suspects and sometimes used guard dogs on the suspects without recourse to the laws of Ghana. There had been situations where some suspects had died or become permanently incapacitated as a result of gunshots.

The release then lamented the reported fact that Kwesi had been shot in the back, an obvious indication that he was fleeing and posed no imminent threat to the Ghannatta head; thus, any claim to self-defense must fail.

The statement likened the shooting to an extrajudicial policing attack several years earlier, which already had garnered much national and international media attention. This was a case in which another alleged galamsey trespasser had been fleeing mine security and was shot from behind in such a way that his intestines burst forth. As he writhed on the ground, incapacitated, he alleged that the mine security personnel approached and said that they would only take him to the hospital if he would agree to their story that he was an armed robber and that they had apprehended him on the run. In public statements subsequently issued, the mine insisted that this man had not been shot. Rather, he had fallen on the spike of a fence while fleeing security personnel. Only later did they admit to the security violence and provided a reparative surgery.[1]

In the statement concerning Kwesi, the Wacam head excoriated the unconstitutional assumption of mine security's doling out the death penalty at whim, sidelining the rule of law. Armed with constitutional provisions, the NGO director lambasted the mine for its groundless claims to a sovereign-like purview, its ability to employ shoot-to-kill mechanisms in the name of protecting their concessionary property: "Article 13(1) of the 1992 constitution states that, 'No person shall be deprived of his life intentionally except in the exercise of the execution of a sentence of a court in respect of a criminal offence under the laws of Ghana of which he has been convicted.' Similarly, Article 15(2a) of the 1992 Constitution of Ghana states, 'No person shall, whether or not he is arrested, restricted or detained, be subjected to torture or other cruel, inhuman or degrading treatment or punishment.'"

The Wacam statement decried the inhuman behavior of the Ghannatta security head, who apparently had left Kwesi on the ground, writhing in a pool of blood, presumably to die, abandoned and alone. The statement detailed that "it took some community people who heard Kwesi's groans to rush him, first, to the Obuasi Government Hospital and then to Komfo Anokye Teaching Hospital in Kumasi where sadly, he died on Sunday [several days after the shooting]."

Interestingly, this was a different version of the events than that which I was to uncover through talking with those galamseys who were out working with Kwesi that day. When I first visited Kwesi's home village, Binsere, soon after his death, I had expected to have short, private conversations with his family, particularly with a couple of his aunts and uncles, and his wife, with whom he already had had two children. Instead, I found myself surrounded by around seventy people from the community: the local elders, district assemblyman, and chief's linguist instantly assembled a village meeting. The chief was conspicuously absent. Indeed, he no longer stays in the village, has fallen from legitimacy, and usually does not even return to preside over ritual events. He is viewed now, as the community members put it, "as having his soul with the mine," as with many similarly situated chiefs.

While the chief was absent, other customary authorities were present. Notably, the chief's *okyeame* (the chief's spokesperson and frequent ritual officiant) was allowed to speak very little. When the question of the chief's collusion with the mine arose, the crowd clamorously shamed him, imploring that he proffer—to them and to me—the information of the chief's collusion with the mine to which they assumed the okyeame was privy. None of this was forthcoming. Cowed yet firm, the okyeame—poignantly adorned in a bright orange AGA shirt, a gift from its local environmental director—insisted he knew nothing.

The wife of Kwesi was present yet mute. Shrouded in silence and a dusty, pale blue headscarf, she sat on a shaky bench in the inner circle of the village meeting. Even when Kwesi's name was spoken, she remained like stone, transfixed on something beyond the group, despondent and silent. She appeared markedly absent. And the village authorities did not turn to her at any part of the discussion. It was unclear whether she simply could not be engaged—too bereft, too devastated to speak of anything, not least her traumatic loss—or whether the male community authorities were bent, instead, on staging a different conversation for the meeting, one that they would lead and dominate.

This was a community matter, the district assemblyman said, and it had to do with the community's loss of farmland and streams to the mine in the early 1990s, with the onset of surface mining. This was not merely about Kwesi's death: this was about unfulfilled promises that the mine had made, in the wake of the destruction. "We were to get electricity, boreholes for drinking water, a school. And you know what we want above all of this?" he asked. "Jobs."

The moment he mentioned jobs, many of the surrounding male youth started to clamor, "Yes, jobs. We have nothing. They took our farms, and we have nothing. We do galamsey because we have no alternative."

Over and over, they repeated that their burning demand from the mine was jobs. What they wanted more than anything, even beyond fulfillment of these promised compensations, over a decade overdue, were jobs at the mine. They both detested the mine for their community's devastation and longed for employment there above all else.

Amid this clarity and resolve among the leaders, I quietly noted my position. I felt as though I were being addressed as a conveyor of information to the mining company. Perhaps I was, as a white American lawyer and anthropologist. This was my first time in this particular community.

"Galamsey mining is our only alternative," one young man thundered. "This is our only answer to ourselves, our futures, our families. And to the mine, what it has done to us. And they say we cannot be stopped. That is because we are driven to this. No matter how much we are beaten and killed, we will return. If they kill us, we are ready for that. Galamsey is all we have."

I was surprised that the discussion of Kwesi's death had been so submerged by the demands for jobs and farms. And yet I understood: all foreigners are treated as possible receptacles for delivery of messages to the mine. And this was their resounding message, above all else: they wanted to be formally employed at the mine. Additionally, I had entered this meeting with a prominent Wacam activist from town. It also may have been that they were hoping that some journalists who write statements for Wacam would voice their demands in the press.

I had apologized, embarrassed, that I had not had time to buy the customary drinks and some biscuits to present before I had arrived. In fact, I admitted, defensively, that I had not realized that the occasion would be a full community meeting.

The district assemblyman answered, without irony and through the thick of poignant silence from the group, "We were eating our biscuits before you came. We want jobs."

Upon notification of the shooting, the mine, for its part, actually had sent personnel rushing to Kwesi's body to help transport him to the hospital. AGA also immediately released a statement denouncing the act of the Ghanatta security guard, attempting to cleanse the company's image of it. The security personnel of AGA are not permitted, by company policy, even to carry firearms, the mine insisted. This whole matter arose from an unfortunate breach of company policy. This was a particularly important moment of public disavowal for AGA, as earlier that year, in January 2011, it had been crowned with the ignominious Public Eye Award.

Reports quickly abounded in the local press that the company's contract with Ghannatta was terminated. AGA promised to issue monthly reminders and demand compliance statements from its security contractors that no security personnel were to be armed. They also regularly would be briefed on AGA's allegiance to global human rights and security standards, as well as on the international soft law norms of corporate best practices.

Police swiftly apprehended the Ghanatta head. He was ultimately tried and convicted of murder. He was then imprisoned in a high-security facility in Kumasi, where he remains. This, of course, defies portrayals of the mine and its security forces as sole arbiters over life and death within its shadow sovereign purview. Yet, while this executor function has never been wholly unqualified in the case of the mine at Obuasi, the mine's purview in this respect decidedly had been diminished in the wake of AngloGold's merger with AGC in 2003 and, especially, following AGA's Public Eye Award.

People now say of the imprisoned Ghanatta man, "He is only a shadow of the man he once was." Formerly strong and heavy, he sits weakened, emaciated, almost vanishing to bone. And pale, looking almost bloodless. Lifeless, indeed. Many speculate that he ultimately will go mad, tormented by spirits wronged or merely possessed by the spiritual sovereigns he can no longer feed and pacify. The last I heard, this remains to be seen.

The galamseys of the village, for their part, declared the Ghannatta man dead on sight. Many said that, even if he were able to bribe the police and judges and be set free, he likely would never return to Obuasi. He was a marked man and would be killed by any of the galamseys at first spotting. And he knew it.

What had gotten into this man? What was he thinking? Had he already gone mad? Was he possessed by spirits he had been propitiating for undue profits?

Various explanations abounded. "He was in the military under Rawlings, and so he had that in him. The *juju* [a potent, often destructive, spiritual force], the killing capacity, the torment, everything," said one policeman, who knew him personally. Another former friend of his told me that the man was possessed by akpeteshie—a local gin, a possessive "spirit" in its own right. Very potent, cheap, addictive.[2] "He has always been drunk these days. He must have been drunk."

But there is the crucial element, one that illuminates much of the shadow regime in play at the instance of this murder. This facet also bespeaks a much more complex constellation than those found in the unequivocal shaming of the NGO packaging, on the one hand, and the mine's self-exculpatory narratives, on the other.

As I walked away from the village meeting in Binsere, toward the dusty, sun-soaked road and the waiting car, one of the village residents—also a galamsey—followed me. I was not fully understanding the situation, he said. He wanted to help me understand, to give me information; he asked for alms in exchange. He was part of the group that had been out the day that Kwesi was murdered. In fact, he was the one who ran back to find Kwesi bleeding on the ground. This was somewhat contrary to what the Wacam statement had claimed, that "it took local community people's hearing his groaning to get him help." This galamsey had triggered the rush to get Kwesi to the hospital.

This galamsey explained that the Ghannatta security head had been collecting regular rents from the galamseys working in his patrol zone. It was the same with the people from Binsere that the security contractor had hired on, on direction of AGA, to try to enlist local support in policing and informing. A former NGO activist himself had been selling the slots that the mine offered, through its security contractors, collecting rents in turn and inciting many local tensions. Local politicians also were involved in the selling of labor slots—the chief, again, being largely out of the picture, unable to rule in the community.

The Ghannatta head, the day before the murder, had been complaining that he was not collecting his regular rents from the galamseys, which he declared were due in order that he look the other way. The galamseys said they had not been winning gold to pay him. Not accepting this, the Ghannatta head had told an assemblage of galamseys, including the late Kwesi and also this galamsey who had rushed to his body, that he would take the life of one of them the next day, to collect his debt. The galamseys, undeterred, went anyway—said to be common form when they are determined to mine. To the Ghannatta head, this galamsey intimated, it was a form of sacrifice. A blood debt. Part of the idea being an offsetting of abstract monetary debt, yes. And also a penalty inflicted, to be sure. But, perhaps, also a sacrifice. This reading also could render more legible the excessive nature of the bullets—sixteen, in excess of an economical killing. The more blood spilt, the more some lower spirits might be charmed into hastening the manifestation of gold for quick riches.

Moreover, it became clear that this murder was actually lodged within the larger territorial shadow system of the Gentleman's Agreement. This concord had come into force in 2009 between the Central Committee of the galamseys and mine security personnel, if not other mining officials. This agreement established a shadow agreement over informal property rights—at least, effective use rights—and respective laboring jurisdictions between the galamseys and the mine within AGA's formal concession. In turn, the galamsey leadership promised to police its laborers—spatially, tactically, and spiritually—in order to control and diminish the various forms of violence that the galamseys had routinely leveled at mine personnel and production sites. Mine officials—in public, at least—vehemently deny the existence of such an agreement. They insist that they are only "dialoguing with the galamseys" to control the violence. Nevertheless, it is commonly accepted in town that this agreement exists. The site of the murder was shadow rule territory for the galamseys; the security personnel tacitly agree to allow them to mine, in exchange for payment.

What undergirds the tenacity and the fierce resolve of these galamseys, with their precarious terrains of labor? Often, galamseys invoke ancestral and customary rights to the land and the gold. They also lay claim to entitlement born of the sacrifices they have given—through the devastations of their communities, lands, and livelihoods—to make the AGA mine as profitable as it is today. They register these sacrifices as both natural and profoundly spiritual. Most significantly, everyone wants to ascend to the ancestral realm and, thus, enjoy the possibility of reincarnation. A person devoid of a livelihood is not seen as fully adult or even, in many ways, fully human. One cannot marry or have children, and hence cannot be properly mourned at a funeral ceremony. Without these things, one can never become an ancestor or reincarnate. Death becomes absolute. These deep-seated motives—revolving around cultures of death, temporality, and vitality—help to account for the bold spirit of many galamseys, who regularly stare down violence as well as an injury or fatality that may await them in the mines.

Even going underground into sinuous, shaky tunnels is terrifying. The constant threat of collapse and suffocation looms. What is more, the underground is an enigmatic and treacherous realm of the netherworld in Akan, wherein Nyame's aspect of death reigns supreme, symbolized as a scorpion[3]—though perhaps this aspect is more accurately personified by Asaase Yaa, despite this deity's ordinarily being heavily associated with the attribute of fertility. In the past, many Asante and other Akan would flatly refuse to enter the subterranean levels for this reason alone, the close spiritual association with death.

Since the 1990s, with the initial burgeoning of the galamsey shadow force, there have been many violent and arbitrary crackdowns, beatings, and even killings of these laborers. These have happened at the hands of AGA's security forces or of the state military, there to back the mine. In the course of what are called "operation flashouts," the army arrives at the worksites and villages of galamseys to intimidate and humiliate them, to loot their homes, and to disrupt their operations. There have been periodic reports of underground burials, during which police bulldozers have sealed mine openings with soil and rock while some galamseys remained trapped underground. This book's introduction relates one such harrowing episode.

In another chilling incident in 2006, state military personnel reportedly swept up several galamseys at their mines and then stripped them naked, bound their hands and feet, and drove them through their home villages. The military personnel displayed the galamseys on the backs of trucks and whipped them in front of their wives, children, other kin, and fellow villagers. A number of these galamseys subsequently reported that they became impotent for some time. Others were ashamed to face their families and to continue living in their villages. Yet others said that they felt broken, no longer fully human. Similar language is also used to describe the severely dispossessed and destitute—so downtrodden, that they no longer feel fully alive, without *sunsum* (or personal, conscious "spirit"), or with diminished *kra* ("fire," light of the soul, life force). These flash outs, it seems, are intended to serve as a deterrent by way of nightmarish spectacle. But they bespeak a much deeper rage, as well as a sense of both corporate and national insecurity. They literally embody a desire for the emasculation and enervation of the whole galamsey enterprise. They inscribe, in bloody script, the naked force and raw power that drive the policing of these labor phantasms. This force, that power, is carved into the flesh and souls of the abject laborers, rendered superfluous by the formal industrial landscape.

In yet another dramatic example, in the fall of 2009, there was an explosive clash between company private security personnel and galamseys operating on one of AGA's abandoned sites. Allegedly, security personnel nearly buried alive forty artisanal miners, having closed a tunnel passage with a galamsey group underground. Disturbingly, though not uncommonly, the bulldozing burial is reported to have been deliberate, an informal policing punishment for trespass and theft. According to most accounts of community members and local advocacy organizations, frantic community members succeeded in persuading the AGA personnel to reopen the tunnel, but the haunting event rattled through Ghanaian civil society groups and media outlets as only the latest eruption of tensions, a particularly grotesque episode in an extensive legacy of violent conflicts over land and gold in town.[4]

As one prominent mining activist and Obuasi native told me:

With these flash-out techniques, I can remember hearing [a mine official] come on air, to Shaft FM [a local radio station], and announce that the mine was going to "smoke the galamseys out like rats." They would burn tires at the openings of the galamseys' tunnels, and then they would be waiting at the surface opening with cutlasses [*nnade*], as though they were literally smoking rats out of holes. And I would object, sometimes on air, "These are human beings! They are not rats!" And [this particular mine manager] would reply, "These boys are thieves, coming to steal from us. What do you expect?"

In response to many such reports and rumors, the UNDP funded, in 2007, an independent governmental inquiry into the allegations of human rights abuses in mining communities in Ghana. This study was conducted by Ghana's Commission on Human Rights and Administrative Justice (CHRAJ). Among the most disconcerting confirmations of CHRAJ's final report were such repeated instances of brutality against the populous galamseys in Obuasi. One highly publicized piece of the report was confirmation that the mine previously ran private detention facilities (also functioning as makeshift prisons, by popular allegation) within mining company compounds, where mine security personnel deployed various forms of holding, handcuffing, interrogating, torturing, and disciplining of galamsey suspects.[5] This element of heavy-handed territorial securitization practices, confirmed in the CHRAJ report, was especially highlighted in Wacam's nomination of AGA for the Public Eye Award and in its related press coverage—and, perhaps, even led, in the end, to AGA's receipt of the award over other noteworthy contenders, including BP. The policing brutality against galamseys is one element of corporate history that AGA has sought to disavow in its recent image-cleansing campaigns.

AGA officials, while generally acknowledging past occurrences of brutality against the galamseys, tend to argue that they have been exaggerated or misrepresented in civil society and journalistic reports. For example, AGA officials responded to the CHRAJ report findings on private prisons, and to my later inquiries, with an explanation that the detention rooms were merely places inside the mining compound where mine security officials would hold the apprehended galamsey suspects—in handcuffs, at times—until the local police arrived to take them to the police station and, then, to the local jail or court. AGA also has officially acknowledged a previous company history of releasing attack guard dogs on galamsey suspects who had been discovered on AGA's concession. By some allegations, the guard dogs even killed some of the galamseys during their attacks and, often, would deliver serious injuries. However, this is a practice that AGA claims was only conducted under previous corporate ownership—and only in the early 1990s.

Despite the denials, my field research with current and former galamseys, as well as with others from their families and communities, corroborated many of the allegations of previous brutal flash outs, beatings, torture, guard dog attacks, and other highhanded modes of policing and extrajudicial punishment or killing.

STRUCTURAL VALENCES OF THE SHADOW FORCE

In 2009, after fifteen or so years of such violent conflict with the mine, the galamseys mobilized to establish their organization, the Small-Scale Miners Association (SSMA) and to negotiate the Gentleman's Agreement with AGA personnel. The Association now functions as a key shadow sovereign in Obuasi, a counterpoint to AGA's role as shadow sovereign. Both are involved in sovereign-like rule over territories and subjects, in the shadows of the legal regime of the state. Both the mine and the galamseys manage their subject populations through enforcing coercive shadow property regimes and through administering biopolitical projects aimed at fostering life. Their leaders also exercise exceptional decisional force in domains of death or abandonment, deploying violence, at times, with impunity—or, at least, with some degree of legitimacy—within their respective realms of rule.

The galamsey Association boasts a Central Committee with a hybrid institutional form, at once drawing upon the models of corporate governance, of state district authorities, and of traditional political offices. The Committee has a president or chairman, a vice president, a treasurer, a secretary, and an assembly of board members whose practical protocols resemble those of elders' councils. The Association also has a tax-collection arm, internal adjudicatory bodies, and a police force. When its internal mechanisms fail, the Committee can enlist the aid of state police and even the state courts and prisons. The Committee members, although presiding over territories and populations of an illegal realm, take great care to maintain cordial relations with formal legal and political authorities. As the gold price soared following the global financial crisis of 2008, with the gold price's peaking around 2012, galamsey activities became much more lucrative. Accordingly, the Association's leaders have succeeded in gaining significant capital from private investors, domestic and foreign, which has further enhanced their power.

The Association also has various internal task forces, for which they at times receive funds or technical assistance from local NGOs. They have an occupational safety task force, a medical task force, an environmental task force, an educational task force, and a task force to ensure that children do not labor. Many measures aim to reduce and to regulate the levels of vulnerability and exposure to bodily assaults from toxic substances—including mercury and cyanide—and to other unsafe mining conditions, such as deep underground tunnels that lack adequate infrastructural safeguards. The Association also sometimes will provide housing, clothes, and food for newcomers to Obuasi who labor within their ranks. Should an injured or infirmed galamsey need to go to one of the local hospitals, the Associaton may cover the bill. It also will make public donations and gifts, covered in the town's media—of, say, computers to local schools, or food and books to a local orphanage.

The Association's leaders are all male, although an estimated 40 percent of the laboring force is female. Women of all ages are involved, especially as carriers of gold or as cooks and washers at overnight campsites. Those few women who do participate in the digging tend to be masculinized, addressed as though they were brothers or sons of those leading the excavation. During work, gender relations tend to be actively desexualized and routinized, almost mechanized. In accordance with embodied cultural codes that govern symbolic pollution and spatial segregation, menstruating women are forbidden from entering the mining sites. The transgressive presence of menstrual blood near the sacred gold could invite injury, death, or other calamity. Likewise, laborers are prohibited from entering worksites if they recently have had sexual intercourse without proper subsequent bathing and ritual purification.

The Association, now in full force, has a robust system of surveillance and readily receives news of any notable gold find within their informal territorial realm. Many involved in the galamsey operations explained to me that the Central Committee of the Association learns, usually within no more than a day or two, of a gold find, and that they send their security forces—very strong and heavily armed—to the site of operations. The security forces then announce that they have effective rule over all galamsey operations in and around Obuasi and that they, acting on behalf of the Committee, have arrived to take over. The Committee usually demands no less than one-third of the gold product—actual rock, as opposed to the final proceeds that are calculated after processing and sale to a distributor. The distributor is either the single official governmental Precious Minerals Marketing Company (PMMC), or other unlicensed independent buyers. After this cut is taken, the general distribution of proceeds within galamsey operations is such that one-third of what remains goes to the sponsor or financier of the so-called "ghetto" (the local term for the galamsey pit operation, used in English and in Twi), another third goes to the manager of the pit, and the rest is used for the cost of production and the payment of the galamsey laborers.

I first met the leaders at the site of their very modest office in Tutuka, a neighborhood of Obuasi in which many galamseys reside. As is common in the area, we arrived impromptu and unannounced. A friend, Thomas, a local politician, had brought me to the place, so that he could introduce me to the Committee members present.

Thomas was rather trepidatious, as he hailed from a rival political party. His party, the New Patriotic Party (NPP)—the party that tends to be more accommodating to foreign capital interests—had been in power since 2009. The previous NPP municipal chief executive (MCE), akin to a mayor in the United States, was quite brutal and antagonistic toward the galamseys. At the time of my research, the in-office MCE was affiliated with the National Democratic Congress (NDC), the other dominant political party social democratic in orientation. The national NDC candidate had become president, and then he appointed the NDC candidate who had lost the Member of Parliament (MP) race in Obuasi (traditionally, an NPP stronghold MP seat) to the position of MCE for the town. This NDC MCE, himself formerly of AGA mine management, is the one who helped the galamseys to negotiate the shadow agreement with the mine.

As we entered the Central Committee headquarters, Thomas trembled with nerves, cautious in every step. He later explained that he basically "was on enemy territory." He ended up leaving midway through the conversation, as soon as I asked about the political power shift and the origins of the Gentlemen's Agreement. He suddenly stood and invoked a vague, urgent matter at the office that had just arisen. At first irritated that he had left me alone, stranded without even the driver waiting outside, I soon became at ease. It was clear that the leaders were much more open to speaking to me in his absence. The stultified and tense mood immediately lifted, and we carried our conversations more informally.

Many members of the Committee were present, and they sat in a semi-circle in chairs along the perimeter of a spartan room. There was one desk in the corner, with only a couple of lone papers. There was not even a clock hanging on the wall or a computer on the desk. This was the whole of their official headquarters, this one room, wedged between other small shops on a narrow, congested side street in Tutuka. When I asked about the taxes they level on their subject populations, they immediately cited the need to pay rent for the office, to settle the electricity bill—a small ceiling fan rattled above us—and to take care of other sundry operational costs. In a shade of irony, Thomas had pointed out the brand new model of a very expensive luxury vehicle sitting out back, a car that everyone in town knew belonged to the chairman. "That's his. They recently hit a big rock in one of the ghettos, and there you have it. See how much they are eating?"

Throughout my initial conversation with the Committee heads, they kept emphasizing what small business they do, how they only use small pick axes, and are desperately in need of access to more capital investment. They asked me if I had capital, if I were interested in investing in the galamseys. I replied that I was only a student and had no money for investing. I was only there for research, I explained.

One of the key spokesmen at first kept reiterating, "We don't have a problem with AGA," especially after I asked about the history of violent clashes. "We don't have a problem with them," he insisted. "In fact, we are working on their waste dumps."

When I asked about the Gentlemen's Agreement with AGA personnel, another leader present finally admitted, "It's true. It's not legal, formal. Legally, AGA can't even give us the land if they wanted to. It would have to go through the Minerals Commission. But we [the Central Committee] are working with [AGA] to try to control the violence. This was part of the agreement."

I asked about a rumor I recently had heard, about AGA's bringing in independent contractors from South Africa to mine the waste dumps. The waste dumps and abandoned pits were supposed to be clearly demarcated as zones that fell within the Association's shadow jurisdiction. A more strident member of the Committee immediately demanded to know who had told me that, asking aggressively whether I had heard that from AGA. I said no; I had only heard that from friends in town.

He then continued, partly disingenuously. "Listen, we are supposed to have the waste dumps. That is really all we have. With these new South African companies there, we are praying, *praying*, they do not take these from us. Because then we will have nothing."

He then proceeded to utter many of the refrains the leaders kept issuing to me, assuming, I think, that I would report to the mine or local government officials. "We don't use child labor. We ensure that the children who come to try to work are sent to school." "We don't go underground in AGA's mines." "We don't allow our guys to operate unsafely. We train them. We have a Safety Task Force." "We don't go on other people's farmlands, and we don't destroy their waters. We are environmentally conscious."

Of course, all of these were preemptive responses to the heavy accusations leveled against them by unsympathetic media reports and townspeople. As one of my friends noted on the ride away—the most belligerent leader had followed me to the car, to inspect who awaited me in it—"These guys have been very marginalized, demonized, for a long time. They're going to be guarded."

THE RISE OF COLLECTIVIZED CASUALS

This first encounter with the leadership did not yield much by way of backstory. I was later to gain a much clearer view of the Association's rise and its internal governance, along with the contested architecture of their shadow economy. A longtime prominent mining activist in town and a local assemblyman, Peter, gave great insight. Peter was the assemblyman for Sansu, a community that lost all farmland to AGA's surface mining and is now mostly ruled by galamseys. He resolutely denied that it was primarily the savvy efforts of the current MCE that gave birth to the galamseys' current organizational structure and the striking of the Gentleman's Agreement with the mine. When I asked about the role of the MCE, Peter (admittedly, of the rival political party) insisted, "*We* initiated it. I did, with Kofi [another prominent activist], and these small boys. It has *no* political background. It has *nothing* to do with political interventions. I initiated it. Later, we also had to consult so many people. That's when Wacam, TWN [Third World Network-Africa, another key national NGO], and some other organizations came in. But we started it. Not anybody else."

Peter explained that the galamseys really began to organize and informally enter discussions with mine personnel in 2002, when Wacam and other NGO advocacy was really picking up, and the activists had gained much access to local and national media outlets. At this time, the mine officials also said that they were eager to stop the violence, which had been escalating, particularly with increasingly violent galamsey invasions of the mine's underground shafts. Peter explained:

> Yes, I first organized their meeting in 2002. Then, there were around 3,000–4,000 galamseys around Obuasi. Now, of course, there are many more. . . . The galamseys were scared. Some of them even ran off. We met in Tutuka. There's a school there, where we had it. And I asked them to select some people, a delegation, for them to meet. They selected sixty people. Well-built, macho people. And I asked them to meet me at AGA, opposite the security reception. I went there, instead of sixty, there were about twenty. And I said, "Where are the rest?" And they said, "Oh, AGA, they just want to place marks on us. They just want to identify us." . . . So the first meeting day, there were five. I psyched them, I assured them, that nothing would happen to them. We met, and then after the deliberation, AGA said, "Oh, then we can meet again next week." So, the next week, there were about 100 of them. That's where they were able to put their grievances on the table. And one of them was, if you could

allocate some of your abandoned pit, we will also stop going underground. Because the galamseys, they were going underground. Fighting the workers underground. Some of them did not survive. . . . Some would go mad!

I replied that I had heard that some miners and mine security personnel would cooperate with the galamseys, and others would not. Peter retorted:

Ah! If you think you are not going to cooperate, they will force you to cooperate. And during the start of the negotiation, with the underground, I would say, the galamseys took over. So, the mine called the executives of the galamseys, and said, "Look, your people have taken over the underground. What do you do?" Then, this is what you do; you go down there and make sure. . . . What they used to do is go down there, underground, and bring them out. But the soldiers were afraid. They couldn't do it. . . . So, the galamseys said, "Look, if you give us this, we will do that for you." So, they took a portion of land [from AGA], and [mine officials] told [the galamseys], "If you are able to bring them out, then we will also work. . . . We will get someplace where, [out] from underground, [the galamseys] will go to work, without disturbing the people."

Then, according to the assemblyman, the Gentleman's Agreement was finally reached, in 2008–2009, releasing some AGA territory, informally, to the galamsey operations, under the shadow rule purview of the Small Scale Miners Association. Peter insisted that the current MCE never could have done anything with respect to helping to devise the Agreement if it were not for "my guys' invading the underground."

Further researches into the origins of the Association revealed partial truths on either side of the explanations. The MCE was instrumental, but things were long underway prior to his even taking office in 2009.

The Association heads during my fieldwork in 2012 were not without their internal detractors. They had to fend off not infrequent attempts for coups, out those who were informing to the mine, or discipline those who were otherwise undermining from within.

I had a long conversation with the head of one such rival faction, Samuel, one day in Sansu, when he had been passing by Peter's house in an effort to get the assemblyman's permission to break off from the Association and to start a separate organization, which they would call the Obuasi Miners Union. A Wale elder from the North of Ghana, Samuel claimed to have been the first to organize the galamseys to work on the open surfaces in the early 1990s. Many of the local unemployed youth then had been resorting to stealing, and they had been angrily cutting the company's cables and things of this sort. He at first had high hopes for the leadership of the new Association, but those were quickly dashed by the realities of rule. According to him: "[The current chairman] doesn't listen to anyone during meetings and doesn't take advice. He will just decide. . . . And the Association is not doing enough for Obuasi. Obuasi deserves better. We are paying all of these dues. We don't see anything. Maybe even for one month, we can come together as an Association and donate to the local orphanage. Then, people can look and see that the galamseys have done something to give back. We have even gotten to the point, I think, where we should have a hospital in town built by the galamseys."

Samuel also told of how the current members of the Central Committee were growing very concerned on received information that they may break away. Some of them, including the chairman, had taken to traveling everywhere surrounded by bodyguards.

These nascent plans for the breakaway union were short-lived. The proposed Obuasi Miners Union heads delivered a formal letter to the Obuasi divisional police commander announcing that they had formed an organization and would be present in town. The commander, I was told, replied that the Obuasi police would not be able to recognize the union as a local labor organization, as they would be illegal; this, of course, aside from the fact that the Small-Scale Miners Assocoation works hand-in-hand with the local police, with the Central Committee even calling in local police forces when in-house adjudication and policing mechanisms fail.

One galamsey boss, Raphael, elaborated on the operational changes among the galamseys since the onset of the Association, which included, among other things, attempts to control the violence and also the frequent injuries and fatalities in galamsey operations:

Formerly, it was something, they were in a rush, those days. They were dying. Because, as they were working, they would be afraid of the soldiers and the police bumping on them [during the flash outs and more routine arrests], so they do the things in the rush, because the men are coming, and then before you realize, boom, they are dead. They have been trapped. At times, twelve guys, maybe six guys, because they were not following the safety rules. But this MCE, he came, and he pleaded with the AGA, and the land has been demarcated for them to mine. And then, they asked them ... to have the task force to move from site to site, to make sure the right thing is done. So, if they should come over here and the safety is not being practiced, they will tell you, "My friend, stop. Do this, before you will be allowed to work." The place that has been apportioned to them, they call it, "ghetto-ghetto-ghetto-ghetto-ghetto." So maybe this man will be having his ghetto here, you will be here, I will be here. But we will be chasing the same rock, the rock is lying down. It travels far away. So, if you get the chance of blasting, you are okay. . . . Then maybe, this is the belief, take this to be the land, and then the rock will be some meters underground. So, we have to dig all these things, a hole, and then get into the rock, and then have the expert to come and dig around the rock and then position the piers so that it doesn't fall on you, after the blasting.

Prospecting knowledge, spiritual and practical, is sold for a percentage of the proceeds of the mining, often about one-third. Many of those formerly employed at the mine have knowledge of plentiful, unplumbed reserves. If the possessor of the knowledge also holds crucial skills to harvest the gold—especially blasting, which is very dangerous and potentially fatal to the unskilled—then the negotiated cut of the proceeds can be even higher.

Raphael, who was formerly an AGA security man who was retrenched during the days of casualization, recalled the previous violence and the galamseys' forceful takeovers of the formal AGA laboring sites:

> Others, too, they were going to the site to steal. Some of them will be young, and they will go to the AGA concession. As I was saying, this guy would sneak, and also go there and work with them. They go there, and they threaten them, and they are armed. AGA workers aren't armed. They go there and say, "Massa, we know you are working. Where you're working, it doesn't belong to me, but get off." At times, they're talking in a way, just to convince you. But if you don't agree, then they'll have to apply the force.

I mentioned that I heard that the intruding galamseys would often offer percentages to laborers and security personnel, before taking over. Raphael replied:

> That is it. And if you don't take care, you will be caught by AGA. You are fired, and then you have to lose everything. . . . Normally, you have to take into consideration, your family. . . . You need not to be taken for granted by the galamseys, because if they should be arrested, and they are sent to the court, the next day, you will see them. They have the money to go and pay the judges and all that. As a worker, you have to consider the consequences. Why not do your work, and forget about those galamseys, because they are doing their own thing? . . . At times, they will put some galamseys in jail, just to serve as a deterrent to others. At times, too, the [law enforcement officials] are given some funds. At times, the galamseys are asked to sign a bond that they will not go there again. But Ghanaians are human beings . . . because that has been their source of income for the day. If you don't go there, you are not going far. You are going no place. So, if you should go there, at least, at the end of the day, you get something for the family. So, if you jail [a galamsey], and if you tell him not to go there, the next day, he will be the first person that you'll meet.

Raphael also explained how the galamsey forces often absorb local laborers, who otherwise would be living in destitution:

> When many of [AGA's laborers] have been sent home, then life becomes very unbearable for them. Some of the galamseys now, as we were saying, have even been given the mandate to go and mine [under the terms of the Gentlemen's Agreement]. These people who had worked at the mine, they know all these places, so they lead them to where there is the booty, or the gold concentrate. Others, they will contact the Association. They will say, "Hey, I know a place, we were doing the surface mining, there was a big rock over there, there was gold. Due to the insufficient safety aspect, we were asked not to blast. But the rock is there. I can just lead you there, to the place,

because the rock is there." Maybe he will be an excavator, using a bulldozer, or maybe even one of the drivers. For others, he was one of the blast men. Of these blast men, in particular, most of them have been sacked. Most of them are in the house. They are not doing any work. So, if they should come and do this, go and tell them, "There is a big rock over there, there's a place over here, let me sit down with you, I am ready to go and show you." And it becomes something like a contract. So, then, after giving him what he demands, he has to go there and show him where the rock is located. They go there, and they also mine. They have their own means of mining.

Raphael echoed many others in lamenting that this lucrative activity was not regulated or systematically taxed by state authorities, so that benefits were not won for the more general population in that way. However, he was quick to note various community philanthropy efforts in which the Central Committee recently had engaged, in contrast to many who complain that they merely eat most of the money for themselves and do not contribute to the larger community. Raphael noted that the leaders had pledged that 1 percent of their earnings would be spent on contributions to the development of the town: "I just heard from the news the other day that [the galamsey leaders] had presented some computers to some schools. And they told them that they are ready to put up something like a school hall, an orphanage, and all that. . . . Last time, they went to the orphanage. The other time, they sent computers to other schools. They just want to develop the area, as they are working over here, because that would also serve as a good moral."

Raphael also spoke of the customary rights and informal social contracts drawn with the chiefs and elders of the lands on which they operate. Asking permission is not only a matter of gaining the chief's consent, and of performing the necessary rituals—with libation (*ohwie*), sacrifice (*aforebo*), and prayer (*asore*) to supplicate the principal earth deity (*obosom*), Bona, the ancestors, and other gods and spirits in the area. The consultation of traditional authorities also often involves negotiations concerning ways in which the galamseys' proceeds will contribute informally to the material and social life of the town. As Raphael details it:

Normally, when we get the land, we sit down with [the chief and elders]. . . . There is something called fast-tracked thinking. . . . "If things go on smoothly, maybe our structures are dilapidated," and they ask, "Would you please also help with cement to put up the building? We don't have any place for our priest over here, if things should go smoothly, would you please help us to put a nice place for our priest over here?" . . . And if things go well, we make sure that we do it. Sometimes, I will just call my guys, and say that the community is doing something—say on Tuesdays, we don't work on those days, why not go, join hands with them, and work? . . . We the workers mingle with them, and they will see.

Some of the galamseys' work is conducted in the gaping holes in the earth left by AGA's surface mining. Other galamsey production is based on underground blasting, for which galamsey forces often enlist the prospecting and technical extractive expertise of the large labor force of blast men in town who have lost their jobs at AGA. Others dig deep underground tunnels, which are winding shafts (*amena peaa nkron*) that typically go to the end of the gold veins or until they hit the water table. Some pan in shallow streams or dig on shallow gold-bearing lands (*mmoaboa*).

Many of the galamseys work in alluvial mining—that is, mining stream beds for minerals—which involves several steps. As Raphael explained to me:

> Let's talk in terms of alluvial mining. . . . We have to go there [to the land], and the excavator has to go and take all the soil out of the land. You go down there till you meet some gravel. You have to take the samples. We have our own way of doing it. We have something like a pan to pan it and see the contents, and it works, and although it is not technological, we have our own means of getting it. This is the local means of getting it. So, if you do all these things, the excavator has to dig all the gravel and put it at a place, and we [place] all of our washing plants at a station, in a group of maybe ten, eight, or so. Every tank has one washing plant. So, what is there, we've got all the gravel over here, and we've got the washing plant over here. So, normally, we take something like the head pan, we fill it, we pour it in the washing plant. It will be a vibrator, and then the gold residue passes to one end, and there's something we call net, or a blanket. We put this thing on it, and then the residue, the bigger ones, will just go away. And the small, small particles will remain, and this is normally what catches the gold for us. And then you put the waste away, and the small concentrate will be there, and you will take this and put the mercury, and through, through, the gold will come.

Speaking of the difficulty of theft in such circumstances, he added: "It's something very complex, so you cannot just go to somebody's site, position the machines, go and take the head pans. But there are some areas where you have the nuggets, and in these areas, they can easily come and take the nuggets and put them in their mouth."

Raphael also celebrated the Committee's enhanced welfare provisioning mechanisms, particularly with regard to safety. Here, the Committee is resonating with AGA's own "zero injury" campaign, in which mine safety has become a paramount concern. He explained the development of the Committee's new "Safety Department" task force:

> In their own wisdom, they have formed a Safety Department. They are doing these things. Other things, they are doing these things for their family to be cared for— they [the Committee members] are driving the big cars, having the big mansions, in town! I'm telling you. . . . But before they allow people to work, they make sure that whatever they are doing conforms to the safety rules and regulations over there. If they go, and you are not doing the right thing, they will go and tell you, "My friend, stop. . . ." And if they go the next time, and they're doing the same thing, they'll make

sure that this place [the pit] will be covered, and it will not be given to you, because it has been apportioned to them in a way.

I replied that I had not realized that the safety regime had been so centralized. Raphael answered, "Yes! Because of this man, the MCE. He is doing a marvelous job for them."

INVASIVE FORCES AND ACCUSATIONS
OF PROPAGANDA

The broader public's concern about the safety of AGA's mining operations is also a matter of vociferous controversy that swirls around the galamseys. AGA alleges that the galamseys pose grave threats to the economic viability, longevity, and safety of its operations. The mine currently cites the illegal operations of small-scale miners as its highest—and its longest-standing—threat to mine operations, to mine security personnel, and, sometimes, even to mine laborers themselves. As indicated, galamseys sometimes arrive at the company's sites, including its underground mine chambers, heavily armed and announcing that they will take over by force, if necessary. Especially problematic, from mine officials' standpoints, is when galamseys invade underground operations, either digging tunnels that link to extant shafts or cavities (sometimes threatening the integrity of underground pillars and safeguards), or even dropping down elevator cables, deep into the earth (and, not infrequently, meeting an untimely death).

Mining officials tend to dismiss the galamseys' rationales for their operations (loss of farmlands, mine labor retrenchment, and casualization) as deceptive. These common refrains, according to one mine official, appear undermined by many of the arrests made on-site. "We keep finding, again and again, that when we arrest the galamseys, many of them do not even speak the local Twi. They cannot claim to be indigenous to Obuasi, to be from villages that have lost their farmlands to us."

The AGA official continued that the now rather organized leadership of the small-scale miners has been sending envoys to actively recruit laborers from the North of Ghana, where degrees of poverty and unemployment are much more drastic:

We have been hearing that, at times, they even go around, telling the potential recruits that there are jobs at AGA, and they will bring them down to start work in Obuasi. And then, once they arrive in Obuasi, they say, "Well, there are no jobs at AGA after all." And then, the people are stuck down here, without their families, without much money to go home. And then they tell the northerners, "But we can employ you in galamsey operations. Just work with us, and we'll take care of you— feed you, give you clothes, everything. AGA won't do that, and there are no jobs there, anyway, it turns out." We've been hearing that's how they're doing it. And in this situation, they obviously aren't all coming from villages that lost farmlands.

This mine official did say that some arrested have been identified as former employees of AGA who had been terminated, though they are by no means the majority. He also noted concern over the increasing presence of Chinese galamseys and Chinese-run galamsey operations: "They are even now coming onto our concession. We just arrested about 30 of them a few weeks ago [spring 2012], and we sent them to the prison in Kumasi, where they were immediately released. I don't understand how it is that these galamseys—and Chinese ones, at that, they're not even Ghanaians—seem now to be operating with near impunity! They just posted bail and immediately got out. It has never been this way before, with this level of impunity."

According to Central Committee members, it is a major misconception in town—and one likely propagated or at least encouraged by unsympathetic mine officials and politicians, and their colleagues in the media—that the Association is involved in territorial agreements, labor contracts, and other business deals with the Chinese miners who have been arriving in heavy waves in recent times.

In this sense, Kofi, the key journalist and activist, concurs:

The bosses detest the Chinese presence. They think that, more than anything else, the Chinese presence is giving galamseys a bad name, yet again—especially in destroying people's farms and encroaching on sensitive mine areas. People think that the Association leaders are actually giving out property to the Chinese, or investing in them, or giving them some of their own guys to work, but they're not. Ghanaians do work for them on their sites, but this is not the Association's doing. And most of the Ghanaians who go for these concessions and front for the Chinese, illegally renting them to the Chinese, they are powerful businessmen and politicians, most of them living in Accra, who have the money to do such things.

Whatever the truth of direct Chinese collaboration, galamsey groups now are finding themselves with rival foreign investors who supply heavy machinery for clearing land. According to Asante and state officials, Ghanaians will front for the foreign financiers, allowing for more systematic evasion of property, permit, and taxation regimes. In a July 2010 press statement published through the Manhyia Palace's website, Asantehene Otumfuo Osei Tutu (king of Asante) called for the Ministry of Land, Forestry, and Mines to "find a way to control" illegal galamsey activity, and noted that "if it has become necessary" to give galamsey groups concessions so that they may mine legally and more safely, then they should be required to apply for a license from the state Minerals Commission. The Asantehene also remarked that large state and private police forces at times will swell to "clear" galamsey operations, only to discover afterward that they have reappeared in short order. He particularly noted complaints from management at AGA's Obuasi site, where galamseys threaten company security.

More recently, with the breakdown in the shadow balances of power with the Association's galamsey forces and with the nation's attempted "upward adjustment" reforms for the fiscal regime, which would enhance state takings and lead to further costs to the mine, AGA and other major transnational mining companies operating in Ghana have been threatening to halt investment and even entirely pull out.

Prominent members of Ghana's Chamber of Mines, which serves as the industry mouthpiece and representative organization, often issue such threats in public fora and national newspapers.

According to Kofi: "What the Chamber of Mines has been doing over the past four months [spring of 2013] is going around, region to region [across the nation], and the main thrust of the engagement has been to make a lot of noise about how the government has to reduce these new taxes, how the tax increases are posing such serious obstacles to the companies' operations in the country, how we must work to curb the illegal mining problem. It's all propaganda, to avoid the higher taxes."

Kofi also mentioned that he recently had been part of an advocacy dialogue conversation with the mine, in which mining officials were blaming the galamsey issue in particular for the mine's reported fall in productivity and profitability at the Obuasi operations:

> Just a few days ago, we had a dialogue meeting. . . . At the meeting, AGA was blaming the galamseys for fortunes of mine going down, saying that, if we're not careful, then the company could collapse and shut down in three months. But this is their propaganda. After the meeting, [a mine employee] took me home, and I asked him, "Do you sincerely think that the problem of the mine losing its profits is one of illegal mining?" And he said, "No, honestly, the galamsey problem is nowhere near even the top five threats to the mine." So, that is not the main problem. It is the propaganda to try to shift the focus. [The mine employee] said that the reason the mine is collapsing is because the South Africans have rejected indigenous knowledge of underground mining. The locals have rich experience. And when AGA came, they did away with all of this indigenous knowledge of the underground mine. It has affected production levels. There are people with so much experience, who know the system of underground mining. It has been going on in Obuasi for over 100 years. But AGA is ignoring this knowledge and bringing in all their machines and so forth. . . . This is a mine with very rich ore. . . . A simple question community people have asked—these are people without any schooling, raw indigenous knowledge: if the mine is not rich, if the company is not making profits, why don't they pack up and leave? They are hanging on because they know the mine has potential and can easily recoup their investments. A lot of this is just propaganda.

Whether or not the mine's issuances have been merely propaganda, such threats have been striking fear into the hearts of those who inhabit the town, where the mine is the core mainstay of the economy. In light the recent severe retrenchments at AGA and the subsequent temporary shutdown, these popular fears have been at fever-pitch. Many retrenched AGA workers continue to seek the solace of alternative livelihoods in the galamsey work.

Only Ghanaians can legally obtain concessions from the Minerals Commission for small-scale mining. Foreigners can apply for permits to provide machinery or services on such concessions, but only seventy-five Chinese in the country are currently registered to do so and, according to Ghana Chamber of Mines figures reported in 2013, there are thousands of Chinese involved. Indeed, government officials now say it is hard to measure the scale of Chinese involvement and financial backing in Ghana's small-scale mining. Government officials say that not all Chinese can be passing through customs in Accra. They must be entering illegally, across the borders, through neighboring countries—Togo, Burkina Faso, and Côte d'Ivoire.

The effective illegality of the Chinese operations is also what furnishes their cover for operating with serious degrees of impunity. This implicates those who front for them and get the concessions, those who work for them as miners, and those political authorities and customary leaders who receive their payments.

As Kofi explained to me, with unmistakable agitation: "Yes, this is how, basically, the Chinese can act however they want with how they run the galamsey sites, how they treat their laborers, sometimes with weapons and everything. Because they know you can never take them to court [if you're somehow linked with them]. . . . And the Chinese who run these galamsey sites will be as bold as to tell you openly that if you dare try to give them problems, it won't work, because they've already heavily bribed the police and all the local officials. It's madness!"

In April of 2013, violence and debates surrounding the intensifying Chinese presence in Ghana's gold fields—which has led to much property destruction, water pollution, farmland dispossession, spiritual disruption, and compromised traditional and state political authorities—culminated in the launching of a governmental inter-ministerial task force. The force conducted military sweeps and mass deportations of Chinese involved in illegal gold mining across the country. This social drama attracted attention from prominent media outlets across the world. Many of these Chinese miners, whom local Ghanaians often view as comparatively powerful agents of a national and racial Chinese project of incursion, previously had been living as impoverished peasants in a southern province of China and had arrived as part of the (at times, coerced) laboring forces for financial sponsors of the latest gold rush.

Here, again, the mining encounter serves as a privileged register for the staging of broader popular discourses, national anxieties, and sovereign controversies concerning the novel—in some ways, neocolonial—formations of power, wealth, race, and rule in Ghana's new constitutional democracy. Amid soaring global mineral prices and ever-rising Chinese demand for raw resources, Ghana—Africa's second-largest gold producer and also a site of recently discovered key oil reserves—has resurfaced as a critical site of geopolitical competition. In fact, China recently surpassed the United States as Ghana's largest trading partner, and, according to Fitch Ratings, the total amount of loans from China's Export-Import Bank to Ghana exceeded the sum of loans from the World Bank to the nation for the period of 2001 to 2010. Intensifying public debate over the heavy sovereign indebtedness to China has proceeded alongside this tumultuous local conflict over gold, which culminated in the military sweeps of galamsey operations in which Chinese were involved.

As the terms of the galamseys' Gentleman's Agreement with the mine seem to be faltering—as the spring 2013 military flash out portrayed at the start of this book vividly attests—both the precarity and the gravity of the shadow balances of power in town are thrown into high relief. This underscores the more dramatic implication that a group of casual laborers—informally assembled, and often from dispossessed communities or groups of retrenched mineworkers—have succeeded, if unevenly and uncertainly, in making significant material demands on a transnational mining corporation. They have done so through informally collectivizing—against state law, and in its shadow—their forces in the Small-Scale Miners Association, which is underwritten by spiritual and practical powers. These powers, in turn, establish their capacities to mobilize, coerce, and unleash violence, often at the decisional whim of the Central Committee leaders.

2

Spiritual Sovereigns in the Shadows

In a long November in 2012, dry in air and drenched in gold, the Chairman of the Small-Scale Miners Association, Baba, met an untimely death in a fateful motorcycle accident. He had risen to local fame and amassed great fortunes. No one seemed quite sure why he had been chosen as such a grand beneficiary to the whims of wealth (*sika*), but so it was until he met his sudden demise. The proximate cause was clear in the form of the accident. Baba was dodging a pothole in the road without a helmet. According to his associates, he had been rushing from Obuasi to nearby Kumasi, to catch a flight to Accra. He had been racing to receive his wife, who had just returned from a holy trip to Mecca.

The circumstances were so senseless—and sudden and unexpected—that there was an almost immediate, general consensus in town that the death must have been spiritually produced.

Kwaku, a friend of mine and also close to a dear friend of Baba, received the news in short order, by way of a cell phone call while we were riding in the back of a car, en route to fetch food for supper—rice and groundnut soup—with a group of friends. As Kwaku put it:

> If I'm quoting my brother correctly, his brother [a close colleague in the Central Committee] was with him in Zongo [an Obuasi neighborhood] before they left, and he said, "Oh, Baba, you're our big boss. Let us send you in one of the cars with one of the drivers. One of them will take you and drop you at the airport in Kumasi." And Baba said, "You foolish boy, you want to kill me?" And then Baba insisted that his friend let him use the motorbike. And then they were trying to get him to wear a helmet, and he refused, saying he didn't want to. And then, he rode with my brother's brother.... Soon after they left Obuasi, they had the accident, and Baba died.... It

seems as if he had been spiritually deafened. He couldn't hear the warning about the helmet.

Also, Kwaku continued, Baba's insistence on taking the motorbike—not even his own motorbike, but his colleague's—did not make sense: "You are filthy rich. You have the most expensive, latest model of a Toyota four-runner. In fact, you have a whole fleet of cars. Why would you take a motorbike—someone else's motorbike—to run to catch a flight in Kumasi? And anyway, even if you did miss the flight, so what? There are flights leaving from Kumasi to Accra every hour, and you could have just caught the next one. And you are rich, so why should it matter if you have to buy another one? It just doesn't make any sense, how he died."

Various explanations of Baba's death abounded. Some suggested that envious or power-hungry fellow Central Committee members had gone in for spiritual powers to bring him down, to produce his reckless behavior and early death. As Baba was so central to the organization, the sacrifice of his life would be very dear, hastening the flow of gold, some reasoned.

Others in town speculated that the source of spiritual attack on Baba rested with the leaders of the separatist faction within the galamseys' Small-Scale Miners Association (SSMA). These separatists allegedly had engaged in ongoing spiritual and practical contests with the Central Committee leaders for much of the past year, commissioning powerful ritual authorities in Obuasi and also from the town of Walewale in the Northern Region of Ghana, an ancestral home of one of the separatist leaders.

In casual conversation not long before Baba's death, the head of the separatist faction, Samuel, had talked to me about the spiritual dimensions of the tensions within the galamsey ranks. This man also told of how the current members of the Central Committee were growing very concerned on received information that the disgruntled group might formally break away. Some of them, including Baba, had taken to traveling everywhere surrounded by "macho heavies," or bodyguards. They would not move an inch without spiritual and physical protection.

On this nondescript yet somehow premonitory day, in banter on the side of the road in the village of Sansu, Samuel grew rather solemn. He dismissed these security precautions, assuring me that they were senseless and excessive. "There is no need for these," he insisted. "Even when I was young and had my strength, I didn't use it. . . . We heard that even last night, they [Baba and other Central Committee members] went to visit a *mallam* [here, meaning Islamic ritualist] in a nearby village. They were going for protections, thinking we would attack them. And then, on the way home, blood was even spilled. They hit a man on the way back to town. But they are taking care of him, paying his medical bills."

Samuel and his friend sitting in the next chair, another galamsey, concurred that the spilling of blood was reckoned as an effective offering for spiritual services rendered by the *mallam* and any conspiring *jinn*. This was so, even though the vehicle collision was apparently unintentional and accidental, on the part of the driver. Nevertheless, they apprehended the event as spiritually generated. Spirits merely had brought it about—or that was the understanding that Samuel proffered.

As for Baba's final fatality, others blamed his wife or other family members. Still others said that his principal presiding spirit had come for his dues, to collect the heavy debt incurred for Baba's vast riches. As chairman, Baba, of course, was seen as heavily armed spiritually—backed with protection, perhaps, by at least one powerful deity and with access to multiple prominent diviners. Most rumors in town appeared to settle on the explanation that Baba had done this to himself by going for craven blood money rituals (*mogya sika aduro* or, simply, *sika aduro*) in order to bring hefty, accelerated wealth.

In the reckoning of local norms or moral economies, such deeply unethical spiritual engagements would by design, almost inevitably, generate his untimely demise.[1] Although any such ritual gains would be contrary to the highest divine laws of Nyame, the concentration of ritual energy may produce short-term wealth or other gains. The catch is that these riches or results do not endure because they run so contrary to the laws of the cosmos, which are right, proper, just, and true. The fruits of unethical enrichment always dissipate, ordinarily within six or seven years, and sometimes sooner. Higher-order divine law, almost in self-executing fashion, will exact eventual downfall upon those who have engaged in selfish, nefarious rituals. The punishment of the fall can extend beyond economic impoverishment or the emotional depression of the wrongdoer. The consequences can include tortuous madness, ceaseless hauntings, or even death, which often arrives abruptly and under peculiar circumstances. Additionally, any objects acquired with the blood money suddenly will become unusable. A car will not run. No one can inhabit a house with peace. Expensive jewelry goes missing or comes to carry a curse.

Interestingly, many galamseys—who must have been steeped in envy of Baba, no doubt—privately said that they even were rejoicing at the accident, at their leader's bloody death. Losing someone so central and precious to the Association only could be calculated as a significant sacrificial offering to the relevant spirits, who, in turn, could reward struggling galamseys with hastened and more plentiful manifestations of gold at their sites of operation.

The various speculations that vied and swirled around the death of the chairman bespeak a wider cognizance of the forms of spiritual authority that the galamsey leaders wield. It is popular knowledge that they enlist spiritual surveillance in their shadow rule. It is also commonly understood that galamseys at times recast ostensible losses as projected productive gains, as symbolic expenditures that assume the forms of spiritual supplication, sacrificial offerings.

The leaders of the galamseys—both at the level of the association's Central Committee and also at the level individual laboring groups—routinely draw upon their own diviners to charm some of the spirits who interact with gold, to pacify the other local gods and ancestors, and to secure safety and prosperity for themselves and for the precarious labor of their subjects. In so doing, they anchor their claims to rule in transcendental spiritual realms.

Typically, the leaders consult either indigenous religious spirit mediums or Islamic *boka* (or what many in Obuasi call merely *mallams*, meaning "teachers"), the latter dealing in spiritual contracts with *jinn* (genie spirits).[2] Even those galamseys who are practicing Christians—and thus, by the book, forbidden to engage in traditional spiritual engagements—by and large, must engage in ritual pacts with fellow laborers and in sacrificial offerings to ancestors, to the spirits of the earth, and to other relevant spirits with jurisdiction over their laboring sites.

Lands in Akan kingdoms are owned or ruled over by principal deities of the territories. Traditionally, this typically was Asaase Yaa (supreme earth deity) or a local earth deity. Obuasi sits almost entirely within Adanse territory, which is now incorporated into the Asante kingdom. The highest-ranking deity in Adanse territory with a living priestess is Bona. Bona presides over hunting, fishing, farming, and mining in Adanse. Accordingly, miners and others regularly visit traditional priests and priestesses (*akomfo*) to propitiate Bona and other relevant spirits with libations and sacrificial offerings (typically, particular drink and food items), seeking permission and also blessings for work upon the lands. Without the permission of Bona and other deities, many believe that gold will not even appear for the taking.[3]

Gold occupies a pivotal place in Akan cosmology. It is held to be at once a sacred symbol and a physical reflection of the light of Nyame, the supreme creator (Absolute Consciousness of Being and Wisdom); in turn, powerful divine spirit governs gold in the ultimate analysis, though lower-order spirits may temporarily intervene in order to increase or diminish the appearance of gold for miners. The pinnacle throne of the Asante is the Golden Stool (Sika 'Gua), venerated as the seat of the collective soul or spirit (*sunsum*) of the people. In everyday conversation, one often hears "*sika*," the word for gold; it is also used for wealth or money. One also hears "*sika kra*" (or, at times, "*kra sika*"), meaning "soul's gold." This latter usage indexes the metal's sacred status as a close material aspect or manifestation of the ultimate Nyame. This understanding of gold's sacred properties also resonates with much wide-ranging, deep spiritual alchemical wisdom from throughout history and across many cultures, which reveals gold's transmutative capacity, helping to propel a being into the ultimate state of divine union or enlightenment in human form and in the afterlife (as well as in potential future lives).[4] In Akan society, gold occupies a paramount place in the sanctification of authority, in circuits of gifting and reciprocity, and in systems of general valuation. As Thomas McCaskie argues, it "is located conceptually and materially at the very core of the historical experience of [Asante] society and culture."[5] Its centrality is at once economic and sacred, substantive and metaphysical. In many ways, this remains true today.[6]

What does the significance of these forms of spiritual authorization, underwriting, or undermining for galamseys reveal about the centrality of transcendental or numinous grounding for powerful moral economies of labor forces? This significance is amplified for those who informally labor amid dire and perilous conditions, regularly facing risks of death, violent repression, madness, destitution, or other forms of physical, psychical, or spiritual injury. Potent forms of fantasy and terror, dreams and nightmares, ambivalently mediate the subjection of galamseys to state and corporate violence, as well as to new forms of shadow rule, such as the Association. How do the galamseys' sacrifices—literal and metaphorical— effectively serve as sites for a powerful renegotiation of cultural justice in the realms of the city, the soul, and the sacred?

This chapter examines the practical logics of mining sacrifices and the spiritual powers they channel to examine how galamseys crucially harness sources of vitality and propitiation to navigate interchanges of desire and death. They do so in the governing and disciplining of bodies that perilously labor with purpose, fealty, even senses of honor. These ritual practices register ambivalent aspirations and devotions beyond rational communion-of-wills spiritual contracts, shading into the uncanny spirit of sacrificial obligations and ritual pacts honored unto death.

Within the realm of these ritual pacts, blood serves as a particularly critical locus of vitality and excess, and its sacrificial deployment is an index of the incorporation into natural orders of that which exceeds these earthly laborers and furnishes their activities with transcendental grounding. Yet, while blood is one of the most significant symbolic fluids in communing with the spiritual realm and in differentially empowering laboring subjects, it is only one among many. Alcohol is the other chief offering, of course, but so, too, are clothes, jewelry, money, or various specially prepared food items—especially, eggs, mashed yam, various herbs and spices, and plantains.

Indeed, not all deities and spirits demand, enjoy, or even accept offerings of blood. Each deity has her particular tastes and requests, and it is for each deity's channels—who often also function as the "sacrificers"—to interpret and communicate such preferences and requirements to the "sacrifier," the human who commissions the sacrifice.[7] Some deities in Ghana actually outright detest blood and refuse even to take part in exacting revenge or dolling out death on account of this. As Emmanuel Akyeampong has shown, rampant warfare during the precolonial period fostered the rise of war deities (*abosom abrafo*) above nature deities. In Asante, specifically, the Asantehene (king of Asante) possessed all war deities, and their channels reported to him. The war deities required human or animal blood, and they also preferred golden rum—as opposed to white rum—on account of the former's perceived likeness to *kokoo*—the color red—and, by extension, to blood.[8] Brandy also could be used as substitution. On the other hand, nature deities and ancestors preferred lighter colors in alcohol libations—in the form of gin, white rum, schnapps, or palm wine. Some gods also refuse alcohol. In the event that the god does not accept alcohol, the rituals may use water for libation.[9]

For galamseys in Obuasi, I argue, it is sacrificial obligations and ritual pacts—allied with acute deprivation, unemployment, and the strong desire for livelihood, marriage, and, one day, perhaps becoming an ancestor—that converge to underwrite their bold spirits and moral economies of labor. More broadly, spiritual backing also furnishes with vitality and perseverance those who labor in what the galamseys call "the womb of the earth" for AGA. Likewise, AGA itself invokes, beseeches, and partakes of transcendent power in its various rituals of communing with the divine for fortunes and protections in the mine, as we will see. Spiritual sovereigns have come to stand behind and to anchor claims to power, authority, and legitimate rule that official sovereigns *and* prominent forms of shadow authority draw upon in their attempts to harvest gold, mobilize and govern labor, and stake claims to territorial jurisdiction.

Sacrificial imperatives incite forms of violence and rapture, fear and adoration—possessing, transporting, and seizing the mind by force. In local cosmologies of labor, blood and other offerings serve as tactile hieratic or sublime substances that craft connections to spirit that transcend those earthly beings who wield the seals of spiritual authority, who purport to rule in their names. This is especially so for galamseys, who systematically enlist sacrificial rituals, draw pacts, observe local prohibitions, and even—in contrast to AGA mine operations—refuse to mine on Tuesdays, the day of the week on which local gods and ancestors proscribe work. Galamseys also forbid mining during other taboo times, such as sacred festivals. As Emmanuel Ababio Ofosu-Mensah explains, regarding the traditional taboo of working during one such festival, the Adae, "It was believed that the ancestors would punish a miner who flouted this custom by causing him to be buried alive by the earth."[10]

The members of the galamseys' leadership confirmed for me the current observation of sacred days as internal ritual and labor policy for the galamsey forces. Galamsey bosses state that to allow laborers to work on Tuesdays or other sacred days—or to refuse to make the traditional sacrifices and engage in the other requisite rituals—would be very irresponsible to their financial interests but also to the lives of their laboring forces. As one galamsey boss, Tim, explained to me in an impromptu conversation in his living room, as he sat beneath a hovering, florid, life-sized portrait of Jesus:

Tomorrow is Tuesday, and it has been generally accepted that we don't go and mine on Tuesdays, especially those who are doing the galamsey. You see, we have the belief that the gods of the rivers have a special day for their meetings, so that date has been consecrated for the gods. So, tomorrow, for instance, those who are going for the galamsey, they don't go to work. . . . If you should go, if you don't take care, you may go and hurt yourself and die. And maybe you bring a curse to your family. . . . And if you try to go and work on that fateful . . . Tuesday . . . before you know it, a snake will be chasing you. The spirits, they put the snakes as their guard, and they tell the snakes, "Hello, we are now coming to work here tomorrow. Nobody should come over here. If a person comes here, you are the guard over here, don't spare the person." The snakes, they will chase you, spiritually.

This galamsey boss also explained how he enlists the diviners' aid in planting spiritual surveillance mechanisms on his site of operations, usually in the form of possessed snakes, a seemingly stray dog, a cat, or even rocks and other natural features. Things like surveillance cameras would never work outside of the electrical grids of the town, but the spiritual securing of the terrain is enough to keep many would-be thieves from trespassing in the night. Likewise, the ritual pacts are often sealed with spiritual surveillance mechanisms that ensure that the laboring groups honor the terms of the pacts and their obligations to each other under them. Should a transgression be detected, spiritual sanctions would result. The force of this all-seeing gaze, many galamseys confide, is ordinarily enough to ensure adherence to the terms of agreement within laboring groups and with respect to the proceeds of the gold.

If the galamsey leadership and its security interlocutors at the mine lay conceivable claims to property and rule through spiritual power, then the seeming resilience and fortitude of the galamsey laborers in the face of repeated trauma, of physical and spiritual violence, would seem to draw from beyond the natural realm as well. The ritual lives infuse with force and resolve these laborers, who work amid extreme terror, peril, and, often, possible death. In such worlds, an interplay between what Victor Turner describes as two modes of anti-temporality—namely, the eternal, continuous divine and the iconoclastic, individualistic "cheating" of proper temporal sequencing—can yield powerful yet also grievous results.[11] As noted earlier, in an extension of related works in this vein, Obuasi offers a situation in which industrial labor has been heavily casualized, and smaller groups enlist spiritual power to foster intragroup loyalty but also to vigorously compete with each other, both within and between groups.[12] As formal legal and political authority have become disaggregated, and as labor power has become ever more fragmented and casualized, the pluralities of spiritual jurisdictions, forces, and powers increasingly have come to the forefront of cultural consciousness. As I argue throughout this book, religious authorities—whether traditional, Islamic, or Christian—often step in to govern where formal legal and political mechanisms of rule are inaccessible or fail to bear much salience to people's everyday lives and innermost concerns. Spiritual authority is crucial on a most basic level for the underwriting of the moral economies of miners who relate to gold, land, and much else as backed by or imbued with spirits in need of proper propitiation and supplication.

This is not to say that all indigenous spiritual governance is endogenous, native to the land, or autochthonous, at least in any straightforward sense. Deities and other spirits (and their human channels and traditional authorities) in town have long come from elsewhere, especially from the north of the country. They often have followed the routes of forced and free labor migration from the north. As mentioned in the introduction, during the eighteenth and nineteenth centuries, the Asante Empire employed slaves, many of them captured from groups in the north, to work in the mines. Later, in early colonial times, Ashanti Goldfields launched a campaign to recruit—at times, coercively, after the company adopted the South African model of forced labor recruitment—underground mine laborers from Ghana's northern region.[13] Many from southern Ghana view groups from the north as more in tune with nature and its powers, with enhanced auras of a sort of sublime spiritual power and mystique. Oftentimes, people in Obuasi will tell me that they most fear those deities and spirits who travel from the north of Ghana or from the south of Burkina Faso.[14]

Many deities in Obuasi originally hail from places in the northern region. Some have been in the Obuasi area for centuries; others have arrived more recently, according to their priests and priestesses. Yet even in view of these deep histories of transcendental pluralism in Obuasi and throughout Ghana, the cosmological terrain of Obuasi recently has become even more complex. New migrants are bringing their own priests and priestesses, sources of spiritual power, ancestral connections, and practices of ritual rule. Often, prominent galamsey bosses and others roam great distances outside the nation—even, for example, to East Africa and to India—in search of the most potent powers for charming the gold, both spirits and human spiritualists. At times, the galamsey leaders travel to find and to secure these foreign powers; at others, they hire people to go in their stead.

GALAMSEYS, SPIRITUAL ARMAMENT, ENIGMATIC SIGNIFICATION

Within the wider popular consciousness in town, galamseys are a sort of enigmatic signifier. Their presence is haunted by the restless ghosts of dispossession, abjection, and, at times, improper sacrifices. The popular ambivalence flows, in no small part, from competing elements in the local representational repertoires pertaining to the galamseys. On the one hand, galamseys are said to make significant contributions to the local economy through the wealth they generate and spend in town, and it is believed they would face destitution if they were to be forbidden to do their work. On the other hand, there are countervailing, much less sympathetic accounts of their activities that emanate from the mine and from others. AGA sources flood media portrayals with harrowing images of reckless, spectral artisanal operators. These cast the galamseys as a grave threat to the environment, to public order, and to proper moral codes. Perhaps most critically, the company claims that they jeopardize the profitability and productivity of the mine and, by extension, the jobs it offers to local people. Many in town say that galamseys also bribe local chiefs for access to peasant farmlands. As such, the galamseys also destroy resources, disrupt livelihoods, and displace people from their lands.

Many townspeople are also ambivalent about the galamseys' heavy enlistment of spiritual backing, sometimes extending into sources with dubious moral valences. In particular, many fear ritual transactions involving *juju* or *sika aduro* (blood money). Such rituals are said, ordinarily, to include the siphoning off—or even the wholesale consumption—of human vitality, executed in the spiritual realm. In such quick-money rituals, the sacrificial demands are said to increase until one will not or cannot meet them. At that point, the spirit consumes the person, her possessions, her freedom of will and consciousness, her lifeforce, her vitality.

Raphael, a galamsey boss, described to me, in typical formulations, the ways in which some enlist powerful but ultimately destructive spiritual forces in calling the gold:

> So, if you go to the spirit [interacting with the gold, through occult channels], you go on with some rituals, and this will start from an egg, and then jump to a fowl or something. Later on it will be a sheep, maybe a cow, and the next day, if you don't take care, before you realize . . . it will come to a human being [spiritually]. If you don't take care, it can even take your life. It might not kill you, but it will dwindle your light. And you will become sick and weak, and they will have to send you to a shrine. . . . It involves so many negative effects, and the positive is maybe you are being given the amount of gold, as maybe you want it, getting the gold, and after it, or maybe along the line, or maybe midway, you will be asked to do something to pacify the gods, or maybe do things so that it will come. In a way, that is the point of no return. If you don't do it, if you say no, you are going to get crazy, or something like that.

As an example, Raphael invoked a case he had just seen the night before, of a man who had gone for the fast money rituals and had arrived at his spiritual recompense—a sudden onset of madness:

> Just last night I was here, and in this area, there was something like a traffic jam, and this guy was there, and he started blowing his horn. Beep, beep. There were so many cars in front of him, so they had to park for him to go, because we were thinking of something urgent. . . . He started, vroom vroom, while parked, and he opened the

door, got out, and he started disrespecting his car. What had come over this man? He started gazing at the skies and started laughing, and since he was very hot, he took off his shirt, and he started laughing, started dancing. Ah! What has come over him? He started kicking his own car! He started beating it! . . . They had to put him in this store, to ask him, 'What happened?' To put it in a nutshell, he went in for these kind of fishy riches. It has come. So this man has enjoyed for a period of more than six years. These are the results. For all that, you got it. You have your own stores, your own cars, big mansions. Look at the consequences. You got mad. . . . He's done this without the consent of the family. The wife is not aware. The kids are not aware. And then it happens that you have to call them, go and put this man at AGA Hospital. And according to [what neighbors were saying], they had to refer him to a psychiatrist at Cape Coast [where there is an asylum], for mad people [abodamfo]. And since then, I haven't heard anything else. So normally, when they go for this, the consequences are awful. But sometimes when they go there, different spirits, they will help them. Maybe they wouldn't help me. Others, they go there, and they are okay, in life.

The rituals, as with the labor itself, involve grievous and often fatal risks and dice-throwing.

The galamsey presence itself in Obuasi—irrepressible and growing—is, of course, partly generated by a broader structural economic problem of unemployment and the heightened prevalence of the so-called informal economy.[15] Thus, their desperation and determination to labor at all costs. No matter how heavily these miners are policed and repressed, they return to the bloodied sites, and in short order. This leads some to claim that they are "inhuman." A popular phrasing is that galamseys "think with their feet," alluding to the belief that they are animated by spiritual allegiances more than mundane, everyday concerns and affects. Yet this phrasing is also a commentary on the galamseys' acute earthly desperation: they labor unto death for the chance merely to survive amid acute deprivation and devastating unemployment levels, particularly among the youth.

The galamseys often enlist local spiritual authorities, but they also will commission their own diviners, deities, and spirits from outside the lands. At times, the very wealthy galamsey bosses even will relocate their favored indigenous priest and the priest's family, either to live in one of their own homes in Obuasi or to live in a nice nearby home that the galamsey boss will build for the priest.

As Raphael explained to me, citing practices of some of his colleagues: "This is to make sure that [the priests] will be closer to them at any point in time. Instead of them traveling to the north [of Ghana, from which many of the most powerful diviners are said to come]. . . . They will be calling [the priest], 'Massa, please come over here. We have your accommodation, your food, bring everything. We are ready for you to come and do this thing over here. We are waiting for you to protect us spiritually.'"

Raphael also explained that it is very common for the higher-level galamseys routinely to consult the priests and priestesses for spiritual armament and protection: "Because others, they can go through these occultic channels. Even your own guys can kill you. If they are working, and doing the same thing, and they see you are progressing, they can envy you to the extent that they will just kill you off. It can happen. So, many people will go in for protection."

Many of these spiritual authorities now advertise themselves on billboards erected throughout town, or on radio airwaves, in newspaper advertisements, or on local television programs.

Raphael also spoke of this new mass advertising phenomenon among local *mallams* and *akomfo* (Akan priestesses and priests): "They normally go on air, and they tell people who are going for the gold ... the fetish, the mallams, the priests ... if you believe them and trust them, even if you are not ready, they will tell you that you have to pacify the gods, you have to talk to them in this way. They can also heal you, tell you that this thing will be coming. And some of them, the priests, they can even call the gods for them to talk to you. You will hear them."

The advent of promotional tactics for these auratic powers appears, in part, to be driven by competition from recently flourishing Christian Pentecostal and charismatic pastor-prophets, who advertise massively, claiming to use only the Holy Spirit in their divinations.[16] These Christian preachers tend to roundly demonize and excoriate "traditional" practices and practitioners.[17] However, the phenomenon of the commodified priest also seems to be a result of the fact that informal mining has become such big business in town—measured both by the number of people engaged in it and by the yields, which had grown amid the rising gold prices (around 2012) following the 2008 global financial crisis.

GOLD IN THE PURVIEW OF PROMINENT AKOMFO

The Akan priests and other diviners who provide services for beckoning and charming the gold do so at the pleasure of their tutelary deities or spirits. Often, purportedly on behalf of the deities, they demand a cut of the gold proceeds. One of my principal interlocutors regarding gold and spirit, a prominent local priestess, Okomfo Akua, now uses extensive record books for the spiritual contracts she draws up with galamseys, as well as with a wide range of other clients—local judges and lawyers, pastor-prophets, chiefs and politicians, farmers, and those selling in the markets.

In her natural state, Okomfo Akua has no memory of the deliberations and transactions conducted while she is mounted by one of her two *abosom* (Twi: deities).[18] Her *okyeame* (Twi "spokesperson")—also, in her case, her earthly husband, Kwabena—assumes the role of chronicling the agreements in the record book. If galamseys fail to produce the agreed-upon amount of the cut of the total value of the gold—often around one-third, though sometimes a specified lump-sum monetary payment—then the priestess's deities can consult with the local spirits and deities to conduct spiritual surveillance of the territory to assess the nature and the extent of the breach. Where a breach is found, Okomfo Akua and her husband often issue warnings. If the galamseys do not heed the warnings, the priestess can interfere spiritually with the operations such that gold no longer will appear at the site for the taking. The priestess says that she never commissions her deities to visit curses or other severe punishments upon the transgressive galamseys, though the local deities and spirits may elect to do so, independent of her activities and even her wishes.

One of the most important rituals that Okomfo Akua performs for many local galamseys is for prospecting. Alongside Kwabena, she requests that a sample of soil, often no more than a handful, be brought to the consulting room of her palace, which is also her shrine. It is an open-air room, walled on three sides and opening on a small clearing for parking, beyond which are expanses of brush and vegetation. White sheep are often tethered to a nearby tree, and black cats roam freely about, often weaving in and out of consultants' legs—with unsettling effect, for some. The walls of the shrine are painted in mint green, lined with white trim. Okomfo Akua's bejeweled throne is positioned against the back wall, facing the opening, next to a carved wooden stool, her spiritual throne. Kwabena will often sit to Okomfo Akua's right, on the bejeweled throne chair. If he does not sit there, he will sit on a chair against the opposite side wall, facing the okomfo's consultants.

Once the galamsey prospectors bring the requested sample of soil from their potential mining land, Okomfo Akua orders them to place it in the center of the floor. As Kwabena explains:

Assuming you get a concession, and you want to know if there's gold in it or not, and you come to her, then she will tell you, "Go and bring either soil or dust, from that particular one." So, assuming this place is my concession, I come to her and ask, "Is there gold?" She will just say go and bring either soil or dust. And when you bring it to her, she will call the power that she works with. But then she also asks you to bring a leaf, so you put the leaf on it. . . . So, she will call the power that she is working with [one of the two deities], and then [the deity] will come and see the soil or the sand. So, if there's gold in it, [the deity] will tell her that there is gold in the soil. . . . So the *mmoatia* [dwarves, or short helping spirits] or the abosom will come . . . and if there's gold in the soil or the sand they've brought, it will light for everybody around to see that it has lit. If there's gold in it, it will burn, for [the deity] to say there is gold. Anybody around can see it, with the naked eye. . . . No matches, no kerosene, no petrol, anything. You bring it yourself and put it there. . . . So, when [the sample, the spirits, and the mmoatia] come together, anytime they will meet, there's supposed to be a difference, and the difference is the fire that lights. When the gold and the mmoatia or the abosom meet, the fire is something that is supposed to happen for you to see that there's a difference.

Although this Okomfo Akua and Kwabena work with two principal deities, one of them being the second-highest-ranking deity in the lands of the Obuasi municipality, the okomfo also works with many other spirits, who often appear as mmoatia. She would not disclose to me how many there are in number. She said they are many, but they come as one. Another okomfo who worships at the nearby River Fena, Okomfo Kwaku, who serves as a prominent priest for the river deity, disclosed to me that he directly works with ninety-nine spirits, and that they each speak in different tongues to him. Okomfo Akua says that she communicates in Twi, and in some English, with her deities, but that, once she is mounted, she can fluently speak many other languages—including those that she does not know at all in her natural state. And her voice changes. The deities speak through her.

Okomfo Akua says that her deities will come whenever she calls them, as is the case with every true okomfo, according to her. As well, she says, a true okomfo does not need to rely on an external medium in the form of some sacred object, as is the case with many priests and priestesses. For example, many akomfo summon their tutelary spirits with particular waters in certain calabashes, or with specific carvings or drawn shapes or symbols, or with certain types of sacred mirrors. Okomfo Kwaku uses a calabash and also a small mirror, lined with cowry shells, which he said came from the bottom of the sea, delivered by the spirit of a mermaid via mmoatia carriers.

Okomfo Akua said that, despite popular understanding among spiritualists regarding the need for such objects, one need not use such instruments. Rather, she pours libations and utters summoning calls or incantations. Then the deities come and dwell within her. The abosom directly communicate with her in the spiritual realm. Yet they also temporarily take over her body, as though using her natural body as a vessel, and they speak their word and work their services through her. I asked her where her soul, or her consciousness—or her *sunsum*, her conscious spirit—goes when this happens, and she answered that she does not know. Many other priests say the same. It is as though they just go blank, black out, and when they resume consciousness, they cannot recall what had happened over the duration of their channeling. This is where the crucial role of the okyeame, the spokesperson or mouthpiece for the priest, comes in.

This interpretive and mediating role of the okyeame is particularly important for the discerning and recording of the next steps. For example, if the soil sample lights in the middle of the floor, then the spirits will direct that certain offerings be made and other rituals performed on the land on which the galamseys or other miners will labor. As Okomfo Akua explained during one of our initial conversations:

So, assuming [the soil sample] lights, there are some rituals that the spirits will order or direct. And then, the galamseys will go and do them on the land. So, the gods will tell me, "Go and do this ritual on the land." So, we [Okomfo Akua and Kwabena] will go with the galamseys on the land, and then go and do the rituals for them. We will go and pacify the spirits on the land. It may also be that there is a river, closer to the land, so I also have to go and pacify the river obosom, and tell the river deity, something like, "Nana, even though you are taking care of this land, your son or daughter is hungry, and she wants to work on this land to get something to eat, so please, allow him or her to work on this land."

Okomfo Akua, echoing many others with whom I spoke, also insisted that if the galamseys do not properly conduct these preliminary rituals and then perform the necessary sacrifices and other rituals as the spirits order, they will never hit gold in the ground. It even can flee, moving like a snake or a ball of light. She explained, "If you don't pacify the gods, you will work on the land, but then you will never see the gold. Even though there is gold in the land, it won't appear."

As for the specifics of the offerings that the deities and the other spirits demand, they vary from land to land, falling under the sovereign purview of the local spirits. However, there are broad patterns. Okomfo Akua explained:

At times, we have to shed blood. But then, it's not always the case. Every land has what it wants. Some of the lands think goats are okay for them. Others think dogs. Others also use the cock. So, the abosom will tell you the kind of animal or what you should use as a sacrifice. . . . We can also use eggs. But at times, you will not shed blood. The spirit will direct you to use something that is quite costly or more expensive than even shedding the blood. . . . At times, you will be directed to look for some herbs, like the leaves, and you go and search for all the leaves. And [you come with them] and then you use a spirit. The spirit will direct you to a certain [other] spirit or leaf, so you go and bring that one. So, when you mix all of them, you have to sprinkle it and just thank god that it is on the land.

"Are these sorts of herbal concoctions ever ingested by the miners themselves?" I asked.

Kwabena replied, "Not necessarily that, though that is for protections. As for this mixture, the galamseys are meant to just sprinkle the herbs on the land. It can be that the gold is far away underground. So, it will just attract the gold to come up. So, as you sprinkle it on the land like that, it will attract the gold to come up, so you only need to dig a few feet, and you see the gold."

The prospecting ritual with the flames in the shrine can even indicate the level of gold that may be harvested on the land, how plentiful the deposits are or how abundant the gold's manifestations will be. Kwabena detailed the determination of gold levels, along with the ways in which the spirits will usually dictate the proportion of the mining proceeds that should come back to the hands of the okomfo and okyeame, on behalf of the deity:

At times, galamseys will ask, "How much do you think that I can even get on the land?" It depends on the lighting [during the prospecting ritual]. Assuming the flame is high, that means you are going to get a huge sum of money over there. But when the lighting is small, that means probably that you won't get enough [to justify operations or certain levels of investment]. . . . In most cases, it is the spirit that tells us how much the galamseys should give to the deity. So, assuming the flame is high, that means that there is enough money on the land, and then the spirit will tell you, "Because there is enough gold on the land, afterward, divide the money into three. Bring me one, and you keep two."

As mentioned above, the spirits also may police the galamseys' subsequent operations. If galamseys later breach or otherwise fail to fully honor the terms of a spiritual contract made with the deities of the okomfo, the gold will cease its manifesting on the land. Additionally, other spiritual penalties may be inflicted on the laborers or those close to them. As Kwabena explained:

> It happens that someone can even pay part of it [what is due to the deity], but then they'll come and tell you that the work is bad. It doesn't go. But the spirit will go there in the night and see that, oh, the work is still going on. When it happens like that, they will cease [your] getting the gold. . . . Most of the spirits will not curse. Most of them do not curse. But then, they think, they will allow you to work on it so that you will give as much as is due to them. So, assuming that they gave you the authority to go and do it, and you are not giving [back to] them, they will not curse you, but they will stop you from getting the gold.

Many galamseys harbor serious concerns about nefarious witches (*abayifo*) in the area who may try to interfere with their operations; they may also worry about jealous family members or people they know from other domains of their lives. As Okomfo Akua is a medium for such a high-ranking deity, I asked her and Kwabena about whether, if the proper rituals are done through them, witches are able to interfere with the operations. They supplied a fascinating answer. They explained that there is a "vast interval," or a "vast difference," between witches and the deities of the land, including the two deities that work through Okomfo Akua. The witches operate on a much different—and much lower—energetic frequency and cannot even approach the deities in the spiritual realm. The deities are much higher in rank and of different spiritual constitutions altogether. And the witches know this, Okomfo Akua explained. She added:

> It can never happen like that [where a witch interferes with a deity or approaches a deity in the spiritual realm]. But then, if a witch still wants to challenge, when she wants to do something on the land, the deity will probably just get a hold of her, the witch, so that she will be disgraced. [. . .] She may go mad, she may fall sick, or she can even die. It has just happened, that the deity has killed someone. The witch who died, before she died, she confessed that, indeed, she wanted to bewitch somebody. The family will come and then have the normal discussion to solve the problem, over here tomorrow. Later tomorrow morning, we will work on it. . . . The witch was in a

different place, but because she wanted to bewitch somebody who has come for protection over here, she couldn't. Before the person died, she confessed that indeed, she wanted to bewitch somebody. But then the person has come for protection from this place, so we have to come and then pacify the gods over here before anyone can even work on the corpse. Because when it happens like that, nobody can work on the corpse. Anybody who might want to work on the dead body might also have the repercussion [through principles of spiritual contagion].

Okomfo Akua also clarified that, for this or any witch to be successful in her attack, she must make a spiritual agreement or transaction with a witch of the target's *fiefoo*—household people or extended family. Indeed, an Akan adage that many often take literally admonishes that "there is a witch in every household," meaning every extended family in a matriline. The witches' intrusions upon the lives or fortunes of galamseys or anyone else are delimited by this condition, because in order to intrude in a person's life, they must cajole or charm that person's family witch—or one of the family witches—into "selling out" the family member in the spiritual realm.

Even though Okomfo Akua concedes that witches wield some extensive powers, her tutelary deities make prompt arrests of any witches they spot. According to her, the apprehensions happen in the spiritual realm, but they manifest in the physical realm.

Kwabena added again, however, "There is no way that the witches can even meet the gods in the spiritual realm, because the god supersedes the witches. They see themselves as at a distance. There is a *vast* interval. Assuming you even have a witch pass by, the god has to arrest the witch."

Thus armed with the sponsorship and patronage of a deity of the lands, one who can override any interference of the witches, galamseys are emboldened in the face of meddlesome witches who may have attempted to render even more perilous their pit operations.

When galamseys initially go to make the sacrifice, all of the laborers, by custom, are to be there for the ceremony. They propitiate the spirits, make sacrifices, often spill blood, and eat together in a ritual feast. As Kwabena explained:

It is only the blood that the gods need. We offer the blood, and then everyone gathers around in a circle and cooks the meat and eats together, on the land. . . . The meat cannot be taken off the land, even if people feel too full and satisfied to continue eating. The gods taboo that. So, if it is the case that everyone is full, then they must return the next day to continue. If they still don't finish it, they have to make sure they continue until it is finished. . . . They can call others [from outside the laboring group] to join and eat, just that it must be on the land.

The customary authorities, perhaps chiefs or queen mothers, of the lands also must attend such rituals or at least send a delegate. Kwabena continued: "Some of the lands, when you go, you have to go and greet the chief. At times, the chief can just delegate someone to go with you on the land and do the pacification. But when it is dearly necessary that the chief be around, he will go with you for the sacrifice, and sometimes the chief's okyeame, too. It's either the chief himself, or his okyeame, or the chief will delegate someone else to go with you.

In conversations about their regular rituals, galamseys often stress the importance of spilling blood. They will ritually prick their fingers to drop blood every time they hit gold-bearing rock, so as not to offend the spirits by taking the ore without making a sacrificial offering. Okomfo Akua and Kwabena insist that, with the sacrifices of animals at the ritual feasts, it is only the blood that the spirits want.

"What is it about the blood? Why the blood?" I asked. "Some people tell me that it acts as a tonic, an 'energizer,' to the spirits."

Kwabena replied:

> The blood is not bitter. It's not sweet. It's not like a tonic. But then, there's the belief that, assuming you want to build, you need your roofing sheets, you need your ingredients that need to come together, before you can put up something that you call a house. So, what the gods need is the blood, so before they can do it, they have to call upon the supremacy, which is Nyame. There is nothing that you can do on this earth without god, which is the supremacy, giving you the permission to do it. . . . Anything that you want to tell god, you have to tell the spirits. So, suppose I'm sitting here, and I close my eyes, and I say I'm praying. Who am I talking to? I'm talking to a spirit. The spirit will take my prayers to God in heaven.

Both then went on to insist, as they had done many times over, that their forms of worshipping and calling upon Nyame are the same as the Christian prayers to God the Father and to the Holy Spirit. They argued that it is the same ultimate creator god that is addressed in prayer, and they invoked many blood sacrifices found throughout the Old Testament of the Christian Bible. This was much to the vocal consternation and protestation of my Baptist Ghanaian friend who was there with me during this conversation.

Kwabena said: "Even in the Bible, before Jesus Christ, at times when the Israelites sinned against God, and then God might want to punish them. Then, he says, 'No, I won't punish you again, but use a sheep, take a sheep to the altar, make a sacrifice.' To them, God does not take the meat of the sheep that has been taken to the altar. He takes the blood. . . . Even Jesus Christ came to shed his blood for us."

It is through this form of world-spirit reckoning that many galamseys and their spiritual authorities ultimately apprehend the reliance on blood for pacifying the gods and other spirits in the course of ordinary rituals on the lands of the mining operations. This is the case, often, even if they are practicing Christians, whose usual religious authorities tend regularly to rail against practices such as blood sacrifices or the pouring of libations.

Some galamseys reported to me that, when types of selfish juju rituals are executed, it is often that a spell is placed on one or more of the miners. As one young galamsey told me, following a death he had just witnessed, "I have just seen one the other day. The guy went to mine on a taboo day (*Dabone*), when no one else was there, and he died on the land. They killed him, spiritually."

I asked him whether he thought the man had just been trying to get gold while others were not looking, and perhaps that is why he ventured to mine on that day.

He replied, "No, you see, galamseys just don't do that. You don't do that because you don't know what might happen to you. You can meet the gods and ancestors there on those days, and you can die. It was that he was possessed, or that he had this [spell] over him. This spiritual thing led him there. That is how these things work."

At times, one galamsey group may attack another through spiritual means. However, the rules of metaphysical equivalence in these lands state that accidents that occur on another's land will not bring riches to one on the site of one's own operations. The accident must occur on one's own land. Some galamseys are said to go, out of envy or spite or competitiveness, to a local priest or priestess in order to propitiate spirits to block or to otherwise stop the appearance of gold on a rival group's site. Significantly, the leaders of the galamseys' shadow rule Association are said to sometimes deploy such spiritual policing and penalty mechanisms.

However, Okomfo Akua said that she does not perform such rituals: "People do it, but over here, we don't do it. Because with the gods . . . there's a belief that everybody is supposed to earn a living. So, why should they prevent someone's source of livelihood? It's too greedy."

Okomfo Akua and Kwabena also, increasingly, have been helping Chinese galamsey operators who are coming to seek their spiritual support. At first, they said that they refused out of hand to assist the Chinese artisanal miners because they were doing so much destruction to local farms and streams, were flouting local customary authorities, and were treating Ghanaians so disrespectfully. However, as the Chinese miners started to interact more with local authorities in a more appropriate way, some local priests and priestesses would see them, including this couple. As Kwabena explained:

> The Chinese also come now, but they mostly come with their own stuff. If it's a matter of mixes, they come with their own things—perfumes, incenses, talismans. They have it already. They have the powers, so they only can top it up here. . . . They don't carry the gods here, but the gods follow them spiritually. So, when they come, they also have to come and seek the permission of the local gods over here, so that they will protect and guide them. Because they don't know the land, so local deities will protect them to make sure they do their work successfully.

I asked about the rumored rampant destruction of local lands and streams, often at the hands of Chinese-run or Chinese-populated galamsey operations.

How were the spirits responding to this, given that so many of these destroyed things are sacred, and given that the land, gold, waters, trees, and so forth do not even belong to the foreigners or to the foreigners' ancestors?

Kwabena answered: "Yes, in most cases, they work around a stream or a river. But mostly they disturb the stream. . . . So, when it happens like that, then probably the deity of the stream or river will let your machine break down. So, when the machine breaks down, it might not work again. I believe that a time will come that [the Chinese miners] will not work around streams or river bodies, because they believe that, since they disturb the streams or river bodies, their production does not go."

They also regularly provide for individual ritual protections for the galamseys and AGA's underground miners alike—and for AGA management personnel and for many others in town, for that matter. They provide services for purification, sanctification, and pacification (*asubo*) after one has sinned or offended the gods. They also advise on ways to ensure that miners do not approach the gold with an impure body or soul. For example, a man who sleeps with his wife must bathe before going into the mine. Otherwise, he enters the mine impure, and presiding spirits may well kill him—a penalty that they inflict, ordinarily, within two to three months after the infraction.

As opposed to spiritually charged, protective talismans, which tend more to be instruments administered by the mallams and the boka, this Asante priestess and her okyeame tend to prescribe herbal concoctions used for ingesting and bathing.

As Kwabena explained:

We will give them something that they eat into their bodies, and those that they also bathe with. We can give you something that you put in your water, so you are not bathing with a shower, but then you bathe with plastic. You have to pour it into the plastic so that you are going to mix it, and then you bathe with it. And then, mostly, the way it happens [is this]: it may be that you're working there, but you'll be feeling uneasy. You won't be feeling fine. The moment you leave this place, you will see that there is a rock fall. So, because it is within the body, you have the sense that probably something bad is supposed to happen here. When you just leave it, you leave the place and see that a bad thing has happened over there. So, that's why the Christians, they'll also tell you, "Oh, I could hear a spirit, the spirit was telling me." What they call the Holy Spirit. [. . .] Everybody on this earth has a spirit, so if you don't sin, if you are not someone who has sinned against god, at times, you might be doing something and then something will tell you, "Oh, pass this way." You never know if you had passed at where the spirit was telling you that something would have happened to you.

Galamseys and others, whatever their primary faith or spiritual orientation, often will invoke a sense of being guided by such intuition, by a guardian spirit, an ancestor, an angel, or another being of the ethereal realm. In this connection, they are able, at times, to have a presaged sense of their own accord concerning many things but especially impending danger.

It bears noting here that many of the charismatic and Pentecostal pastor-prophets who perform divinatory and other intuitive functions—as they claim, on the pleasure and grace of the Holy Spirit, by and in the name of Jesus—often, like many akomfo, later cannot recall anything that they foretold or intuitively read in conversations with those who consult them. Of course, many in town allege that these pastors channel indigenous spirits or deities and draw upon other more traditional powers. In many instances, powerful pastor-prophets—in Obuasi and beyond—have been found to have buried potent spiritual herbal mixtures in black plastic bags or *asuman* (talismans, objects infused with special qualities for conferring powers on persons and spaces within the vicinity) beneath the floors of the churches, much like the bone relics traditionally buried beneath Catholic altars. They will also use these spiritual powers to help protect and advise.

Such is a common understanding of the veiled traditional powers that, many say, help to power the public displays of prophesy, healing, or other gifts among Christian leaders. Alongside these pastor-prophets, Islamic authorities and healers also continue to play an important—though contested—role in commissioning jinn. This is especially so for those laborers who hail from the much more heavily Islamic northern part of Ghana.

In these ways and in many others, Christian and Muslim authorities, like the traditional authorities, exercise forms of spiritual jurisdiction that support the laboring lives of galamseys, AGA workers, and town denizens writ large. It is the broader spiritual reckoning of dispossession, destruction, loss, accumulation, and reconstitution—this "spirit of the people"—that renders otherwise mystifying and diffuse trauma at least partially legible within local social orders and representational economies. This same collective spirit, or consciousness—however internally fraught with dissonance, ambiguity, heterogeneity, and uncertainty—suffuses the flesh, blood, and soul of informal rule in Obuasi. The numinous and transcendent dimensions may confer pronounced power and authority on informal sovereign realms. The same powers may also enervate or undermine leaders of such groups, as illustrated at the beginning of this chapter, with the untimely death of Baba. Let us now turn to a fuller examination of the informal rule of Christian authorities in town, with their various—at time vying, at times complementary—forms of spiritual jurisdiction over lands, lives, and spirits within their purviews.

3

Pray for the Mine

In May 2009, AGA announced that it was formally disavowing and declaring satanic the corporate mine's long-running practices of pouring libations and making large annual blood sacrifices with prominent chiefs, queen mothers, and *akomfo* (Akan priestesses and priests). Henceforth, the mine would abdicate the traditional ritual responsibilities. In so doing, it would further marginalize those who remained, as most in town believed, the pertinent custodians of the local lands and the principal divine conduits to the relevant spirits and deities. The reason, mine officials explained, was that these traditions in fact courted demons, resulting in meddlesome and, at times, calamitous results for operations. This was at once immoral and counterproductive, as the purpose of the rituals was not only to maintain ties with local tradition, but also to garner safety, security, and prosperity for the mine and for those who labored within its domain.

Why this sudden shift, which was very disconcerting to many in town? Mine officials had heeded the spiritual guidance of prominent authorities from within the Obuasi Fellowship of Churches, the group of Pentecostal and charismatic religious leaders in town. They had joined in prayerful alliance, foregoing much sleep and food, to discern the causes of calamities occurring at the mine. After arduous endeavor, both communal and communing, they reached a collective comprehension of the predicament. The epiphany came after one particularly charged all-night prayer event. It was a matter of received revelation, as opposed to volitional verdict. God had revealed to them—through visions (seen with inner and outer eyes), through speech (heard with inner and outer ears), and through transmissions of the sensations of innate knowing—that AGA must cease its traditional sacrificial rituals at the six major mineshaft openings. These ceremonies that

engaged the customs, ancestors, and local deities *appeared* to function as traditional honorifics and pacification of local traditional rulers, in incarnate and in
spiritual forms. However, the charismatics insisted that God had shown them how
these traditional sacrifices, in effect, were commissioning demons for spiritual
contracts. These dissimulating-yet-nefarious agreements, the church leaders
maintained, were generating gold at the dear prices of short-order injuries and
deaths at the mine. In short, the gold was given in exchange for sacrificial compensations.

The president of the Fellowship, Joshua, explained to me the discernment process over a long, quiet conversation in his family's living room one evening. Kofi,
the key mining activist and also a friend of Joshua through local Christian networks, had brought me to the president at my eager request. I had learned how the
Fellowship was behind AGA's formal disavowal and was determined to learn more
about the spiritual jurisdictions and the contests behind the shift. I also sought to
learn more about the popular understanding that the *galamseys*, so much a threat
to AGA's governance of the mine, were steeped in the traditional rituals. Was
AGA's shift another way to demonize galamseys, with this formulation of a ritual
conversion—the Christian (and, later, Muslim) sanctification of the mine? Would
this spiritual renunciation of tradition and reinvestiture through God the Father,
or Allah, help to tame the spiritually empowered galamsey forces, in the eyes of
AGA managers and of those pastor-prophets who counseled them?

As Joshua, a Ghanaian and longtime resident of Obuasi, described the revelation, his voice morphed in tone and temperament, growing at once firmer and qui-
eter. He was soft yet unretreating in his resolution. He elaborated, with solemnity:

> What we were witnessing was that every time AGA would do the sacrifices, this
> would be followed by so many deaths and other accidents underground. These would
> happen within two or three weeks after the rituals. So, God revealed it. So, it was
> apparent: these acts were the work of the Devil. We spoke with people at AGA, and a
> few of the executives, in particular, listened to us. See, they are also Christian and
> worship at our churches. Thank God they listened, and they changed the company
> policy about these sacrifices. Instead, we installed the Pray for the Mine ceremony,
> twice each year, where we would pray to God for protection, for prosperity.

He further elaborated on their collective interpretation of the deceitful tactics
of the Devil:

> From experience, we realized that any time such rituals were performed, by two
> weeks, into three weeks, after the rituals, there were terrible accidents. Yes. Terrible
> accidents. And sometimes, several people were just slaughtered, were killed, under-
> ground, and the kind of blood that spilled out. . . . We are ministers of the gospel, and
> we know that if you sell your soul to the Devil, sometimes he may deceive you to
> think that he is on your side, that he's rendering services to you. But we know that,

when he stretches forth his left hand to you and declares peace, the right hand will be ready for terrible actions. That is exactly what was happening.

Joshua explained how AGA's chief executive at the Obuasi mine at the time of the transition to Pray for the Mine was a Christian. "He was an Australian, a very good man. And then another man took over, a German. Then, when he left, Kwaku [a Ghanaian] was appointed to take over."

"And they are both Christian?" I asked.

"Yes, and the current one, too," he added.

I was able to speak directly to an executive, Kwame, at the Obuasi mine alone in his office one early evening, after his slew of meetings had ceased for the day. I asked him about Joshua's relating the story of God's revelation about the traditional rituals and the turn to the Christian ceremony.

Serene yet with a wry grin on his face, Kwame pressed, "What did Joshua tell you?"

I explained how Joshua had detailed the all-night prayer circles among high fellowship members, along with the visions, intuitions, messages, and signs whose combination culminated in the collective conclusion: the traditional rituals conjured demons and spelled ill-fortune for the mine and its laborers. God commanded a turning away from them and a migration to the Christian rituals for the blessings of the mine.

Kwame smiled and said, simply, "We just asked them to come together to pray. Pray for our prosperity, our safety, our people. Pray for the good fortune of the mine and of the town. . . . You don't always see it directly, but there is so much behind the scenes. I am constantly fielding calls from the MCE [municipal chief executive], saying the District Assembly is asking for water, fixed pipes, patched roads. More electricity. Free electricity. It is endless. You don't see it directly, but AGA gives so much. It basically runs this town and makes it work. The government does not. . . . We ask for the blessings of God to make all of this happen, to keep it all running smoothly."

Kwame himself is an active participant in one of the most populous Pentecostal churches in town, where he regularly worships with his family.

Kwame offered me a ride into town, as he had to leave the office to get home. On our way out of the AGA compound, once in the car, I asked him about the accusations of dispossession and destruction, and about AGA's recent receipt of the Public Eye Award. He answered swiftly and firmly, "We have done so, so much in these communities, not only town. We have spent very large amounts of money putting boreholes into these more rural communities around the mining operations. We bring them electricity, roads. We are in constant dialogue with their chiefs and elders, who come to us with their demands. We meet them whenever we can. . . . We bring them together with us to pray during these ceremonies. We are all part of one system."

The Pray for the Mine services are a key site where this fictive drama of a truly interdependent and mutually beneficial town–company relationship is displayed. The ceremonies are interdenominational, though most ritual authorities who preach and lead the worship are from charismatic and Pentecostal churches.

I attended one such service on a Sunday evening, after sunset, in May of 2012. The ceremonies and celebrations involved much festive music and dancing, and they took place outdoors at the Lenclay Sports Stadium in the heart of Obuasi. AGA had built this stadium for the town some years ago, and all major sports matches in town are held there. The theme for this "Pray for the Mine" was "Persevering to Attain God's Promise," a line taken from Romans 8:24–25. Various pastor-prophets, local politicians, and mine officials spoke to the gathered crowd, as did the acting Adansehene, the highest-ranking paramount chief for the Obuasi area—although many of the traditional authorities are furious that the mine has abandoned the customary annual sacrifices to the local spirits, ancestors, and deities. They say it is causing so much social disruption and spiritual precariousness in town.

As the highest-ranking queen mother for the area told me, during an informal conversation at her palace's receiving space in the neighborhood of Akrokerri, where the pastor Joshua had introduced me to her:

> AGA formerly would come for us, the traditional custodians. They would come with a bus, for us leaders, and the akomfo. We would do the libations, sacrifices, and other rituals. They would bring sheep, cows, goats, fowls, tiger nuts, and other certain amenities. The gods and ancestors demand these. This is a deep part of culture. You cannot just throw it off and ignore it. . . . Furthermore, AGA never told us why they were stopping. They just stopped the rituals. This is disrespectful to the custodians and the spirits of the lands. We have jurisdiction over the land where they are mining. . . . Now, they [AGA personnel] are saying the Christian ministers say they cannot do the rituals. I am charging my elders to rise up and speak our voices on the matter, to inform the mine officials that we will cite the mine proper if they do not resume the rituals, as we used to do in the old days.

I listened intently and then asked, after a full pause, "Are the ancestors coming to you in dreams? Are they coming through the akomfo? Are they expressing upset about all of this?"

She replied without hesitation, her eyes fierce and resolute as they leveled with mine. She also issued a threat, which she appeared to assume that I might personally deliver to complicit AGA personnel: "It is clear the ancestors are angry. Our *abosom* [deities] are angry. The strongest, Bona, he is angry. . . . We can even remain here, on this land, and do the rites, and our ancestors and gods can still take charge over there. It might come to that."

The queen mother of Akrokerri was not in attendance at the Pray for the Mine ceremony I attended, nor had she ever attended one before. In fact, she said that AGA had always failed to invite her, another flagrant offense against clear customary rules. However, the acting Adansehene (king of much of the traditional land, Adanse), stood on the stadium stage, stolid and restrained. He bore a comportment that may have functioned as a silent protest. He stood solemnly throughout the ceremony, silent and looking somewhat bemused. He was adorned in brilliant traditional cloths befitting a customary king (and not a Christian in such a ceremony), ornamented with very large golden rings and gleaming armbands. He stood stoically beneath the customary umbrella that his royal attendants held over him. He spoke only when the emcee of the event summoned him for remarks—and then with but few words and much regal decorum, as though his cynical participation in the event were just another iteration of the long effort to transfigure the age-old customs, laws, gods—efforts that always, by many accounts, eventually met with futility.

A common plea among all principal Christian speakers in this ceremony was for God to realize that the time has come for him to "glorify himself" by "glorifying the mine"—restoring the Obuasi mine and town to their "lost glory." By turn, many speakers argued, God would glorify the whole nation.

The featured speaker was the municipal chief executive, appointed by the president of Ghana and functioning much like a mayor does in an American city. His speech followed the opening prayer and blessings, along with the readings from scripture, all of which were spoken in English and readily translated into Twi for a jovial audience of around two hundred people from across Obuasi. In his speech, he exemplified the remarkable interweaving of spiritual vitality (especially the Christian valence), economic prosperity, the struggles and symbiosis of the mine and the communities, and ways in which divine forces interact with the political sphere to ensure and safeguard Ghana's international stature as a model democracy. Surprisingly, he invoked the perseverance of a famous American president, Abraham Lincoln.

The MCE greeted everyone with great resolve, bellowing thunderously:

> I greet you all and welcome you to this Pray for the Mine ceremony. You are a great many, including the acting president of Adansi Traditional Council, members of the [District] Assembly, Members of the Obuasi Union of Churches, AGA executives, Nananom [traditional chiefs and queens], presiding members, fellowship assembly members, staff and wives of AGA, members of Shaft FM [the main local radio station], brothers and sisters in the Lord, distinguished ladies and gentlemen, media friends. I begin with this prayer:
>
> > "Trust in the Lord with all your heart
> > And lay not on your own understanding
> > In all your ways, on your way to . . .
> > And he shall direct your path."

It is for this reason that Obuasi Union of Churches has for three-and-a-half years now consistently organized this prayer session for AngloGold Ashanti, in particular, and Obuasi, as a whole. To invoke God's blessing and protection upon us. I therefore deem it a divine privilege to participate once again in this prayer session. [Amens erupt.] This is about the sixth time, and I must testify that each session comes with special lessons and directions. [More amens arise, followed by waves of claps.] And I believe with today's program, everybody gathered here will go home totally edified. Ladies and gentlemen, many a times in life, we battle our doubts and insecurities. We wrestle our fears and hesitations and fight against the disparity between the promise and the current reality. We try to do everything we can to try to keep from getting discouraged. Sometimes, there are things that drain our energy, steal our joy, stretch every inch of our faith, and leave us worn, battered to the point that some don't even make it to the other side, that are missing the mark and foregoing the rewards of their labor. Nananoum [traditional rulers], ladies and gentlemen . . . I believe the Union of Churches could not have found a more appropriate theme for this year's interdenominational intercessory prayer session—"persevering to attain God's promise." You have probably heard this. . . . Try again, and if at first you don't succeed, try again. The dictionary defines "perseverance" as persistence, steadfastness, determination, or resolve. But I like to think of it as *only* a determination of the Holy Spirit. The Bible talks a lot about perseverance, because without it, we will never fulfill our God-given purpose or potential. Even the story of legendary Abraham Lincoln epitomizes the very essence of perseverance. As a young man, Abraham Lincoln went to war . . . and returned as a private. . . . As a lawyer in Springfield, he was too impractical and temperamental to be successful. He turned to politics, and was defeated in his first try for the legislature. Again, defeated in his application to be commissioner of the general land office, defeated in the Senatorial election of 1854, defeated in his effort for his vice presidency in 1856, and defeated in the Senatorial election of 1858. Around that time, he wrote in a letter to a friend, 'I am now the most miserable man living. . . .' But then, in 1860, Abraham Lincoln was elected President of the United States. [Loud claps and cheers resound.] He didn't give up, when it looked as if God gave up on him. He didn't throw in the towel when his life didn't turn out the way he wanted. He didn't whine and complain and throw a fit when God didn't give him what he wanted, when he wanted it. He persevered and received God's promise. . . . For AngloGold Ashanti as a company, you will be confronting newer challenges in the areas of productivity, safety, and community issues. But you have to remain focused. . . . Endure till you pass the finish line. . . . I know you have sunk a colossal amount of money into your mine, and you are looking to reap the full benefits. However, don't be discouraged by the different moments you encounter, but be guided by the words in Galatians chapter 8, verse 9. I quote, "Let us not get tired of doing what is right, for after a while, we will reap a harvest of blessing, if we don't get discouraged and give up." [Loud claps follow.] . . . Staff and workers of AGA, continue in the face of the daunting challenges and remain poised to increase production. We solve community grievances, target safety issues, and enjoy the blissful coexistence with the community. [Amens arise.] In the same way, I wish that the people of Obuasi would be a little more *patient* and support the company to meet its targets, increase profitability, and inspire growth, so that we can realize the development we so much desire. Ladies and gentlemen, 2012 is an election year, and Ghanaians will once again vote in the polls, to be witness to the whole world that Ghana is indeed the beacon of democracy in the West African subregion. [Loud applause resounds.] We have the responsibility to ensure free, fair, and peaceful elections, and the onus lies on us as politicians, political parties, public servants, students, civil society, and citizens to ensure that the whole nation is not brought into unnecessary violence and bloodshed. You may sometimes be pushed to the limit and tempted to react, but let's just remember that we must not be guilty of wrongful deeds in the process of articulating our opinions and fighting for our rights, and let us not seek to satisfy our thirst for power by drinking from the cup of bitterness and hatred. We must forever conduct our struggle on the high bed of dignity and discipline, keeping in mind the story of Lincoln. He endured deception . . . in all this, he persevered, and got elected. . . . Don't ever forget that what matters most is not how many times you fail, but that you never stop trying. And there's a reward for persevering. On this note, I want to acknowledge the wonderful work of the Obuasi Union of Churches to ensure the development of the municipality—spiritually, economically, socially, and all that. . . . I wish everybody gathered here a wonderful evening filled with abundant blessings. Amen. Thank you.

Despite the politic tone and carefully wrought language in the MCE's prewritten speech, relations among those in town, of course, are far from harmonious. Nevertheless, the fervent appeal to faith and perseverance in the face of threats from AGA to diminish investment at the Obuasi mine—or even to temporarily shut it down (which it eventually did in fall 2014)—seemed to breathe new life into the body politic of town denizens, so disenchanted by the declining jobs at the mine, the looming threats of closure, the destruction of lands and streams, and the violent clashes with and among the galamsey forces.

The chairman of the Obuasi Union of Churches spoke next. The Union includes all of those leaders in the Fellowship, but it also includes Christian denominations that are not charismatic or Pentecostal. The chairman is a laconic yet towering presence, seemingly quiet yet very forceful when he begins to speak. He is an Anglican Archbishop, related to the Asantehene (as noted earlier, the king of Asante), and the brother of Sam Jonah, the former Ghanaian chief executive of the Obuasi mine. He also is a former executive of the mine, though, as he told me in a private conversation, his position at the mine became increasingly untenable as the Anglican Church pressured him to swear allegiance either to the mine or to the church. The church prevailed, after a protracted inner struggle that the chairman endured.

In the chairman's speech at this Pray for the Mine ceremony, he resonated with the MCE's injunctions to persevere, work hard, and mobilize across faith lines to preserve and restore the glory of the gold, the mine, the town, and the country. He began quietly, in staid traditional white Anglican clergy garb and with a very restrained, dignified demeanor. His voice rose to a powerful pitch as he spoke:

> I am very humbled to give the welcome address to such an important gathering of such prominent and eminent personalities for the important prayer festival for AGA, Adansi Traditional Area, and mother Ghana. This year's prayer festival is a special one, special in the sense that we are on the verge of winning the battle against poverty, injury, casualties . . . to defeat the enemy completely and attain the promise God has desired for those who persevere. About three years ago and beyond, there were all witnesses, losses of fatalities on the mine, and it was by the grace of God that AGA management found a solution to their problem. That's when they shifted to prayer. . . . God has answered our prayers, and the results have been very, very, very favorable. . . . It is worthy to note that for the past two or so years, things have improved very well. Gold production has improved. Gold price is constantly going up. There has not been much casualty on the mine. I think, for two years, there was not a casualty at all. And we give praise to the almighty God for that. When we look back to the past achievement, then it means the laity of Obuasi and their brothers, Muslims, have been wonderful. We are seeing a lot of mercies flowing even within these men of God. These men of God have persevered and they have attained promises from God. There have been many promises within their ranks, due to their hard work and perseverance. . . . The theme for this year's prayer festival is a special one: perseverance. You attain the promise of God and it is then. . . . Persevering to attain God's promise. What Abraham has promised for all of us, he had to persevere for us. Dear people of God, it takes perseverance to unlock these promises. It takes perseverance, endurance, hard work, and pain to attain the promises God has given us. You must endure and work very hard for it.

When the chairman finished his speech, applause and cheers roared throughout the stadium grounds. The ceremony's band piped up, and almost all of the participants attending entered the open space in front of the stage and danced around in large circles, almost in concert, jubilant, exultant, and praising. This continued for about ten minutes until the event was called back to seated order so that the next few speakers could deliver their thoughts and blessings.

Next to speak was a mine executive, a vice president. He is a pacific and towering presence. He is a Ghanaian who was born and raised in Accra and Kumasi. He is also a staunch Pentecostal Christian and fervent supporter of AGA's renunciation of the traditional rituals. He addressed the audience, appealing to divine blessings and a notion of restoration as multiplication or amplification of the boons of a previous state, rather than a simple return to a previous state. In this way, he obscurely invoked notions of divine bounty and the divine itself as ever-expanding, much like the known universe. He also explicitly linked the potential prosperity of the mine and of the town to that of the nation:

> Stakeholders of ours through the times. I think about three years ago, we started this process, and you fully supported it. And we want to thank you so much for standing

with us. This theme has been chosen for a simple reason. We believe, as a company, that God has given us a promise. And that promise is about restoration. Restoration of the mine's glory, restoration of Obuasi's glory, and, by extension, restoration of our country's glory. And when you talk about restoration, it goes beyond getting back to your former state . . . You read the scriptures and it says that when a man takes one item of yours, and he's restoring, he gives you four times [the amount back]. . . . So we believe that God intends to take this mine way beyond its former glory. If you agree with me, say Amen. [A rush of amens.] So our work is quite simply cut out for us. We want to pray until that promise is fulfilled. Somebody say, we want to push, pray until something happens. Hallelujah! [Amens.] And that is why we are all gathered here tonight. Let's keep praying here, in our churches, and in our homes, and wherever we find ourselves, till this promise of total restoration is achieved. We believe that, as a company, it is not just about our success. We actually only truly succeed when our communities succeed. And that is why we want you to keep standing with us. Occasionally, we pick up hiccups and things in our safety and in our production and all of that, but we also want to state that a bend in the road is not the end of the road. We believe that at the end of it all, God will glorify himself. So, we thank you once again, and let's pray tonight, and let's trust God to fully and completely restore us. Thank you very much, and God bless us all.

Applauses and cheers coursed through the crowd, which was feeling more and more like a congregation.

Next, a discordant moment occurred, when the acting resident of the Adansi Traditional Council stood in his highly colorful and ornate royal regalia. He was next to assume the microphone. He spoke with precision and authority, interlaced with touches of skeptical aloofness. The traditional authority appealed to a more general tenor of thanksgiving and invoked an "Almighty," which, as discussed earlier, is also present in the traditional Akan religion, as the figure of the all-powerful creator, Nyame. Significantly, he also implored all to remember that the galamseys are kin, and that they need the community's help and support:

On behalf of the Adansi Traditional Council, and on my own behalf, I am happy to be part of this important event. This is my second time in two years to attend this event. I thank the almighty for his mercies, kindness, and generosity. First, let us thank the almighty once again, and also commend the organizers of the thanksgiving event. Well done, well done again. [Claps.] Thanksgiving is a communal ritual celebrated all over the world. The significance of Thanksgiving Day serves on a deep spiritual avenue through prayer, gifts, gift-giving. Thanksgiving [Day] originated in America and has spread its way to other continents of the world as well. The idea behind it was to spread peace, harmony, and prayer-hood. For us in Obuasi, I think it is befitting and fair. . . . Everybody, young and old, is taking increasing interest in AngloGold Ashanti. . . . The company employs more than 9,000 engineers, including [independent] contractors, making it the biggest employer in the mining district. It indirectly [employs] more than 50,000, and also I must add that the company adds substantially in the local economy.

AngloGold Ashanti has so many programs, such as rewarding medical care, and it also builds roads and bridges to properly link us. . . . Although our focus today is Anglo-Gold Ashanti, it also means that the thanksgiving event is for all of us because of our stake in the gold. However, there is a certain issue which you know already—that nagging issue of illegal mining. . . . It is an activity that is disturbing everybody. I take this opportunity to appeal to the government to help these small-scale miners to legally set up their own mines elsewhere. I'm urging you all to educate the people on the cause of illegal mining, in your homes, workplaces, churches, and wards. These miners are our sons, parents, friends, and relatives, and they are operating with no regard for safety, and are dying in numbers. . . . Ladies and gentlemen, today's thanksgiving ceremony offers everybody a wonderful chance to set aside time to spend with our families, to enjoy each other's company, and reflect on things for which we are thankful, today, almighty god. Thank you, and thank you once again.

The president of the fellowship, Joshua, was up next, offering blessings and directly invoking the name of Jesus, reworking and constricting this more ecumenical formulation:

Praise the Lord. I salute everyone gathered in the presence of God this night. Father, the time has come for you to glorify yourself. The time has come for you to favor your sons and your daughters. Paul said that the letter of the word came, but the spirit gave it light. He asked the Lord, as your word comes upon your people in the form of showers of blessings, that they will understand the revelations of his word. Although the word brings information, may your spirit so embody, that by understanding, he will be able to write with it. How that we know that which he wants us to know, and cause us to love you more, and as the chief direction, be able to apply that way, and in the end, we'll have a cause and a reason to give you praise. We thank you, in the mighty name of Jesus. Can everybody shout a big amen? [Amens.] Perseverance to attain God's promise. . . . Corinthians chapter three, verses 10 through 15. The challenges of this present time are quite enormous. And the child of God must know that some of the conditions will be favorable, whilst others will be very harsh. But no matter the outcome, God has a sure word for his church and for his people. . . . There's going to be an open door, and, therefore, we should live as those people, and make the most of every opportunity. It is very important for us to understand that in the midst of all of these challenges, that we develop the attitude of perseverance, if we really want to attain God's promise, which will also be the fulfillment of our dreams. . . . In the name of Jesus, through the sacrificing, power, and the spirit, and through the energizing power of the Holy Ghost, that your people will be refreshed, they will be refined, and that from this day onwards, they will spring up from the word, and they will run. They will run! And never faint. And know that in the name of Jesus, that from this day onward as well, whatsoever, by the end of the day, everyone here will have a cause and a reason to give you praise and glory. We thank you, in the mighty name of Jesus!

One last reverend, another Pentecostal pastor, spoke in fiery and imploring tones. He echoed many of the prior messages, but emphasized the sovereignty of

God over the gold and the ever-present need to counteract the manifold machinations of the Devil in the mines:

> Our production goes down, just as the preacher says, never give up. Let's press on. We will get our valuables. Amen. And know everything belongs to the Lord. Gold is a metal. People have the belief that it's a spirit; it's not a spirit. It's a metal. In everything that the Lord has set in place to be useful to man, there's an operation by the Devil. That is why it's also important . . . to break down the values, manipulations, and devices of the Devil on the mines. Amen. The Bible says, when you come to the Lord, and you make a covenant with the Lord, you stay in that covenant. So, I implore the executives of AGA, stay in the Lord. Never consult *any* source for any power apart from our Lord, Jesus Christ. And because you have done this and it continues to be done, the Lord will bless you completely. The Lord, he knows where the gold is. He will lead us there; he will lead us! . . . We have a lot down there to develop. Pray that the eyes will be open, the signs will be out there, so we can get all the riches on the earth that will be there, waiting for us to see it there. . . . Pray for production, unto God, pray for production. Let us enter into the deep ore, and let Jesus pass through. Pray for going underground, and [for] where all the riches are! Pray for safety, of all the workers!

The crowd cheered most animatedly at these final rallying cries.

The evening ended with a decided charge, with many of the attendants saying they felt the strong sense of the Holy Spirit descending upon them throughout the event. Many said that they felt renewed and revitalized. And so the ceremony seemed to serve its intended function, generating a sense of collective effervescence and of greater empowerment toward the causes of perseverance and connecting more strongly to the power and the providence of the divine as the ultimate authority to govern the mine and people's everyday lives.

Shortly after dawn on the day following the Pray for the Mine ceremony, I attended the chairman of the Union, the president of the Fellowship, and other key member pastors as they performed the Christian substitutes for the traditional rituals, making rounds to the major mining portals into the earth. The principal leaders from the council of the local Obuasi Union of Churches, numbering about 20, ventured inside the AGA mining areas. The primary enterprise was to conduct a "blessing of the shafts," conducted with Christian prayers and anointment of holy oil at the six principal shafts. They appealed to God for the prosperity and protection of the mine. As one Pentecostal pastor-prophet explained to me: "This blessing is also most certainly for purification. We must sanctify the mine each year, cleanse it with the Holy Spirit, so that none of the territorial demonic spirits can inhabit the place and cause any deaths or calamities, or affect the production. After we sanctify, they can't even come here. The power of God is absolute. We cast a spiritual fence around the territory by the power of the Holy Spirit, in Jesus' name." This blessing of the shafts ritual closely mirrored the displaced sacrificial rituals with symmetrical timing, placement, pouring of waters and oils (instead of blood and gin), and incantational prayers. According to mine officials and members of the Obuasi Union of Churches, the transmutation and purification of these mine rituals were a resounding success. At that time, Pray for the Mine had been in full swing for three-and-a-half years. Over that time, church authorities and some mine officials maintained, AGA had only lost one worker to a fatal underground accident, in stark contrast to the terrible accidents that would trail the use of the traditional sacrifices each year.

The president of the Fellowship, Joshua, explained much more of the granular backstory, as I sat next to him on the bus ride, with all of the church leaders, proceeding from the center of town into the mining compound for the blessing rituals. He repeated earlier explanations: "Each year, with the sacrifices, terrible accidents would just occur. Sometimes, a lot of people were killed. . . . There would be collapses."

"And those were spiritually related to the sacrifices?" I asked.

"Yes, because if you go there, and you perform these sacrifices, you are stirring up the spirits to work! So they love blood."

"Why is that?" I continued.

"That is what the demons like. It keeps them vital. . . . They always want to see people hurt. So things that are related to blood, things that are related to, you know, pain, anxiety. These are things that forces of darkness like. It stirs them on, it makes them so happy. . . . Certain accidents that are incomprehensible, you know that they can be traced to demonic activities."

"So, there is a territorial spirit behind the gold, but it is not one unified spirit?" I asked, alluding to the traditional beliefs of a deity or multiple deities having prime access to the governance of the gold in any particular physical and spiritual jurisdiction.

"It is believed that in the mining areas, wherever there is gold, demonic spirits will want to take control of it. Yes. Similar incidents occur in locations where they mine. That is what the Devil does. He always wants to take control over the natural resources of any particular area. Because it is gold, a metal . . ."

"And he's possessive?"

"Yes, very, very possessive, because it is gold, a metal. Anything that is related to value, the Devil likes it," Joshua explained, adding that it is the same with oil, gems, other precious metals, or anything else related to wealth.

I inquired further with Joshua and the others about the Christians' absolute prohibition on blood sacrifices. Joshua continued for the group, with several other pastor-prophets listening, "Jesus has already done it. He spilled blood for us. . . . Jesus became the sacrificial lamb. Insofar as he sacrificed for us, there is no need for any sacrifices to be done anymore. So, we operate by faith, on the basis of the word of God, and the name of Jesus. That is it."[1]

I added that I had heard that many miners were still engaging in furtive sacrificial or other propitiatory activities for the gold and other aspects of their labor. Joshua conceded, explaining, "These are their private activities, and they hide when they do these things."

"Do these things compromise the integrity of the sanctification of the territory?" I asked.

"No," he answered definitively, amid a soft chorus of agreement from those surrounding us, within earshot. "Once we sanctify the place, it's sanctified. Whatever you do. . . . Even the sanctification will destroy the rituals and the sacrifices that they do."

CONTENTIOUS COSMOLOGIES AND
SPIRITUAL DOUBLES

Yet all is not so duly settled and serene in the spiritual terrains of broader popular consciousness in town. Local traditional ritual authorities countered that the mining deaths absolutely were still happening; AGA just has not been reporting them. Moreover, several told me that they held troubling and relevant information regarding one high-profile fatality that had just happened, one acknowledged by everyone in town to have happened to a miner working in AGA's underground operations. This happened right before the Pray for the Mine ceremony that May. The traditional authorities maintained that the spirits revealed to them that this death was actually a punitive measure meted out by prominent local deities who felt disrespected and neglected by AGA's recent turn away from them and from the public performances of customary duties under the spiritual jurisdictions.

Others in town argued that the circumstances of the death read more like witchcraft. One woman from the deceased miner's home village told me that the community's rumors held that his death resulted from a spiritual attack issued from within "the house" (fiefoo), meaning from a suspected witch from within the victim's extended family. According to those underground with the miner, this man even voiced a premonition that a rock overhead was loose and could dangerously fall. He told his manager, who disregarded the matter. Only a bit afterward, the rock fell and killed him. Those who were underground with him said it was as though the rock had "chased" him; it was not a normal fall at all, subject to the usual laws of gravity and directionality. As this woman explained to me in a private conversation in a mutual friend's home, "It was also how he died [that gave rise to witchcraft suspicions]. One of the boulders slashed the waist, and the way he was slashed, he was almost slashed into two. And he was on his way to Kumasi, when he died on the way."

Further, she and others added, this miner had had the intuition that something could happen, either through his own ritual practices for spiritual protection, or merely through messages from his own spirit guide, which most believe every human has. It could be a Christian, Muslim, or traditional notion of a soul with intuitive faculties. The essence of knowing is the same, but with varying mechanisms and prisms, different paths into oneself and into connection with the absolute that exists within and far beyond the mundane, earthly, physical realm. This miner's intuition combined with the curious element of the strange, almost animate "chasing" of the rock. The concatenation of socially established facts led most people to conclude that his death was spiritual in provenance, whether it was an offended deity or a bloodthirsty witch who produced it.

The Pray for the Mine events continued in earnest until November 2014, when AGA shut down its Obuasi mine for its temporary maintenance period, which persists. AGA never officially returned to the traditional sacrifices. In addition to the Christian ceremony, the first cognate Islamic ceremony was held in 2013, for the prosperity of the mine and its laborers, many of whom hail from ethnic groups originally located in the North of Ghana, where Islam is much more prevalent. Many of AGA's miners, along with many galamseys, are Islamic, given the long historical and the robust current migratory waves of laborers from northern parts of the country. Many, of course, also remain traditionalist or combine traditional spiritual with these other religious systems.

For those who convert to Pentecostal and charismatic churches, there is usually an active, decisive religious break from traditional spiritual practices—whether from within town or beyond—though, often, residual spiritual ties do remain. As one galamsey boss who engages in customary rituals—though also considers himself a devout Christian—disclosed, in concert with so many others in town:

> Every time I will be visiting the homes of these [Christian] prophets, the ones who will [be] violently shaming the traditional rituals . . . whenever I will visit them, I will come to see signs that they, too, still practice these things. You will see the shrine to the house god and to the ancestors. Even, as so many people will tell you, many of these prophets use the occultic tools, and especially under their churches, or around it, they will bury objects with the spiritual powers. Sometimes, they even will have a deity. A lot of them get their powers of vision from these things. Healing abilities, too. They can do so many things.

Further, the spiritual cartography of the town was very distant to any authentic sense of equanimity and equability. The MCE's speech befogged this critical issue, among others. In fact, spiritual contests and turmoil were appearing to intensify. In many private conversations, Joshua and other pastor-prophets complained to me about the spiritual resistance they endured from many of the miners and the mine management personnel, given the shift to this Pray for the Mine ceremony. As Joshua said to me during one car ride, en route to see the queen mother of Akrokerri, "Some of the miners, too, are very occultic. So, they are not so happy when we go there to pray. They also, in a disguised way, will fight against you. They don't respond so much positively toward you. That is the nature of some of them."

I asked, in turn, "You get direct revelations from Spirit, and then you also will hear from some of the other miners that some of the akomfo and mallams, they were attacking?"

"Yes," Joshua replied.

"But nothing truly bad ever came of it, for Pray for the Mine?" I asked.

"Oh, no, no, no. Nothing! They only sought to sabotage the main program. But it didn't work for them. It didn't work."

"There would be small things, though, right? For example, I heard the lights would go out," I continued.

Though seeming undisturbed by this, Joshua conceded that there had been minor disturbances. "Yes, they tried to sabotage it. And you know, some of the directors and some of the executives, too, some of them are not staunch Christians, and some of them sometimes become afraid of some of these traditional men. So that when they came out with these negative things, it bothered them so much, that they decided to change their minds, and switch back to them [the traditional customary rituals]. That was the strategy. But, thank God, it didn't work."

He elaborated, "The Devil cannot attack the clergy and succeed. These are the vessels of God, and we're standing as ambassadors of the kingdom of heaven on earth."

Joshua also would describe how he and other pastor-healers navigate spiritually treacherous terrains without fear, as they conceive of themselves as one with Jesus, operating as merely a vessel-extension of Jesus's essence. For example, in discussing exorcisms one evening in his home living room, he explained to me:

> It is not scary because you are not doing it by your power. The Bible says [Jesus] gives you power. He enables you. He gives you power when he takes over your life. He translates you. So, when he gives you power, and you cast demons out, you cast demons out in his name. Not in your own name. He is by your side. He takes the lead. So, when you are actually swallowed up by Jesus, you see yourself as a non-performer, that even as you stretch out your hand to touch the sick person, your hand is only an extension of Jesus's hand. It isn't your hand. And if you have that knowledge, and you have that faith, and you know that whoever you are, it is as a result of grace, and whatever you are is because of what God made it, then you depend on the strength of God and the Holy Spirit to cast out demons. Jesus says, "In my name, demons will be expelled." If you cast them out in Jesus's name, they leave.

Joshua had also detailed to me, on several occasions, how the galamsey leadership had approached him and others within the leadership of the Fellowship, asking the pastor-prophets to hold a kindred "Pray for the Galamsey Mines" ceremony for the artisanal miners. It was only fair, galamsey leaders contended, that God's blessings be showered equitably and without bias. Several galamsey leaders also confirmed this request when I asked them. The pastors did not grant the request, however.

As Joshua explained:

They came and asked us to organize a prayer church service for them—pray for them, bless them, and ask God to bless their church and things. But we realized that if we were going to give in, it would be very wrong. Because, one, the nature of their job is such that what they are doing is illegal. They are just encroaching into the lands of AGA. Secondly, AGA is not in support of what they are doing. If you come and ask us to pray for you, and we also pray for you, what is the implication? We realized that we were in support of the wrong things. So, we didn't oblige.

I inquired, "Is it also because of how they usually operate? How they are said to operate very coercively?"

"Yes," he replied. "I just told them it wouldn't be possible. . . . This has happened during the past year."

"Did you tell Kwame [the then chief executive of the Obuasi mine]?" I asked.

"Yes, I told Kwame that these guys came around, and he said, 'Oh, so what was your response?' And he said, 'Thank you, very good.' And I said, 'Oh, so what if we would have done it?' He said, 'Oh, if you would have done it, you would have broken your trust with us.' Because we would have given them even more ammunition to operate. They would say, 'Oh, even the clergy are in support.'"

"I see, because that would give them social legitimacy? Because they're not seen as God-fearing people, generally, right? Even though they might be?" I continued.

"Yes, their lifestyles are even very bad, and they consult a lot with spirits."

"I even hear that they treat it [the spiritual activities] as an operational cost," I added.

"Yes. . . . They consult with the mallams and all these people. They perform their rituals, and they succeed in getting some of the gold and other things."

"So it really does work? Short term?" I asked.

"That is the Devil!" He exclaimed, eyes level, ablaze with conviction.

"Have you ever seen any of the main guys go crazy, yourself?" I asked.

"Sometimes, yes, it does occur."

"So they get possessed?"

"Yes, when they go in for some of these demonic spirits, and they operate with the demonic spirits. And sometimes they hide and perform certain rituals. Some of the accidents that occur underground, I'm told, it is a deliberate action on the part of some of the workers. They do cause some of the guys to die, and by going that way, they offer them as sacrifices," Joshua explained, echoing accounts of many others.

He also detailed some of the harrowing mechanisms of these alleged spiritual crimes. "It is not always done physically, the sacrifice. Sometimes they will. People will go missing. . . . But others, they will do it spiritually. They perform the rituals, the spirits of the people are called, and they appear in their rooms. Sometimes, they appear in water. Sometimes, they appear by the wall, and then, they are asked to stab them, but when you do that . . ."

"To the apparition?" I interjected.

"Yes, but when they do that, they kill them [the persons so conjured]."

"They literally stab the spirit with a knife?" I asked.

"A knife. When the spirits of the persons, the persons you are offering for the sacrifice, appear, either in the water, or in the mirror, by the surface of the mirror, or the surface of the wall, then you will be asked to stab the person."

"Can they go less than killing a person?" I asked, alluding to the many other forms of sacrifice that those throughout town had told me about.

"Yes, and sometimes the people use their own body for the sacrifice. They will give a part of their body for the sacrifice, and when you give that part of the body for the sacrifice, that part becomes affected, negatively. Some use their manhood, others use their fingers, others use their hands."[2]

"What about one eye, one ear?"

"Some can do that, yeah, they can offer any part of their body for that. Those who use their manhood system, it means that, after some time, when you use it, then it means you are not going to produce any children. They will enjoy the money, some of them can marry, okay, some of them can also not marry. But they just enjoy, just for some few years, but later, no . . . it's not lasting."

"They lose their fortune somehow?"

"Yes, at least. Certain houses, after the demise of the person who went in for the blood money, no other person can stay in that house. You can't. Because when you just get in, in the night, you see spirits, moving around, standing there. Or sometimes you'll be hearing, especially those they use for the rituals. Sometimes, they appear, and people complain. We saw them! We saw the spirits! Sometimes you'll be there, you'll hear footsteps in the rooms."

Joshua then recounted his experiences with one such notorious house in Burma Camp, in Accra. The owner allegedly had procured it through blood money. He said a portentous cloud encircles the property. "I've seen the house, but I've not entered before. And I've seen that no one can stay there. So we kept asking, and they kept telling us, that the man used his wife. So, everyone who has stayed in that house has complained that they see the woman. She appears sometimes . . ."

"The wife? He killed her?" I asked, interrupting.

"The wife, he killed her for the money. And sometimes, when you enter the house, you will see the wife seated in front of the dressing mirror, dressing herself, and sometimes, she will just vanish."

"The idea is that they left before their time, so they roam about the earth? They can't rest?"

"Yes, they can't rest in peace. And sometimes, too, the spirits will come after those who used them for the sacrifice."

"To haunt them?"

"Yes."

"So it's a form of retribution?"

"Yes, and even if the person dies, it also occurs that they still remain in the house."

"I've heard that even after death, sometimes they never have peace," I replied.

Joshua explained that, yes, this is true. Even if akomfo or mallams are summoned to do rituals for passing the spirit to a place of peace and respite, the attempts are ineffectual, he says. "It doesn't work."

"So these people are damning themselves to eternal torment, in your understanding?"

"Yes, but they still buy! Why don't you [the person going for the immoral sacrifice] work hard? Pray to God, believe God that he will bless the lots of your hands? Why do you have to kill someone, slaughter someone, for money?"

Joshua then shared, without conveying any names, that many people come to him, confessing such sacrificial sins. When I asked him how he coped with the heaviness of these encounters, he told a story of mercy, embodied signs of spiritual punishment, and the divine scales of justice:

> Well, we only dwell upon the mercies of God. . . . Seriously. We really depend upon the mercies of God. We are God's spokespersons, so we have to speak for God, and dwell on his mercies. Because sometimes it's horrible. There was one guy that we handled some years back at Accra. You could see that the hair on the skull refused to grow. And then, he was also being haunted. And then, one day in church, he entered, and after preaching, he raised the hands. He felt very remorseful. And then he came and accepted Christ. We prayed for him. And after the prayer, he started confessing. His confession was that he was involved in the killings of a lot of people, and then he always was haunted by the spirits of those people, and that has resulted in his hair refusing to grow. So, we counseled him, prayed for him, and then we just believed that God will have mercy upon him. . . . Ever since that time, the hair started growing.

This particular man, Joshua said, had spent many years in the Rawlings regime's security force and conducted many killings, especially during the revolution days.

In fact, Joshua's own father had spent thirty-five years in the military. After Rawlings took over, Joshua's father spent thirteen years as a political prisoner, as he had been serving in the presidential side of the military regiment for Acheampong, who was overthrown during the Rawlings coup takeover. He also had been involved in killings, under order. Every time Joshua would speak of his father, a somber mood descended upon him. Even still, he refused to publicly side with the major political party that opposes the NDC, the successor democratic party birthed by Rawlings when he was elected as first president after the end of his military regime. Joshua refused to declare a political allegiance because, he maintained, it could so easily sway churchgoers in town, and it was not his proper place as a spokesperson for God to be involving himself in political election outcomes.

As Joshua explained to me during a car ride, close to the time of the fall national elections in 2012, "As Ministers of the Gospel, we are careful not to align ourselves with any political party. We have to be neutral. In our churches, we have to be sure to hold a balance, so that in case anyone misbehaves, we'll have the strength to speak to them and talk to them. You know, individually, when we get into the box, everybody has a party that he votes for. But we don't have to come out of the box, just to declare, who we vote for. We're very, very neutral."

Incidentally, many other pastors in town were not so inclined to political impartiality, and they often would host members of one party during major church ceremonies or festivals, promoting them to the parishioners. In fact, it seemed that most pastors had a clear political affiliation one way or another. Joshua was rather anomalous.

Another fascinating facet of Joshua's family history involved his maternal grandmother, who was a prominent *okomfo*. (His family is Asante and Fante.) His grandmother practiced her crafts avidly until close to the end of her life, even after Joshua had converted to Christianity and had begun to avidly campaign for her disavowal of such practices.

He began to tell me the story of his grandmother and his conversion in order to demonstrate to me the necessity of not serving two spiritual masters:

> Once you decide to ignore the ancestral gods . . . . Look, I'll tell you my personal story. My grandmother, she lived up to 101 years. She started as an Apostolic church member. Then, somewhere in 1975 or 1976, she was carried by *mmoatia* away to the bush, and she was kept there for three months. She just got lost. No amount of searching [would locate her]. . . . So, the day they brought her back into the town, they had formally dressed her in their traditional wear, and she was also holding a horse in her arms, and she had become extraordinarily powerful. Very, very powerful, spiritually. She could command things to happen. And when she was dancing, tortoises would be coming from the ground. . . . She could crawl, like the snake, and swallow eggs, and do all kinds of things. Very, very powerful. . . . That is my own grandmother I'm talking about here.

"So, you grew up witnessing much of this? And appreciating it?" I asked.
"Yes, until I accepted Jesus. . . ."
Joshua then recalled his conversion, which happened in a morass of nightmares:

> I was witnessed to by a friend, who spoke to me about Christ. But I didn't accept Christ initially. And I kept experiencing this horrible dream that anytime I slept, I dreamt that I was dead, and I was being buried. Then, when I was put in the coffin and put beneath the earth, and the earth was covered, I felt that this terrible fear was

just all over me. I'd always wake up. Then, suddenly, I would just desire for company. I would want somebody to come around me. There was this terrible fear that waked me, any time I experienced that horrible dream. It was when I was going through such an ordeal that the message that that friend preached to me, some days back, that I didn't accept, started becoming very near to me.

Once he assumed the path of Christ, he also responded to the call to become a pastor in the Church of the Pentecost, which was not even popular in Ghana at the time. He has stayed the course of that path since—thirty-three years in the ministry, as of 2018. But it took him a while to convince his grandmother that she should follow him in converting.

"She had so many powers. Powers to prophesy, to cast spells, to talk to the spirits. She could also cure people with herbs. She had some concoction that was a particular mixture, with so many herbs and things. She would make it in a special calabash. And then, she would place a certain stick into the calabash, and the water would just talk," he recounted.

"What do you mean? You could hear it?"

"Yes, the spirits, she would conjure them through this method, through the water. And you could hear them even with your natural ear, just like we are sitting here and talking right now. I saw all of these things growing up. It was even a source of honor for our family. She would come out in grand ceremonies for the community. People would consult her and even pay reverence to her. It was only later that I came to understand. God revealed how wrong all of this was. I had to tell her that she was working with demons."

"Did she believe you?" I asked.

"Well, not until the very end of her life . . . I got to know God so well, I started ministering to her. She lived to the age of 101. And when she was about 97 years of age, she gave it up, and celebrated Christ."

"And she lost her powers?" I asked.

"Everything," he replied.

He then recalled the story of her casting out the traditional spirit, of her severing the tutelary connection and bond. Joshua was not physically present, but she called him to come to pray soon afterward, and she told him the story of how it had happened:

After she got saved, she asked me to come, so I had to rush down to her. And she gave up this fetish thing and accepted Christ. And I went and prayed for her. At this time, she was lying in bed, and the spirit she was serving manifested itself, and it became a form of man, just by her bedside. Her spirit said to her, "Oh, so you've decided to join these people and that way. If that is the case, then get ready, I'm about to take your life." So, she shouted back to the spirit and said, "You don't have power to take my life. My life, and my soul, my spirit, [are] in the hands of Jehovah." And when she said that, she started shouting, "In the name of Jesus!" And the spirit just exploded, like dynamite, in the room, and she could see smoke, all over the place. And the spirit vanished. . . . After the experience, she called me, to come. And when I got there, she was relating her story to me, and this is what she said. I prayed for her and carried her in the Lord, and I anointed her. . . . She was so faithful to the Lord. She didn't have a Christian name, but upon conversion, she took a Christian name, Grace.

"Wow. And did your family suffer any consequences from this? Did the spirit come to anyone in your family to possess again?" I asked.

"Usually, that is the way, traditionally. These spirits pass down the family line, and, usually, they will come to take another. But it didn't happen this time. We prayed and prayed to banish the spirit and this thing, this line of *akomfo*, from our family. And by God's grace, these spirits have not taken anyone else in our family to this day. This is the power of the Almighty."

As a pastor, Joshua received his own gifts from the Holy Spirit, various forms of spiritual perception and the gift of knowledge across time and without prior information. "As when Jesus was operating what the Bible calls the gift of the word of knowledge. . . . When you possess that gift, God gives you insight into the past and present of personalities. Once it begins to operate, God can use me to say all kinds of things about you. Your present, your past, and the word of wisdom also speaks into the future of personalities. . . . It gives you the gift of healing."

Joshua insists that anyone may receive these gifts, so long as they fully surrender to God. "Provided you will accept God as your Lord and personal savior, . . . Once he becomes the Lord of your life, and his spirit resides in you, he comes to reside in you with a gift. He enables you as a child of god to operate in the supernatural. That is why every child of God, every Christian who has really accepted Jesus as his Lord and personal savior, operates in two dimensions—the natural dimension and the spiritual dimension. Do you understand it now?"

And it is just such gifts that many in town come to tap, for protection, blessings, insights, healings. For resolutions of disputes. For prognostications. Even for locating the gold in the earth.

PASTOR-PROPHETS AS DIVINERS, POLICERS, ADJUDICATORS

As mentioned in earlier chapters, the power of Pentecostal and charismatic Christianity has taken the town by storm since the mid-1990s. This was a time of heightened precarity and much general dispiritedness. Many were losing jobs at the mine and farmlands to surface mining, and there was a general atmosphere of economic crisis—rapidly climbing prices with diminishing opportunities for gainful employment. Many told me that, at this time, there was a prevailing feeling in town of having been abandoned by the traditional gods, ancestors, and other spirits. Where was their protection? Why did they not forestall all of this? Why were pleas for spiritual help remaining unanswered, by and large?

At the same time, the transnational networks of Pentecostal and charismatic churches were flourishing across much of the world, including much of Africa, with ever-accelerating pace and prominence.[3] The churches became prime sites for prophesying and for profiting. Many of the newly unemployed turned to preaching, and new churches of all scales and budgets sprang up throughout the town. Some serve regular congregations of several hundreds of people. Some are solo roadside operations, wherein an inspired pastor spreads the Good News through a crackling, maxed out amplifier.[4]

With this newly garnered pride of place in the community, many church leaders function as quasi-governing authorities for resolving disputes, conducting social policing, and gathering and reallocating resources in town. In these senses, they function as another form of shadow sovereign. Joshua, the president of the fellowship of Pentecostal pastors, explained how many galamseys not only come to him and to others to confess: they also come to the church leaders, on individual levels, for prayers for protection, blessings, good fortune, and counteracting the effects of deleterious spiritual forces. AGA workers and galamseys alike regularly consult pastors for healing, for divine direction (often through prophesies), and for divine revelation to interpret the meaning and significance of certain events.

As Joshua explained, "The galamseys and AGA miners come especially when they are unable to read meanings into the things that happen around them, especially things that are attacking them. And you know, there are certain events that can keep occurring to you, and at specific times, that you find very awkward and not normal at all."

"And they feel it is too much to be chance?" I asked.

"Yes. And so, when the person is not feeling very right, or well, and he feels, 'I will have to find out what is actually happening to me,' some consult the clergy, and they want help from God. That is also the time for you to counsel them, and then give them direction, and tell them what the Bible says about their problem."

The pastors also use connections to the Holy Spirit in order to set and govern territorial boundaries. This can be for forms of protection or for spiritual jurisdiction over a land and operations on it. By the force of the Holy Spirit, pastor-prophets erect spiritual fences or barriers—buffer zones, if you will—against any intrusive, unwelcome, meddling, or evil spirit or person. In this way, the pastors can facilitate spiritual arrests. As Joshua explains:

See, the power of God is such an enormous one, that the Devil cannot stand in the presence of god . . . There are times, you wouldn't necessarily confront [a transgressive person] physically, but even in prayer, spiritually, you can summon the evil workers, and issue commands in the name of Jesus, and they will obey. They will hear, and they will obey. Sometimes you can even erect spiritual barricades, barriers. The minds or spirits will know, they can't go over such barriers. And there have been instances where they have tried to cross, to counter the order, and the Holy Ghost has intervened, and they've fallen. And then, at daybreak, they were exposed. Some of them were exposed physically, as well as spiritually. And they often will disgrace themselves, and then also confess.

In addition to setting and policing territorial boundaries, pastors also routinely adjudicate disputes that arise, in mining and in most other parts of everyday life. The conflicts can be of a spiritual nature or of a predominantly earthly nature.

The role of pastors as shadow sovereigns is especially crucial for those who have turned away from the customary courts and the authority of the chiefs, even where the chiefs have not fallen from traditional rule. The reason is that, from the Christian perspective, all chiefs are possessed by demons who masquerade as stool ancestors and the like. I asked Joshua, during one informal conversation, whether one can ever be authentically Christian and function as a true traditional ruler. He answered without a pause:

> It is very impossible, because of the way that the tradition and the culture [are] set up. You can never be a chief and be a good Christian. Once you are seen to be the chief, even before you ascend the throne, certain rituals and sacrifices will have been performed. A sheep will have to be slaughtered, and the blood, poured on your feet. You have to sit on the blackened stool, and the blackened stool is an ancestral stool that has been dedicated to the ancestral gods. And even the name that you inhabit, as your traditional name for the stool, is given by that blackened stool. It's a demon. It determines your name.

"And then the spirit inhabits you [as the chief]?" I asked.

"It inhabits you. It possesses you," he answered.

"And it's always a demon?"

"Always, always," he replied.

Joshua elaborated on the clergy's adjudicatory functions, pastors as judges with direct lines to the divine, and set within a tiered system of authorities and appeals processes:

> This is one of the chief jobs of the pastor. See, your system [in the United States] is that most of the disputes are settled at the court. Here, in Africa, people will want to take the word of God into consideration before any other matters. And they believe that if there should be any dispute between two Christians, the first person to settle the dispute amicably is the pastor. Not the judge. They would rather come to the church. Sometimes, when you have a problem, you take it to the family elders. You go there first. Then, perhaps, [you] appeal to the presiding church elder. If you are still unable to solve it, it comes to the pastor.

Joshua explained that even those who are not Christian are often disinclined to use the state courts. "Here in Africa, especially in Ghana, people have a lot of respect for the traditional elders. The family leaders, the heads. So, even when they are not members of the church community, they will still want the head of the family to sit them down to settle their disputes. When you come around here, we are not so much into the law courts."

And so, again, we here witness the shadow figures of sovereigns, with all of their pronounced spiritual potency and power. Indeed, in this theater as in the others so explored, these forms of authority largely eclipse the formal legal structures of the state in their centrality and efficacy for most disputes among most people—in the orbit of gold and beyond.

4

Fallen Chiefs and Divine Violence

In December 2011, a much-vilified chief attempted to return to his home village, Sansu, on the outskirts of Obuasi. He was there for the Christmas holiday, he announced, his muffled voice projected through a battery of armed bodyguards. A band of irate youth met him upon his arrival. Many of them were galamseys, heavily armed. Guns, knives, and machetes adorned their rage.

The chief's mere physical appearance was an affront: many in the community had vowed to kill him should he dare return in person. Any time he tries to do so, he comes in a convoy of armored cars, surrounded by guards. On this occasion, livid youth rushed at him. They attempted to remove his sandals, a performative act that would execute his destooling, or formal overthrow. As on previous occasions, violence erupted and ricocheted throughout the village. A small group of those still loyal to the chief counterattacked those who sought his overthrow, brandishing a panoply of weapons and an arsenal of threats. As one villager recounted shortly afterward, "Brother was slashing brother, sister slashing sister. Blood was everywhere, running and running. All because this man had the nerve to try to come."

The sandals remained on the chief's feet, by the sheer force of his heavily armed guards, some say. Others insist that he remains in power by dint of the toleration of the tutelary ancestors and other spirits, who appear to enigmatically underwrite his continued enthronement, despite his transgressions against his people.

Nevertheless, this chief cannot rule the town in any pragmatic sense. He no longer stays in the community, rarely visits, and does not preside over court cases, festivals, funerals, and other principal realms of his would-be sacred office. He hardly even tries any more. Effectively, he has surrendered his reign, although he remains formally installed and continues to cultivate relations with a number of loyal youth in the community, many of them kin or affines. Some of his subjects are less excoriating than ambivalent about him. These latter recall the days of his beneficent provisioning and protection of the village, while also recognizing the drastic enervation of his authority when faced with the might and menace of the mine. They point out that he maintains ties, however fraught or compromised, to the ancestors, on whose authority he was enstooled. As such, he continues to be a pivotal link to the vitality, fertility, and productivity of his people and their customary lands.

This village, Sansu, is the site of one of the most dramatic cases of fallen chiefs in Obuasi. Many of Sansu's residents allege that the chief had enjoyed close ties to AGA and had effectively instigated the dispossession and destruction that followed from AGA's use of surface mining since the early 1990s. They had also charged his predecessor with much of the same. Indeed, many in the village had united to violently overthrow him, burning his palace to the ground. Further, they propitiated the stool's guardian spirits to afflict him with restlessness, insomnia, and other unpleasant maladies for the rest of his life.

None of this is surprising. Sansu had lost much of its farmland to AGA and also had seen the ruination of twenty-three sacred streams, which housed significant deities and spirits. Those streams also furnished fish and, critically, drinking water. In the power vacuum and amid the devastation left behind by the absentee chief, it is the galamsey operators who often perform the customary functions of governance. Sansu is, in many ways, a paradigmatic configuration of the acute social tensions, and the contradictions, that afflict Obuasi. The case of its fallen chiefs is emblematic of broader political, social, and spiritual transformations.

A dramatic shift in customary rule has recently swept Obuasi and its surrounds, in consonance with many of the counterintuitive transformations and resurgences of chiefly politics across Africa. This change has been a somewhat surprising element of many recent neoliberal reforms across the continent, which generally aim to constrain the central state and to delegate authority to nonstate or quasi-state authorities, including chiefs. As Peter Geschiere observes, "There is of course an interesting paradox here: how can one combine a fixed belief in the market as the solution to all problems with far-reaching trust in 'the' community or 'customary chiefs' as a stabilizing anchor? In Africa, this penchant for 'community,' tradition, and 'chiefs' seems to be a logical consequence of a drive toward decentralization."[1] In keeping with these larger trends, Ghana has undergone a revitalization of customary authority with its move toward devolved forms of political rule and the resignification of its bifurcated jurisdictions, a split that is the artifact of colonial and early postcolonial orders of governance.

Far from vanishing from view with a so-called rising tide of "modernization," chiefs around Obuasi have opened up novel avenues and techniques of rule.

Although their positions are imperiled in many ways, changing circumstances have generated the conditions for new channels of patrimony, modes of dispossession, and mechanisms of capital accumulation. Neoliberal reforms have furnished conditions for a new incarnation of rentier capitalist chiefs, chiefs well positioned to bargain with the mining company in ambiguous legal circumstances, often trading land, water, and livelihoods for personal enrichment. Most of the fields and streams in the areas surrounding Obuasi remain under customary tenure. In many of the dispossessed communities, subjects have castigated chiefs for having allowed their expropriation, at times handsomely profiting from it. These subjects allege that their rulers have made unofficial, illicit deals with AGA personnel.[2] Even where this has not in fact happened, accusations persist regardless, undermining the integrity of customary authority.

In the upshot, a number of chiefs have lost legitimacy, although customary legal *authority* as an institution remains legitimate and, largely, observed. Some of the rulers, like the Sansu chief, who have been most compromised, have been formally destooled. While this has been more the exception than the rule, even those who have not been removed de jure, have lost much of their de facto authority. They are seen to have broken their sacred obligations to hold and to serve the stool in trust for the ancestors and for subjects living, unborn, and yet to be reborn.

To the degree that it violates the customary laws of the stool, the chiefs' extraction of rents from both formal and informal mining inflicts spiritual harm not only on themselves but also upon the collective social spirit, including the health and vitality of subjects, ancestors, and local gods. For these chiefs, the lure of riches appears to be *so* strong that gold's auratic, numinous status—as well as the divine imprimatur of customary rule—seems eclipsed by the seductions of private gain.[3]

How can the sacred, dangerous, and enigmatic dimensions of gold help to illuminate the symbolic valence of fallen chiefs, the destructiveness of mining, and communal ruin? How have extractive technologies and shadow dealings led to the decline of chiefly authority in some of the most severely affected communities? To what extent has bodily and environmental assault at the hands of AGA provoked political and spiritual repercussions for indigenous governance and other realms of social life? More broadly, what do mining violence and discredited sovereigns in Obuasi reveal about global forms of accumulation by dispossession under regimes of extractive capitalism with neo-traditionalist banners?[4] As it turns out, an analysis of the sacred dimensions of gold, chiefly power, and the violence of extraction helps to render legible otherwise obscure forms of emergent politics.

The Obuasi case does not involve neo-traditionalist or revivalist political movements, per se, or the creation of the Asante as a newly fashioned economic entity. Yet the commodification of customary resources has borne heavy consequences for the local cultural worlds and for political authority in the penumbra of the mining industry. They have brought new opportunities for a number of chiefs, kings, and queen mothers to voice claims to customary lands in ways that, in effect, commodify them and disinherit their subjects under the ersatz sign of traditional sovereignty. Often, this has had the effect of eviscerating the same customary laws whose sacred authority they purport to invoke. Chiefs effect these forms of dispossession and alienation either through the formal legal system and its land negotiation processes or in the shadows of the legal system, through undisclosed deals with mine management or agents of the state.

The emergence of rentier chiefship, with its political, economic, and spiritual dimensions and consequences, has been facilitated by the most recent incarnation of Ghana's democracy, which emphasizes political devolution and the formalization of land markets—which, in turn, encourage alienation rather than continuous customary title. The same processes that have emboldened chiefs, however, also have weakened them, by leaving them *no real option* to refuse to negotiate with mining companies and their demands for access to land once the state ministry has licensed their concessions. This is to say that what may appear as callous disinheritance on the part of profit-mongering rulers in cahoots with a rapacious extractive sector is facilitated, even encouraged, by the broader economic and legal regimes at play.

CREATIONS AND DISPOSSESSIONS OF THE STOOL

Amid all the devastation caused by surface mining, as I have already noted, traditional authority has retained its significance. This is all the more so because while some land has been sold into family or individual freehold, much of it is still under customary tenure, as is the case with an estimated 80 percent of the surface land of Ghana.[5] The British colonial administration, in collaboration with indigenous sovereigns, established a system of dual legal domains—"customary" and "state," each with its own authorities—as separate, interacting spheres of government under indirect rule.[6] This system remains largely intact to this day, albeit in modified form. As elsewhere in Africa, some features of the customary order were invented.[7]

In Ghana, one of the most pronounced of such inventions concerned land tenure.[8] Under colonialism, a prohibition against alienating stool territory was promulgated and then projected back onto Akan history as though it had been there since time immemorial. In fact, throughout much of the nineteenth century, paramount chiefs gave away stool holdings, and also subjects, to settle public and personal debts. This grew increasingly common with the rise of the cash economy and the emergence of an autochthonous class of merchants and bourgeois proprietors.[9]

There was, however, a deep history of indigenous mining akin to "galamsey." Since at least the seventeenth century, and likely for much longer, indigenous populations collected surface nuggets, panned gold from streams, and dug small-scale tunnel shafts into the earth.[10] Traditionally, there was a clear gendered division of labor, with men digging and crushing and women "washing" the gold, separating it from the other coagulated materials. Indeed, according to many accounts, women—in particular, queen mothers and chiefs' wives—formerly exercised oversight of mining activities.[11]

Mining in the Asante Empire, during the late seventeenth through the late nineteenth centuries, involved some of the most advanced preindustrial underground tunnel systems. They were so dank, hot, and hazardous that it was hard to induce any free labor. Mostly, slaves from conquered neighboring groups conducted such mining.[12] Asante tended to view such hard labor as beneath their dignity. Moreover, the spirits of the underworld terrified most Akan, keeping them from engaging in underground labor in dark cavities in the earth's womb. This gold production fed traders from trans-Saharan trade networks and European coastal exchanges.[13] At times, exports of gold surpassed the violent exports of slaves to Europe. After official abolition of the British slave trade in 1807 and with the dramatic decline in slave exports, the plentiful gold exports helped to offset economic blows and to undergird the continued power and prominence of the Asante Empire into the late nineteenth century.[14]

Gold rested at the heart of the British colonial enterprise, alongside other key commodities. The British Gold Coast was exceptional in colonial history in that its authorities never imposed direct taxation on the population. In the early 1850s, the British administration attempted to introduce a poll tax to cover bureaucratic expenses, but popular resistance swiftly laid to rest any possibility of its implementation. Later, it sought to take possession of the land under an act passed in 1897, but southern chiefs and intellectuals sent an envoy to London to protest it and were successful.[15] Although the state could not impose taxation or control land, it *was* able to levy mining royalties. However, the economic significance of these was greatly eclipsed by revenue from import/export duties, particularly following the rise of cocoa exportation and consumer-good importation in the 1920s.[16] This indirect taxation supported a concerted development initiative, as a result of which the southern part of the country had decent health care facilities, schools, and roads—much better than those in similarly situated colonial contexts.[17] As for the mining sector, the British administration was able to grant concessions to corporations, but *only* in consultation with chiefs, who retained, as they still do, jurisdiction over the surface rights of stool land. Also, of course, this was only made possible after January 1, 1902, when the British formally subjugated and annexed the Asante following the 1900 War of the Golden Stool. At the start of this war, a colonial official, Frederick Mitchell Hodgson, had inflamed Asante by foolishly claiming that he should sit atop their sacred throne, the Golden Stool, an act strictly prohibited by sacred custom.[18]

With the gold industry privatization and the political devolution entailed in recent democratic and neoliberal economic reforms, the position of chiefs and other traditional rulers has been resignified and further entrenched—though not without harrowing controversy, as the start of this chapter attests.

The rule of chiefs is territorial rather than descent-based.[19] However, descent may come into play, and often does, through preferential selection when the queen mother, elders, and ancestors select a successor for a deceased, overthrown, or otherwise indisposed chief. Lower-level chiefs and subchiefs need not necessarily come from Adanse or Asante matrilineages. They may hail from other groups within the larger Akan world. However, the higher-order paramount chiefs, who report directly to the Asantehene, must be Asante. Many of the local chiefs, whether seen as legitimate or not, no longer live in their "traditional" villages, having taken up private residence in various parts of the town. Some live very near AGA's management bungalows or the estates built to provide subsidized housing for its laborers. Some of the wealthier ones even have their primary homes outside of the country.

AGA dominates Obuasi in ways not seen elsewhere in the country, including in the other major deep-pit town, Tarkwa, in the Western Region. Common parlance has it that "Obuasi is the mine, and the mine is Obuasi," also that "the company is like a god" and "a law unto itself." Because it is the principal provider of resources, its informal "social contracts" with town residents and with local chiefs are of great consequence. Not only does it employ a large number of people—both on its own account and through its various independent contractors—but it also participates in the construction and maintenance of roads, schools, hospitals, civic venues, recreational centers, electrical grids, and so forth. Much of the local police force is drawn from AGA's private security ranks.[20] For all the centrality of the mine, however, chiefship—precisely because it has sustained its significance—lives alongside it in an uneasy parallel world. Chiefs and other customary authorities often function as contested intermediaries for negotiations, disputes, and allocations of resources that flow from these formal and informal social contracts between the mine and the town's inhabitants.

In Ghana, indigenous rulers have never been formally incorporated into the state, and thus, in many ways, have never been subject to its direct orders or authorization. Outside of district capitals, their dealings with subjects and with state officials tend to be conducted at "traditional" palaces. Even where their sovereign prerogatives are circumscribed by law, they remain in effective force throughout much of rural Ghana, where the political economies of land use and local governance are central to the lives and reproduction of kin groups. This is true in Obuasi peasant communities, for which chiefs, until recently at least, remained the primary and most accessible adjudicating and provisioning authorities.

Today, in Obuasi and throughout the nation, chiefs control the mobilization of resources, to the extent that they can, through levies or communal labor. They do so either to accumulate wealth in their office, to redistribute it through traditional channels, or to fund infrastructure.[21] They also lobby local, regional, and central governmental bodies, as well as NGOs, for financial support. The more enterprising among them attempt, in addition, to secure venture capital for income-generating projects; some even commit their own personal wealth to these ends. Often, too, they seek investment from development agencies or companies, national and foreign.

The formal division between traditional and state authority is enshrined in the constitution: under Article 22, chiefs exist as *nonstate* sovereigns, holding stools and skins in trust for their subjects. The constitution forbids their involvement in politics, executive activities, or administrative affairs outside of their domains. Likewise, the encroachment of the government into their affairs is forbidden. Although this line is not always clear in practice, there is a popular sense that there *is* one—with very real political and distributive effects for the vast majority of Ghanaians who either live on, or remain tied to, traditional lands. This zone of ambiguity bedevils the efforts both of chiefly subjects affected by mining and of government officials to determine jurisdiction, standing, and regulatory responsibility.

Many of the rulers in Obuasi lament that this dual legacy has sidelined them from participation in the neoliberal economy, especially with respect to land negotiations. In part, this is because *subsurface* rights have been nationalized since structural adjustment, leaving transnational companies to sign concessionary contracts with the state *without* needing first to consult traditional authorities, elected regional government officials (that is, district assembly members), or indigenous communities. When corporations do negotiate with local authorities for surface rights, *after* a subsurface concession is already in hand, they tend to deal more with district assemblies than with chiefs. Further, under prevailing statutory provisions, those who inhabit surface land have no right to debar industrial extraction and its forms of destruction. The law only requires that the mine offer them "fair, prompt, and adequate" compensation, the precise terms of which are left ambiguous, often with tragic consequences for the most vulnerable of the displaced and dispossessed.[22]

Some of the most heated arguments in Obuasi today revolve around what has been "negotiated, agreed upon, and laid to rest," with respect to community displacement and resettlement, claims to land rights, recompense for loss, and the provision of alternative livelihoods. Chiefs are often at the center of these maelstroms. The exact character of early compensation negotiations in the 1990s is contested by various parties, although many people tell a similar basic story. AGA, they say, announced that it had to take over the surface ground so that it could mine; often the company would constitute a committee of local opinion leaders, in consultation with the chief, to preside over the deliberations on behalf of all concerned, but these committees became yet another object of unrest, as many felt unfairly represented. Nonetheless, once an agreement was reached, AGA personnel went about doing the requisite rites with chiefs and ritual experts to pacify local deities and to placate the spirits who govern the gold. Thereafter, the company would come before blasting to deal with the peasant farmers who were about to be dispossessed. Many allege that, committee consultations notwithstanding, in the final analysis the mine dealt primarily with the chiefs, who would walk away with large brown envelopes. Several of the evicted landholders also told me that they did not understand AGA's compensation offers—rather paltry, by their lights—to be negotiable.

AGA officials counter that, after the initial upheaval following the dispossession of Sansu, AGC (AGA's predecessor) enlisted the aid of the state's Land Valuation Board, mentioned in the previous chapter, to determine rates of compensation for the various pieces of land and for the houses and crops that sat atop it. Mine officials told me that the board arrived in 1994 to determine payment for subsequent dispossessions and displacements. AGA officials maintain that the board, then, is to blame for the levels of compensation, which many subjects viewed as inadequate. Mine officials and subjects also alleged that certain chiefs were involved in the valuation process and in the adjudication of contested claims.

Many dispossessed subjects also emphasized to me that, in the early days of destruction, their impressions of the mine as a nationalized organ of state lingered. The mine was, in fact, an extension of the state under early post-Independence republics and under the Rawlings regime into the 1980s, prior to structural adjustment and its denationalization of the mining industry. What the mine decreed was law, backed by the army. Longtime residents of Obuasi often recalled, when I asked about the mine, that soldiers intermittently arrived to "sweep" the town during the days of military rule, especially in the 1980s. As one local politician—a partisan of the center-right National Patriotic Party (NPP), the primary rival to the Rawlings-descendent party, the social democratic National Democratic Congress (NDC)—put it, in casual conversation over lunch with me, alluding to Kwame Nkrumah's mordant text *Dark Days in Ghana*[23]:

> These were the true dark days of Ghana, when the Rawlings military regime would come through. Anyone suspected of stealing from the mine—which often meant anyone that was rich and not a known loyal of the regime—easily could have the house searched and ransacked. The military would take so many things. And the penalties for theft were brutal. The soldiers would take people out in public, in town, and beat them. And I'm not talking normal beatings. They would strap them to wooden planks or platforms and beat them with the ends of their guns. There also were rapes. The military even would rape women in public view, for people to see and witness.

This history of spectacular policing and grotesque violence weighed heavily on the collective memory of many in town, amounting to a "standardized nightmare," a terror rife with spiritual inflections, to be sure.[24] Military personnel were widely viewed as rather inhuman, often possessed by nefarious spirits, malicious powers, or vengeful deities. Such was the legacy of the might of the mine.

These chilling specters were also etched into the psyches of those dispossessed by AGA in the early days of the transition to democracy. One woman from a community that lost all of its farmland—and, ultimately, its chief—to surface mining in the early 1990s told me that, when the company arrived to announce compensation:

> The ghost of the military regime was still heavily with us, hanging over us, somehow controlling our actions. . . . The amounts were very, very inadequate. It wasn't an amount that we all consented to. It was something that the company devised themselves. "We are going to give you this. And it ends there." . . . I was a farmer, and I was depending heavily on the farm. And the farm was the major source of livelihood, so when the farm was bulldozed away, my livelihood was also bulldozed away. . . . Because I was getting money from the produce, and that's what I was using to maintain the family. And when I lost the farm, that source of income also cut off.

This particular community was first affected by violent blasts that left cracks in homes—made mostly of mud and thatch, and sometimes cement—caused by trembling ground or loose flying boulders. Its farmlands also were destroyed by toxic waste leaching from surface mine operations.

In Sansu, the village featured at the start of this chapter, tensions have recently continued to mount. AGA has been constructing a new royal palace at its center, said to cost an ungodly sum. It is unclear how the chief plans ever to inhabit it without its being destroyed. Recall that his predecessor, at the time of his destooling, had his palace burned to the ground. The youth—mostly men, some women— had marched with their heads wrapped in red cloth, like warriors, and encircled the palace, chanting war songs and demanding that he emerge.

"He was not there at the time, but if he would have been home, the youth would have burned him alive," said one man, who had been part of the group. "I'm telling you. The youth. You know, this community is very calm, but when these people start their own thing, you will clap for them. When they decide to do something, nothing stops them."

A local chief insisted to me that the previous ruler of Sansu had *not* actually been removed: rather, in order to avoid the severe ignominy that would attend a destooling, he had elected to abdicate. But his former subjects maintained otherwise. They said that, with the threat of death were he to return, he was destooled. As one explained to me, "We were looking for his life, and he decided not to visit the community again. If he had visited, or if he had insisted that, no, he will continue [as] chief, we would have killed him. By all means, we would have done that."

Many people in Sansu often would tell me that neither the state nor AGA police patrol the area anymore; I never saw a police car in the village. Its residents do not pay for their electricity, and armed youth threaten to deal with anyone who would force them to do so. They say that being hooked up to the company's grid is the only tangible benefit they have seen from mining activity, amid so much devastation, and they refuse to have it taken from them. The local armed galam-seys, in particular, guard the electrical hook-ups. Townspeople view such formally illegal activity as completely justified, a form of what Janet Roitman has called, in another context, "the ethics of illegality."[25] Perhaps the most intriguing thing about Sansu is the emergence of informal governance at the hands of these galamseys, who offer considerable financial support to a community stripped of any reliable livelihood. In filling the power vacuum left by the chief, their leaders, who reside in Sansu, rule alongside the elected district assemblyman and the local council. Together, these authorities occupy the void left by the abdication of customary rule, acting as effective sources of policing, provisioning, and adjudicating.

To add to the tension, the absentee Sansu chief had been asking AGA for jobs for his subjects, this being part of a pitch for the company's social responsibil-ity initiative to hire unemployed youth from communities affected by surface mining. But the ruler has been accused of selling those jobs to the highest bidders in an impoverished nearby community. The Sansu assemblyman told me, "He knows better than to try that here, in our community. So he goes [there, to the other community]. And helps his family. That's all he usually cares to do." Others added that the jobs would last just six months, leaving the laborers "casual," with-out severance rights or other legal entitlements that attach to permanent employ-ment. Needless to say, these rentier practices have outraged the subjects in whose "trust" the chief is supposed to hold the land and other resources under customary and state law.

Another, more recent source of rents is informal mining: rulers extract pay-ments from those seeking access to stool lands—and often to individual and fam-ily holdings that they misrepresent as stool lands—for their own financial gain. Increasingly, galamseys and small foreign companies mine on fields at the out-skirts of Obuasi, citing royal permission to do so. Many of these companies were run and staffed by Chinese immigrants, until the dramatic and violent military sweeps of Chinese operations in 2013. Then, there was a hiatus of many such oper-ations, though they are said to have since returned.

Ordinarily, the rulers, for their part, deny granting concessions to the galam-seys or collecting rents from them. Few believe them. They point out that the chiefs do nothing to stop the destructive activities of these interlopers, who, it appears, hire some of the chiefs' own subjects as poorly paid, badly treated labor-ers. Needless to say, all of this has further exacerbated the fraught relations between communities and their traditional authorities.

REPERCUSSIONS OF THE NUMINOUS REALM

The spiritual realm in Obuasi has registered profound turmoil following the destruction of sacred streams, farms, trees, human lives, and livelihoods. As one would expect in the circumstances, accusations of witchcraft and sorcery have become rampant in the wake of the devastation as people seek to reckon with their misfortune, to find proximate causes for it.

The disruptions run deep. The deities and spirits that inhabit this ecology are said to have grown angry and vengeful. Some of the rivers, in particular the legendary River Fena, can no longer be their home. One prominent priest informed me that it has become so polluted that the gods often do not respond or accept his offerings when he ritually calls upon them. He now gathers cleaner water from a borehole near his home village and carries it, in a sacred calabash, to the side of the river, using it to call the deities. When I asked why they cannot live in the river anymore, he replied, "Can you live in a filthy, polluted place—in toxic things? This is certainly not fit for the gods." The message was clear: that which is not suited for human habitation cannot be a sacred dwelling place for the deities.

Another prominent priestess of a similarly afflicted community told me that the gods with whom she works have also become incensed at the destruction. Some local deities and spirits, she added, have even left the area. Although she does not speak directly with those of River Fena, she communes with the deities of five local rivers, all of which had been adversely affected by surface mining.

"It is true," she confirmed, "that, once a river gets polluted, it is hard for the god to stay in there. So, what happens is that they start moving about. The gods will come out of the water."

She was quick to clarify, however, that the pollution of a river does not necessarily spell the wholesale stripping of its sacred force and spiritual power: "Once a river or stream gets polluted, it is not that it loses all of its power. If you go there, and it's not the time to go there, something may still happen to you. However, there are streams here that we worshipped that have been destroyed as a result of the [surface] mining. We have incurred some wrath as a result."

The priestess, echoing other ritual authorities, stressed the ways in which local gods register their wrath on the bodies of community members, especially those of infants, whose fragility leaves them most open to spiritual incursion. This heaping of spiritual wrath upon the most vulnerable—at times, in fatal script—tends to induce moral panic. The fate of children renders particularly visible the horrors of the violence and destruction wrought on their world. This is not only because elders, chiefs, and parents are seen to have failed to protect the youngest and most vulnerable, itself disgrace enough. It is also because their failure debars them from becoming ancestors in the afterlife, thus also erasing any prospect of reincarnation. In these circumstances, death becomes simple and finite. And, therefore, most terrifying.

At times, the local gods have taken it upon themselves to punish those who have destroyed farmlands, either through AGA's surface mining operations or through galamsey activity. As one priestess interpreted these occurrences:

The gods attack the destroyers. There are cases abounding that indicate that the gods attack those who are destroying the farmlands, especially those who work on the excavators and the bulldozers. Sometimes, they will be working, and the machine will cease for no apparent reason. You will check, and there is nothing wrong with the machine, but it won't be working. Sometimes, too, those who are working, something will just pierce them from nowhere. There is a case where somebody was sitting on an excavator, working, and something, a tree from nowhere just pierced the ears, and he died as a result. There are so many cases. . . . When it happens like that, some of the Ghanaian workers will tell the white guys that it is as a result of this, and so they will go and see the chief, and they will pacify the gods before they will continue the work. . . . Sometimes, the guys will experience slaps. . . . . The operator won't see, but if somebody has a spiritual eye, they will see that that is what is happening. Sometimes, when it happens like that, and they [the persons attacked] go to the god of that respective area, the god will tell them [through a medium], "Yes, I came there to do that."

Despite these spiritual reprisals, many feel that their gods (*abosom*) and ancestors have simply abandoned them. This sense is amplified where the chief has fallen and there is no legitimate custodian of the stool, the sacred conduit for exchanges between the living and the dead. A common formulation is that "the ancestors themselves have changed." People seem to mean this in a broader sense: that ancestors and living elders have not protected the land or prepared the younger generations to navigate the dramatically shifting terrain of the day. Talk of change on the part of the ancestors also seems to index *their* declining capacity to deal with social, moral, and environmental transgressions by means of traditional curses, spiritual arrests, or other penalties. For example, a chief's violations of stool protocols seem not to be cursed as much as they once were; similarly, those who mine or farm on taboo days do not incur the same spiritual sanctions that they are said to have suffered in times past.

In contrast to AGA operations, galamseys *do* routinely observe chiefly labor mandates and customary law in refusing to work during Adae festivals and on Tuesdays (Dabone), a day tabooed for labor by the river gods, Bona (the most powerful local deity, an earth god), the ancestors, and others. As galamseys often work near rivers, this prohibition is crucial. Farmers observing traditional labor taboos also do not work on these days. As Ofosu-Mensah explains, regarding the taboo of working during Adae, "It was believed that the ancestors would punish a miner who flouted this custom by causing him to be buried alive by the earth."[26]

But ancestral wrath, and growing impotence, also has other sources. To this day, those working on stool lands are obliged to render a portion of their proceeds to the local ruler, who receives it on behalf of the stool. This remains inscribed in customary law. The requirement is also part of the duty and sensibility enshrined in an Asante proverb: "Sika pereguan da kurom' a, ewo amansan" (If there is a *pereguan* [a very large amount in the traditional Akan monetary system] worth of gold dust in a town, it is for the whole people).[27] However, miners often flout this rule, to their own and the community's peril.

Traditionally, the spiritual nature of gold was held to possess an all-seeing gaze and to compel honesty in its finder. As Eva Meyerowitz documented, "it was rare for anybody to pick up a nugget on land to which he had no claim, and all gold found was brought to the Omanhene [supreme paramount chief] and the clan chief for the two-third deduction."[28] Each nugget was considered to fall under the sovereign purview of the royals and the spirits who governed the land under which it was found. The land in Akan territories is, in the first instance, owned or ruled by a deity. When a nugget was found, it was presented, by customary protocol, to the state treasurer (*sannaahene*), who divided it into three shares. The Omanhene would then present the blindfolded finder with those three shares in an out-stretched hand. The finder selected one, deemed his "soul's share," which he was allowed to keep.[29]

In current practice, the miners negotiate shares with the customary rulers. These amounts vary widely and, increasingly, are not paid at all. The queen mother of Akrokerri—who, as noted earlier, rules the territory beneath which most Obuasi gold is housed—complained to me that those who mine on traditional terrain tend to give only initial payments and to perform the requisite sacrificial rituals in a perfunctory manner just to pacify the local gods and to call the gold.

"They come, we perform the rituals, and they say they will come back and pay their share when they hit rock, but then we mostly never hear from them again," the queen mother explained. When I asked about physical or spiritual policing, she replied: "We don't have the resources to maintain our own physical police force. We can issue spiritual punishments, and we can send spirits to see what is going on. But usually, the heads of these galamsey groups have hired some of the local youth. These local boys are all my own sons. I cannot be too harsh on them." The queen mother's *okyeame*, her spokesperson, sitting to the side of the queen mother, readily agreed. The flagrant disregard for customary protocols and rituals, they added, had fostered moral decay and resulted in many forms of spiritual disruption.

"It is clear that the ancestors, in particular, are angry. Things cannot continue this way," the queen mother said.

Many traditional authorities invoke the power of the spiritual realm to argue for the sheer impossibility of chiefly corruption. They maintain that while their subjects blame them for misfortunes caused by others or by their own actions, rulers would never misuse funds for private gain for fear of ancestral punishment—especially from the spirit of the stool, who oversees all chiefly activities with a surveillance that cannot be evaded. This is all the more so since, they point out, the chiefs themselves are possessed by these stool spirits, whose personalities they assume.

One prominent ruler, heavily involved in the politics of dispossession, told me how he took on the disposition of a warrior once he was enstooled; this, he said, had been the occupation of the ancestral spirit of his stool during a human incarnation many generations before. In other words, the actions of the chief may be, often are, those of the ancestral spirit who guards the stool in trust for his subjects. Even when his actions are his own, however, he remains under the regulatory gaze of that deity and of other concerned spirits who inhabit the area. If, then, he transgresses the laws of his office—for example, by misappropriating sovereign wealth—the consequences are likely to be serious.

As this same ruler put it, "The ancestors will disgrace you [if you misuse stool wealth]. You might fall sick suddenly, or you might appear in public and start talking nonsense, like a madman. You might be naked. This can happen. They might even ruin your entire life. You might go mad or even die."

I asked him if it were possible to escape ancestral oversight and control. Absolutely not, he said. "They will know, certainly, and you will be punished. Chiefs just can't do it."

By turns, the ancestors are called upon to perform their proper protective and assistive duties. In previous times of crisis, living rulers would sometimes intentionally stand atop stools, thus demeaning or disgracing them. They would do this to rouse the ancestors into action, to cause them to "wake up" to the earthly human realm in order to help their endangered or distressed subjects.[30]

Particularly with respect to ill-gotten gains, spiritual empowerment becomes ever more crucial the more affluent a person becomes. This is not only on account of rampant envy and possible spiritual attacks. It is also because the wealth itself may ultimately consume the holder if his or her spirit is not strong. Given the whims and appetites of wealth—or "hot money," so to speak—there is an inbuilt danger to every get-rich-quick scheme, as explored in previous chapters. The cheating of transcendent time can yield powerful yet also grievous and short-lived results for those who engage it—be they chiefs, miners, or anyone else. Quick-money riches and other ill-gotten gains may swiftly reverse fortunes and may ultimately "eat" the initial beneficiary through death, madness, destitution—or, at the very least, by eliminating any erstwhile gains. Chiefs will invoke this sequence of moral repercussions as the severe spiritual consequences of unjust gains collected under the purview of the stool.

Unfortunately, according to their subjects, many chiefs *are* misappropriating stool funds, all the more so, it appears, over the past couple of decades; *vide*, for example, the Sansu ruler who can no longer return to meet his customary obligations. The current Sansu assemblyman—who, with some galamsey leaders and church elders, now hears cases in his place—explained that "[t]he chief cannot even invite anyone into his house [to hear their disputes]. . . . People take disagreements to us instead. With those things we cannot solve, we push them to the police station." For matters of a spiritual nature, the leaders refer them to a local priest not closely connected to the exiled chief. The misfortunes of the chief's overthrown predecessor, in his later life, are also commonly thought to have been the just result of spiritual punishment, prompted by the betrayal of his subjects, whose lands he alienated to AGA. As one of those subjects recalled, approvingly: "[This chief] was creating problems for people in the community, tormenting them, and people started crying, "Oh, dear god, when are you going to listen to us?" Then, they started calling the gods, "When are you going to hear what we say?" Later, when he was destooled, before he died, there was this boil in the ear for one year. This man couldn't sleep for one year before he died. And he couldn't hear properly."

Other rulers have found themselves in similarly compromised circumstances, with practical, spiritual, and psychic consequences for their subjects. Among the disrupted ritual occasions are Adae festivals, which take place in six-week cycles, each with two component ceremonies: an Akwasidae, held on a Sunday, and Awukudae, held on a Wednesday. There are nine cycles of the Adae in the Akan calendar, of which the ninth marks the new year; these festivals are thought to be critically important for strengthening, renewing, and honoring ties among the living and between them and the ancestors. The latter are fed in the rooms housing the blackened stools that serve as the seats for their spirits. The Akwasidae celebrations generally involve a large pubic feast, though the central ritual feast in the Stool-house—where the ancestral stools are kept and venerated—is closed to all but authorized participants.[31] The chief figures prominently in the rite, representing his subjects in the collective communion with the ancestors. As Emmanuel Akyeampong observes, "The *adae* celebrates one's genealogy. To abrogate it is the equivalent of genealogical erasure or social death."[32] The failure of a ruler to preside, therefore, renders tenuous and uncertain the crucial premonitions, revelations, protections, fortunes, and other benefits that the living enjoy at the pleasures of their ancestors and other spirits. It also threatens their prospects of ascending into the ancestral realm once they die. Such are the complex repercussions of the trauma and violence wrought by the declining legitimacy of chiefship in Obuasi.

What remains of the legitimate reign of the customary in this theater of destruction? Rentier chiefs, violent dispossession, and spiritual disruption abound, largely unabated. To be sure, chiefly authority and disputes concerning it continue to revolve, in many ways, around claims to traditional lands. But these conflicts also throw into relief other facets of contemporary chiefship that likewise are foci of contestation and transformation: notably mining rents, political overthrow, spiritual terror, and the social repercussions of ill-gotten wealth. Chiefship is still very much about land and boundaries, but, especially in extractive theaters, it is about much else as well. The Obuasi world is refashioned by broader cultures of contemporary capitalism, the statecraft of political devolution, and the commodification of ethnic claims and resources. The confluence of these things has begotten a universe of dissatisfied subjects and ruptured social contracts. Those subjects have seized the terms of customary law to unseat or disempower some of their chiefs. In so doing, they have sought to resignify and revitalize, rather than abandon or efface, traditional forms of political authority—centered on the traumatic-yet-productive "vacant stool"—by drawing upon spiritual sanction and the symbolic power of the ancestral realm. People here continue to make appeals to the numinous force that lies behind customary authority, despite earthly betrayals on the part of its living incumbents. Perhaps we might understand these appeals, along with the divine policing of transgressions of the law, as partaking of Walter Benjamin's dictum that "all the eternal forms are open to pure divine violence, which myth bastardized with law."[33] Law, in this instance, refers to manifest earthly laws drawn, in Ghana, from both the jurisdiction of the customary and the jurisdiction of the state.

These new constellations of political life, those that arise in the shadow of compromised chiefs and from the ashes of divine orders, draw upon received sources of sociality and spiritual power. In this way, violated subjects evince their ambivalent fealty to traditional offices, to their transcendent grounding, and, in complex ways, to earthly authority. Through their resistance and their everyday practices, they have begun to forge new futures for customary law, sovereign power, and constitutional democracy in Ghana. They draw strength from demands anchored in enduring moral economies of wealth and in emerging forms of collective action. Here, again, Benjamin's admonition, at once retrospectively insightful and prescient: "Divine violence, which is the sign and seal but never the means of sacred execution, may be called sovereign violence."[34] By revealing the poverty and injustice of so much sovereign violence, wielded by both chiefs and the state, these subjects give voice to a deep-seated sense of entitlement to labor and to a just portion of sovereign wealth—whether they be gained through or in spite of customary rulers.

5

Effigies, Strikes, and Courts

In May 1999, following AGC's successive waves of heavy firings of its miners, a legendary strike roiled Obuasi for ten days. The primary personal object of ire was Sam Jonah, an Obuasi native who had risen from working as a blast man in mines to the top position of managing director of AGC in 1986, with the dawn of neoliberalism in Ghana. He had been the first Ghanaian—indeed, the first African— appointed to the helm of the Obuasi mine. Governmental reformers touted Jonah as one of the heroes of the great financial successes of Ghana's gold-mining industry in the wake of structural adjustment. He had even been knighted by the British Queen for his contributions to African business, in fine neocolonial fashion.

However, Sir Sam Jonah infuriated many in town by, according to frequent accusations, failing to give AGC miners fair pay and benefits, by eliminating much of the workforce with an iron fist, and by instituting the techniques of violently "flashing out" the *galamseys*, the very refuge of so many left unemployed in town. Jonah resolutely opposed galamseys, invoking the uncompromising rule-of-law protection of the private property and profits of AGC, even in areas in which indigenous galamseys already had been operating for decades—and, in some cases, even centuries.

All of this collective fury gathered like a vortex and emerged into the foreground of the 1999 strike. Miners and galamseys joined to erect barricades to the mine's entryways, to bring production to a total halt, and to issue spiritual attacks on Jonah, who was captured in the form of an effigy, if not in his physical person. In the thick of mounting agitation, strikers staged the closure of Jonah's effigy in a coffin. As part of the faux burial, townspeople danced around it, signifying glee in his demise and in effecting his social death. They trumpeted the triumph (however fleeting) of the workers' spirit over his tyrannical rule and his betrayal of the social body of his people. They even took the coffin with the effigy to the graveyard, but did not bury it. Jonah, in physical form, had narrowly escaped the incendiary strike lines, making off to the safety of his opulent home in Accra.

"He would often go and come from his Accra house to Obuasi in a helicopter," one former AGC miner bemoaned, over a lunch conversation with me at home. "When we could barely make ends meet with housing and food, when our wages were low, he would drop in by helicopter, sometimes only for a [football] game. Many of us became furious about this. [He was] one of our own guys, who worked his way up in the mine from the point of a blast man. His mother sold donuts in the market in Obuasi. How could he do this to us?"

In quiet, casual conversation after a church gathering, Kwaku, a brother of Sam Jonah, recounted to me the 1999 labor disturbances and the effigy of Jonah that some of the miners had crafted. "Thank God that Sam was in Accra at the time, that he was able to disguise himself and pass through the strikers and escape. If the miners would've been able to get their hands on him, they would've lynched him," said Kwaku, who was in AGC's accounting management at the time of the strike. Kwaku, having renounced his position at the mine for God's work, is now the local archbishop of the Anglican Church. He also currently serves as the president of the Obuasi Union of Churches, an organization that includes most Christian churches in town.

When I asked him about the stories I had heard of the effigy and ritual burial, Kwaku replied, "Yes, as I said, they made an effigy and celebrated around a coffin. But see, they didn't actually bury it. Okay, he [Jonah] became a little sick. He did fall sick. He was also very stressed and worried. But I don't know what would have happened if they would have actually buried the coffin." Kwaku's tone had fallen low and somber, trailing off, as though to close the topic. The Archbishop, echoing many others in town, also insisted to me that the 1999 strike was, in fact, not really about labor politics but rather about political theater—a pretense, a stage for struggle among elite national party politicians: "[Then President of Ghana] Rawlings had wanted Sam to run as vice president on his reelection ticket in the prior election. Sam refused, because he was busy running the mine and not interested in politics. But Rawlings took offense, and that's how the strike was instigated, and that's also why Rawlings didn't send the military in to crush the strike, as he had in other similar circumstances. The strike was political." Kwaku was implying, in essence, that Rawlings had planted party members to incite the "spontaneous" strike and that Rawlings accordingly declined to deploy the military to quell the strike.

This "unofficial" strike, politically orchestrated or not, had its precursors: informal labor agitation, a rising cost of living across town, and a lack of commensurate wage increases. Miners walked off the job, furious over a package on wage and

benefits that the Ghana Mineworkers Union had negotiated with mine management on May 11 of that year. The strikers understood this new package to contain
no real wage increase, despite a "gift" payment and enhancement of some benefits.
Incensed and mobilized, the strikers blocked access to the mine and, according to
reports of AGC officials, stopped outbound shipments of gold from the mine, disrupted activities at the mine hospital, kept officials from operating pumps that
prevent the underground mine from flooding, and threatened to cut off flows of
electricity and water to nearby residential communities that depend on mine
sources. Stories of the unrest coursed through national media outlets and international industry circulars.[1] Many of the national media sources cited AGC's voiced
concern over sharp drops in production during the strike, which they cast as
$700,000 in daily losses of export revenue to the nation. In a statement that AGC
issued to the national press, the company admonished: "This situation cannot help
government efforts at attracting investment into this country," and "there has
clearly been a breakdown of law and order, a situation which cannot augur well for
the development of the country."[2]

Beginning in 1997, there had been a series of large labor retrenchments, as the
mine publicly lamented large losses, inhospitable institutional and infrastructural
arrangements, and recessionary global markets for gold. Many miners accused
Jonah of engineering this casualization and the mass retrenchments of workers
behind the scenes, largely for self-aggrandizement and to satisfy his seemingly
rapacious avarice. Those loyal to him claimed otherwise, that he was merely striving to conduct good business in a heavily liberalized industry. Despite clear public
revilement of Jonah for specific social malfeasances, he also enjoyed a more
ambivalent stature. On the one hand, miners admired him, even naming a tene-
ment estate after him, in his honor. On the other hand, miners bitterly invoked
him during vociferous strikes as the reason for their hardships and low pay.

In popular coverage of the 1999 strike, AGC was strategically silent on the controversy over the large layoff of "casual laborers," which amounted to a retrenchment figure of around six thousand workers over the course of the late 1990s.[3]
Later in the year, AGC announced that it would "rationalize" its labor force and, in
stages, lay off two thousand of its permanent employees. About five hundred more
casual laborers were laid off over the summer, following the May strike, and then
two thousand of AGC's remaining eight thousand or so shift workers were declared
redundant and received "permanent layoffs."[4]

Both the Union and the mine management called for a halt to the wildcat strike
in May, which Ghanaian labor authorities had declared illegal under Ghana's
Industrial Relations Act. Upon recalling the circumstances of the strike, an Obuasi-
based politician and friend remarked to me, laughing, "You see, the National
Labor Office has to approve all strikes for them to be considered legal. I don't think
they have ever deemed a strike legal, in all the times we've had them."

Others maintained throughout my conversations with them, recalling the events in detail, that this was a political strike and the local Union officials were, in fact, in cahoots with the Rawlings government in instigating it.[5] In particular, many insisted to me that the branch secretary of the Obuasi Ghana Mineworkers Union (GMU) at the time, Afua, had taken a key role in inciting the strike.

Afua, a bold presence with unshakeable resolve, was the first woman to serve as Obuasi GMU branch secretary. I first met her through a mutual friend, a journalist, and spoke with her at length about her work in her living room in Obuasi, where she still resides. She now sells handmade soaps, oils, and other items in town. Afua denied in conversations with me that she had anything to do with a Rawlings-led staging of the strike. "The strike was illegal and unofficial. We, the Union leaders, did not declare it or permit it. It took place despite us, outside of our leadership," she maintained.

However, many involved allege that Afua was acting on behalf of her "political masters" in the National Democratic Congress (NDC), Rawling's social democratic political party. This suspicion was further enhanced in 2004, when Afua was running for member of Parliament (MP) for Obuasi as an independent candidate, insisting that she was not an NDC candidate. However, mysteriously, the NDC later "sacked" her, which publicly contravened her claim that she was not a party affiliate.[6] This was much to the dismay of her ardent supporters, who had taken her at her word that she was not, in effect, backed by the NDC in her candidacy. Her campaign secretary at the time, now also a key mining activist in town, said to me, "We felt so betrayed. I never would have worked with her on the campaign if I would have known she was for the NDC. She claimed she wasn't. I'm not interested in party politics and certainly not in campaigning for the NDC. . . . She's not someone I now should even be talking to."

When I first went to meet Afua to speak with her about the 1999 strike and her role in the Union, this activist was meant to join me, but he cancelled at the last minute without explanation. He later elaborated his falling out with her.

Whether or not subterranean party politics helped to instigate the strike, a veritable maelstrom of public opprobrium swirled around Jonah. As the effigy saga intimates, Jonah, as a symbol of the liberalized mine, has been one of the most divisive figures in the town's popular consciousness. As one denizen of Obuasi put it, "Sam Jonah was ruthless. Just ruthless. All of these flash out problems, they really started with him. He said he would not tolerate [the galamseys] at all. . . . In Accra, they are confused. People like him. They see him as this great entrepreneur. They don't know the realities here. He can't even come to Obuasi without armed bodyguards. And he has to drop in by helicopter."

Townspeople's opinions of Jonah vary, from "opportunist" and ultimate betrayer—some even calling him "the downfall of the town"—to the genius of the resurgence of the mine's productivity, after its languishing state in the early 1980s.

Among the galamseys and the mine laborers, though, the view of him is predominantly negative. Jonah finally left his position in 2004, after AngloGold paid him to do so at the time of its merger with AGC. Many in town told me that his alleged misdeeds have generated an array of curses that afflict him and his family to this day.

The larger atmosphere of the ostensible spontaneity of the 1999 strike bore more than passing resemblances to another seismic strike that shook Obuasi and other gold-mining centers in Ghana in 1947; this strike basically had brought all of the industry's production in the country to a halt. Many who participated in the 1999 strike recalled, in informal conversations with me, that those who were embroiled in it also reminisced about the series of industry strikes in 1947 that culminated in the famous Accra Riots of 1948, which helped to catapult political mobilization for nationalist movements and eventual decolonization in 1957. Many of the songs sung during the 1999 barricades made reference to those days, after which significant gains were made for the average mineworker.[7] Popular memory of the power of strikes in the 1930s and 1940s, in particular, gave force and resolve to miners in Obuasi.[8] This was so even into the 1990s, after which corporate restructuring and new labor legislation had seriously eviscerated labor protections and had undermined formal collective labor power in unions.

CASUALIZATION, INFORMAL UNIONS, AND THE ROAD TO THE SUPREME COURT

Another flashpoint conflict arose around the same time as the strike. Thousands of casual laborers were terminated in short succession in the late 1990s. Many of them were rock drillers and blast men, two of the most precarious jobs. The vast majority discovered, amid rapid termination without benefits and without any union bargaining representation, that they were in fact casual. This was a bitter surprise. Often, these miners had worked the same hours and shifts—indeed, under the same general conditions—as the formal mine laborers at AGC. Over the course of my research, former casual laborers told me over meals and in informal social gatherings that many of them had been working almost continuously for six or seven years. Over this time, AGC had even given the impression to those who *knew* that they technically were on casual contracts that the mine was training them and moving toward formalizing their labor contracts.

The local chapter of the union (GMU) refused to help the retrenched miners—announcing that, as casual laborers, they were not in fact members after all, their histories of union participation and paying of dues notwithstanding. This also came as a shock. A group of the casual laborers assembled an informal (i.e., not legally incorporated) association called the Ashanti Miners Club (AMC), which assumed a shadow governance structure. They elected formal leadership, including a president, vice president, secretary, and treasurer. They also penned a governing constitution for the group. This group took up the case of the casual laborers, and many of them joined the Club's forces. They began with protests against the mine in the streets of Obuasi. The military swiftly quelled these "disturbances." Eventually, in 2001, the Club leadership took their forces in buses to the national capital, Accra, to march through the center of the city. They chanted all the way to the office of the president of Ghana, where they delivered their demands in person.

As Michael, president of the Ashanti Miners Club at the time, explained to me in casual conversation at a mutual friend's house:

> At first, the president's forces deemed us a coup threat and sent some police to arrest us on our arrival in Accra. There were about five hundred of us who had come from Obuasi in buses to march together to the Castle [where the office of the president is located]. I was among those arrested. I learned, also, from the Bureau of National Intelligence officials in Obuasi, who had been monitoring us, that the mine had been trying to portray us as a coup threat, to National Security forces. . . . We had just had the power transfer from Rawlings [the long-time military leader, then twice democratically elected president of Ghana], and the [successor] Kufuor regime was very sensitive to any possible coup threat. So that made them afraid enough to stop us, but once we convinced them that our acts were not for a political coup, but only for our labor demands, they let us proceed.

President Kufuor did not order that AGC and the GMU immediately grant the casual laborers their demands. However, he did commission an investigation by ministry persons working on labor and industrial relations. These forces later produced a report that validated many of the casual laborers' claims of unjust and illegal contractual treatment. The Ashanti Miners Club also made various demands to governmental officials and bodies for further investigation or other assistance for their grievances. These formal complaints to ministries largely went unheeded.

When the political protests and most other formal governmental channels for acquiring redress failed, the Ashanti Miners Club leaders decided to turn to a lawsuit, filed against both AGC and the GMU, the latter for failing to represent them. In an almost unprecedented victory under neoliberal conditions in the Global South, the casual laborers prevailed over AGC in the lower courts. The lawsuit ascended all the way to the Court of Appeals, just before the Supreme Court of Ghana. Fearing defeat in the Supreme Court, the Ashanti Miners Club leaders agreed to a settlement reached out of court in 2010. In accordance, AGA (which inherited AGC's liabilities after acquisition) made lump-sum payments to the remaining 1,217 mineworker claimants in the group. These miners had worked for AGC during the 1990s for various lengths of time, but *all* of them for longer than the periods stipulated by statutory, constitutional, and collective agreement provisions governing limits for the status of "casual laborer." AGC had formally classified them as casual workers, despite periods of continuous employment that sometimes amounted to as many as ten years.

As Michael explained to me, it all turned on locating a matter of simple bureaucratic evidence: "We were able to get the records from the local Social Security office to show that we held continuous employment, that we had been making the regular payments. That was how we eventually got them [in the lawsuit]. . . . AGC had produced record books that documented' shorter work periods, sometimes with terminations and rehires. But most of us had actually been working for much longer, continuously."

The casual laborers were only able to get about a third of their demands, but, according to Michael, the association heads felt as though they had to accept it. Their struggle and various collective efforts had been ongoing since the late 1990s. The case was finally filed in 2003 in the High Court, where the casual laborers won. AGA successfully filed for review in the Court of Appeals. It was already 2010, and the casual workers feared that the litigation would continue for years yet to come.

In a conversation over old case files in his apartment off of a clamorous street in Kumasi, the head lawyer for the case, Peter, told me:

> People were dying. Can you imagine? Dying. They couldn't always eat, didn't have jobs, and often didn't have access to health care facilities. A lot of this was before the new arrangement [the National Health Insurance Scheme and its related enhanced access to medical facilities]. And all of this was still going on. Then, even after the settlement, AGA didn't pay out the money for more than a year—during which, of course, the cedi [the Ghanaian currency] had dropped in value, as it always does. If I have one regret in this case, it is not writing the settlement terms in dollars. I never should have put it in cedis. But I also had no idea that AGA would take so long to pay us. They kept saying they don't have money, and the mine isn't making profits.

Peter trailed off, shaking his head dismissively and casting his gaze downward at the checkered floor tiles. The incessant traffic noise rumbled outside, intermittently leaping through open windows and punctuating our silence. He added, apparently as an aside, "I wish this would have been heard by a human-rights minded court. I would have made so much money. I wish this would have been heard by a court in a place like the US." He then voiced a common idealization of the US court system: "One thing I admire about your place [the United States] is that people take justice seriously. People believe in justice and work for it, at least more than here. And they believe in the system. Here, it's all pretend. People here just go through the motions. And they generally don't care for justice. They care about collecting something on the side, and that's the sad truth. . . . Many of the judges are even drunk.[9]

Michael, speaking to me separately, echoed the lawyer's sentiments about compromised judges and courts. He also related a rationale for the settlement:

We were afraid that, even if we won at the Court of Appeals, AGA would appeal to the Supreme Court. And then, what would we do? We didn't even have funds for living, let alone for the case. We were always taking gifts and informal loans from friends, those who sympathized with us. We were suffering, and we needed to eat. Some of our guys were actually dying. We were fighting for our "human rights" because that is all we had. We tried to bargain for compensation from the mine, we tried to plead with the ministers in government to help us, but no one was listening. We were left with our rights, our lawyer, and the courts. Even our huge public demonstrations didn't really work.

I asked Michael whether they also had been concerned that AGA or the GMU would try to pay off the judges in order to undermine the integrity of the court, an abiding and serious concern among disadvantaged claimants and their lawyers in Ghana. Michael replied, "We could not rule it out. People kept telling us, 'You can't win against AGA. They are richer than the country of Ghana in its entirety. They are a huge multinational corporation and will do whatever it takes to defeat this sort of thing.' They would say that we should just give up [the case on appeal]."

In a separate conversation one evening, riding back from Kumasi to Obuasi, I was able to ask Michael, then a Pentecostal pastor and galamsey, about fearing the company and possible shadow tactics during the drama of the case. He replied without hesitation:

> Of course. And there were attempts to buy us out. They took all of us leaders to the mine hotel, fed us nice food and drinks, and offered us immediate jobs at the mine with permanent status if we would just drop the case. They even offered to move us to a new mine in Tanzania. But I just could not do that, could not sacrifice our men. Our treasurer did cross over, to the mine. We learned he was informing on us. He then cut me off as his friend. I even visited his home, and his wife informed me— after he had me wait a half an hour, can you imagine making someone wait like that?—that he would not like to see me anymore. That was the hardest moment in this struggle. One of my closest friends, turning on me like that.

Peter also told me that, after he had taken on the case, the mine sent someone from the union—which, again, was largely controlled by the mine—to offer him payment to drop the case or settle for lower payment amounts. The man whom the mine sent originally came from the same village as Peter:

> He came and attempted to influence me. The mine was smart. They sent this guy from the same area in the north, and he was from the union, so I could not directly blame the mine for the attempt to influence me. I considered it, as I was in a tough situation myself at the time. . . . But I would have had nightmares, maybe curses. All of that. I would consider it, but then I would look at the list of all these men who were suffering, and I would think, "I just cannot sacrifice all these men." But it was hard. I was not getting paid, and I was just starting out then. I was poor and struggling. But I could not sell my conscience.

Physical attacks and aggressive intimidation were also a central concern. Michael spoke of the general mood of trepidation and caution: "Of course, the mining companies can act in crazy ways, and sometimes, they were doing so. Especially early on, when Sam Jonah was in charge. There was a worry they would just hire people to shoot you or involve you in some accident. But we went on. We were afraid, but we had this saying: You die two deaths—one economic, the other physical."

"Couldn't some people go back to the villages to work the farmlands?" I asked.

"What farmlands? If the guys were from here, and had farmlands around here, most of them had been lost to the mine, too. So, everyone was basically left to fend for himself. And anyway, the money in farming was no longer good. People had become accustomed to the gold money."

Thus, we arrive at the novel cultural politics of precarious labor in the present. Many of the retrenched or dispossessed ended up doing galamsey mining, with loose coagulations of laborers. Even those casual laborers who received payment from the legal settlement between the Ashanti Miners Club and AGA did not gather enough to sustain them for long. The galamsey groups, at first, were relatively diffuse and autonomous, but their ranks were swelling with the rising numbers of those desperate for work in town. When former AGC or AGA miners joined the ranks, they were enlisted as key sources of information as to the location of bountiful gold sites and also for the best means of extracting it with whatever small tools and labor power the artisanal group might have. As we have seen, the galamsey forces and their moral economies of labor have significantly grown in spiritual and pragmatic power, as a novel site of sovereign order and political action. Yet the problem of a fully adequate antidote to the sorrows and trials of contemporary circumstances remains, even in the wake of this uncommon court victory for casual laborers.

Conclusion

Out of the Golden Twilight?

> *Here, Heraclitus, did you find in fire and shifting things the prophecy you*
> *hurled down the dead years; this midnight my desire will see, shadowed*
> *among the embers, furled in flame, the splendor and the sadness of the world.*
>
> —F. SCOTT FITZGERALD, *THIS SIDE OF PARADISE*

The glorification of the mine and Obuasi, for which the participants of the Pray for the Mine ceremony so urgently beseeched the Lord, has not come. In fact, in many ways, things have significantly worsened. In January 2014, AGA announced further, severe retrenchments of the mine labor force and began seriously to threaten possible mine closure at Obuasi. Mine closure could ring a death knell to a town so linked, directly or indirectly, to the economic lifeblood of the mine's activities.

In a deeply disruptive turn for most in the town, AGA announced its decision in April 2014: it would close the mine for a period of eighteen to twenty-four months, during which company officials would put the mine in what they call "care and maintenance" mode, while they "modernize" and mechanize underground operations. In the words of an anonymous AGA management source, quoted in the prominent national newspaper, *Daily Graphic*: "There is still gold but we need a lot of capital and labor restructuring to restore the lost glory of Obuasi. . . . A total of 430 workers were for instance retrenched last year [2013] and it is likely more would be retrenched in the near future."[1]

The Obuasi mine remains closed as of this writing, in spring 2019, though the company recently has announced plans to pour gold again by end of the year. However, all of this remains nebulous and uncertain. AGA has retained only a few hundred employees during this phase.

I had a long conversation with Kofi, the principal mining activist in Obuasi, in Accra in August 2018, several years into AGA's temporary shutdown. Kofi had just finished lecturing at a major interfaith event in Obuasi, where he delivered a talk titled, "Mining the Gold within You," referencing the tapping of the power and the riches of the soul, the golden fire or light (*kra*) of the divine spirit within every human.[2] The poster for the event featured much uplifting, galvanizing symbolism, including the ever-present hashtag that has proliferated on T-shirts, street-side signs, and social media accounts since the mine's shutdown: "#obuasimustnotdie."

As Kofi told me of his event:

> So many of the youth were there, at this talk. Hundreds. And they are so hungry for this message of hope. And everyone is hoping that the mine will reopen. However, I must ask them, "Even when the mine was open, what did it really bring to the community?" We've had this industrial mining in Obuasi for over a hundred years yet we still have terrible roads, dilapidated infrastructure, so much poverty. Why do we expect it to be any different this time, should AGA restart its operations? So, now is the time for people to go within. They must turn inward, and look at their souls, and look at that gold that is already inside themselves, given by God, part of God and his promise. That is the way forward. The only true way forward to freedom, prosperity, and peace. These outward signs of promises, they mean nothing. We must, each of us, tap the gold that is inside of us.

As we spoke for several hours, Kofi unfolded so many stories of the frustration, confusion, and desolation that continuously vex those in Obuasi. Kofi explained that many of the retrenched workers, even though they received payments from AGA for the layoffs, have quickly integrated themselves into the *galamsey* workforce. While the numbers, the organization, and the coercive might of the galamseys have greatly swelled, the violence within the ranks also has increased. Further, the overall enterprise has become much less lucrative, with the rapid decline of global gold prices in recent years. At the same time, AGA keeps entertaining the prospect of reopening the mine, reinvigorating the town with hope, only to return to say, "not yet." AGA roundly denounces the galamseys' work upon the mine's concession as a key factor in its decision not to reopen at this time.

Spiritual repercussions and transformations also abound. Kofi, himself a devout Pentecostal Christian, said that there has been much enervation of the authority of the Christian churches in town. "With all of this loss and poverty, and with all of this rising crime, people are feeling abandoned by God. Many of them are turning again to the *akomfo*, to the ancestors, and to the traditional gods. They are seeking comfort, an easy way out. They feel that God has forgotten them, that God has betrayed them or forsaken them."

"How do the Christian pastors in town interpret all of these changes?" I asked.

"They will often say it is the work of the demons. The galamseys were working with so many demons in their work, and the mine sometimes, too. There has been so much evil involvement over time. In fact, I would like you to speak with one pastor. He has shown me a spot near the opening gate to the main AGA compound, where all of the executive offices are. You know, the one by the gold statue of the miner in the middle of the circle?"

"Yes, of course, I know exactly where you mean," I answered.

"Well, there is a heavy congregation of possessive, territorial demons who are there. They block the entrance and exit of money and productivity. They sap the town and are keeping it down. . . . Even the traditionalists, they say that the traditional gods are angry with the galamseys for misusing the powers, for making terrible sacrifices for quick-money riches. And the same for some who worked with AGA, too. The traditional gods and ancestors are very upset at this misuse, these spiritual crimes. Now, everyone is paying. The town is paying," he explained, with an air of sullen desperation engulfing him.

Of course, this closure has devastated not only mine workers but the more general local economy as well. For example, the suspended production severely slashed the operational budget of the Obuasi Municipal Assembly, the local state-based legislative body. According to a civil society report, the Assembly relies on AGA operations for around 70 percent of its annual property rent mobilization.[3]

As early as 2013, AGA had been hinting at the planned mechanization and retrenchment exercises. In the summer of that year, a mining executive had delivered a public presentation on the Obuasi mine "renewal," in which he explained: "In the short-term, we intend to right-size the operation; and in the medium-term, to transition the operation to a modern, productive mine. . . . The transition to mechanization will, regrettably, also result in a phased process of retrenchments over the next two years due to a combination of decline in gold price, increased overall labour cost, and the increase in other input costs such as power and materials."[4]

Mine management also routinely cited—and still cites—the serious productivity and security challenges that the numerous and often well-armed galamseys pose. The mine officials likewise cite the towering costs of environmental repair and other legacy issues that AGA says it inherited from its predecessor mining company, AGC.

In April 2014, AGA also made a controversial labor-restructuring move in abrogating a contract with a significant local independent contractor, Mining and Building Contractors (MBC), which employed, at the time, around thirteen hundred people in Obuasi, making it one of the largest employers in town. MBC is a prominent underground contractor that had been operating in Obuasi with the succession of mining companies (AGA and its predecessors) for ninety-two years at that time. To the dismay of many in town, AGA brought in a foreign contractor to replace MBC.

In a statement decrying the contract termination, a platform of Obuasi civil society organizations (CSOs) noted that, while AGA complains of falling gold prices and sharply increasing production costs, it continues to employ very pricy expatriates: "The irony . . . lies in the fact that this same company can still afford to employ the expensive services of expatriates, including the payment of exorbitant salaries to them. These costly expatriate employees are brought in to replace the highly efficient locally trained less costly labour that have been executing efficiently the same job meant to be performed by the high-maintenance expatriates."[5]

The Obuasi CSOs Platform also argued that the issue extended far beyond legal contractual matters, into more intimate territories, including social obligations to the workers and to the communities—underscoring, again, the mine's role as a shadow sovereign for the town. Here, we witness the continuing and pervasive pull of the notion of a social contract with the mine in the collective popular political imaginaries in town. As platform members expressed it:

> To us, the fracas between AngloGold Ashanti and MBC goes beyond contractual relationship. It is more of a social obligation which AGA cannot fail to perform. With the current turmoil in the mining industry beginning to bite harder and harder, the people of Obuasi cannot be taken through another round of painful social and economic upheaval because of unfair decisions from AngloGold Ashanti. . . . We appeal to AGA to take steps to reverse their decision to abrogate the MBC contract. Furthermore, workers of the company who have been rendered jobless as a result of the decision should be reinstated immediately so that they will be in a position to fulfill all social obligations to their family and communities.[6]

Kofi, also a leading member of the platform, subsequently said to me, regarding the expatriate quandary:

> Why should AGA cancel a contract with a local company they have been doing business with for the past ninety years or so, and then bring on board a foreign company that knows very little about the Obuasi mine and its complexities? . . . Now they are complaining of a ballooning cost of production. What they have failed to do is to do a breakdown of their costs. For instance, they need to tell Ghanaians what aspects of their operations they are spending the most money on. It will surprise you that while they are complaining of high production costs and therefore [they are] retrenching Ghanaian workers, they are employing expatriate staff [members] in droves. These are expatriates, some of whom earn about $1,000 a day. This money is enough to take care of hundreds of Ghanaian workers every month. More importantly, after a hundred years of mining, there is no skill in the industry you will not get a qualified Ghanaian to handle.

Kofi also complained that most government officials have assumed positions of either silence or vocal support for AGA's retrenchments and plans for the mine's restructuring: "Unfortunately for us all, government officials have turned themselves into spokespersons for the company defending the retrenchment. The Minister of Lands and Natural Resources was on radio last week justifying the shutdown. And then yesterday, the Municipal Chief Executive [of Obuasi] was on the radio rationalizing the retrenchment. I was so angry. Then, the two members of Parliament . . . are silent over the issue."

As AGA is now clearly mechanizing most of its underground operations, most retrenched miners do not expect to be rehired. The redundancy of laborers generated by mechanization is in haunting resonance with the oft-remarked trend of capital to invest and innovate technologically such that, ultimately, much manual labor is rendered superfluous or obsolete—a phenomenon presaged long ago by Karl Marx, among others.[7] Beyond mechanization and the dehumanization of the mine labor, the spectral terrors of a potential future ghost town are weighing upon those in Obuasi. As Kofi succinctly put it, "Many people in town are simply devastated."

This turn of events in Obuasi lays bare the reality that much of the gains won through the collectivized shadow forces—mining advocacy groups, the galamseys' association, and their various religious authorities—are all too fragile, as powerful as they have been and continue to be. Even still, these shadow sovereigns will not fade from view any time soon, of course. The galamseys continue to operate on the mine's concession in droves, the religious and spiritual authorities are as active as ever, and the mining advocacy movements continue, though perhaps in more diffuse forms.

Wacam's closed-door formal dialogue with AGA did result in some compensatory payments for those who were injured or who lost family members to AGC or AGA's violent policing. As Kofi explained to me in August 2018, "This was the first phase: to address some of the human rights abuses. AGA did pay out some money, but then the talks stopped. We were supposed to move to phase two, which would have addressed possible resettlements and payments for people who lost homes and farmlands. Then, the third phase was going to be to find ways to negotiate payments or other redress for environmental damage. However, after phase one, the company temporarily shut down, and all talks with Wacam and affected community members ceased."

Each of these putative gains, of course, now ricochets through a larger structural economic circumstance in which the vast majority of AGA's remaining labor force—along with the majority of Ghanaians in town who worked for AGA's principal independent contractors—have lost their jobs.

Likewise, the "upward adjustment" mining sector fiscal reforms that the national government passed in 2012—in a bold attempt to roll back many of the most severe liberalization provisions and to greatly enhance state revenue from mining—ultimately met with significant and seemingly insurmountable obstacles. This is because AGA and Newmont, two of the three principal mining giants operating today in Ghana, have stability agreement contracts with the national government. These are bilateral contracts that were drawn around 2004, with the administration of President John Kufour, which was generally much more favorable toward business interests. These contracts are meant to shield the companies from adverse fiscal or regulatory reforms that may be instituted by the Ghanaian government during the fifteen-year period of the contract's tenure. Newmont and AGA immediately invoked these contracts, of course, following the 2012 reforms that would have diminished profitability for the companies.[8]

Despite the tenacity (and, often, inscrutability) of these dynamics of raw resource extraction and national revenue diminution, which mirror practices that transnational corporations deploy around the world, the Ghanaian government announced in 2013 that it would force AGA and Newmont to the negotiating table to draw up new agreements that would allow the nation to realize more of the wealth from its gold deposits. The actual renegotiation meetings never truly began. The government did not stipulate a timetable, and, to this day, no final decisions or results have issued from the meetings. In fact, the matter appears to have died.[9] AGA's suspension of operations in Obuasi surely gave much coercive power to its counterargument that it would not entertain renegotiation of the stability agreement contract.[10] Considering the fact that Ghana is Africa's second-largest gold producer, this is a significant loss for national revenue that, in prospect at least, could have been used for the purposes of domestic investment and national development. Exactly how government officials use national revenues is always a separate issue, of course. The point is that corruption, itself a contested definitional category, is often a much less costly issue than these broader corporate dynamics, with significant capital flight.[11]

However, with all of these skilled Obuasi miners—many of them with deep knowledge of ore deposits in town—laid off at once, and with cash compensations from the mine in hand, the galamsey forces have become ever more fortified. Through dialogue and through violence, the galamsey forces succeeded in persuading central government officials in Accra to compel AGA to release some of its concession to the galamseys to labor legally. Yet the galamsey presence continues to be hotly contested, and they are routinely continuing to go underground and into other prohibited zones of AGA's concessions—sometimes furtively, sometimes through openly violent takeover.

. . .

Obuasi remains the site of Ghana's most acute resource conflicts. As this book has detailed, much of this dramatic conflict has been generated by a confluence of processes: the ruination of many local farmlands and streams, the declining legitimacy and power of customary rulers, the extensive (and ever-intensifying) casualization of mine labor, the awakening activities of civil society movements in dispossessed communities, the garnering of the global admonishing gaze of the Public Eye Award, and the rise of the shadow labor force of the galamseys. Crucially, spiritual and religious authorities have served as sources of legitimacy, authority, and power for each of the key forms of shadow rule in their contestations and transformations. Further, the spiritual formations are shadow sovereigns in their own right.

These are the most pronounced features of the shadow worlds forged within the realm of the mine. These critical tensions and forms complicate—and also help to render possible—Ghana's wide reputation as a key neoliberal rule-of-law success story for Africa and for the Global South, more broadly. What appears as sheer violence and devastation in one view, through one level of magnification, appears at another scale—from a distance—to be a comparatively smooth-functioning constitutional democratic order with rising economic prospects. Far from being absent or simply non-functional, the legal orders indirectly help to create and to craft shadow sovereign forms. Shadow sovereigns sometimes enhance the strength of legal systems; at other times, they undermine formally established orders. These shadow forms also serve as sites for new forms of labor, politics, resistance, spirituality, and social revitalization.

This book has examined the many facets of these complex mining conflicts, including the collisions of ambiguous property orders and the ways in which the formal court systems are often rendered inaccessible or irrelevant to those who most need redress. Various forms of shadow authority have arisen to police, adjudicate, supply, and otherwise govern this theater of loss, mourning, and dispossession, fraught with so many forms of impoverishment and death. The key shadow sovereigns of the story have been the mining company, the Small Scale Miners Association, Wacam and related advocacy networks, and various spiritual authorities—African, Islamic, and Christian. Sovereignty has been lateralized, I have argued, in keeping with much of the wider literature. However, within the horizontal, disaggregated forms of sovereign rule (formal or shadow), we see the reinscription and resurgence of vertical, transcendent forms of power that mirror the architectures of the modernist state and also forms of traditional authority.

In contrast to many conventional formulations of the casualization of labor and the evisceration of collective labor power across the contemporary world, we see here a highly original story of casual laborers organizing in the shadows of the law and fashioning formal labor rights to take back some of the wealth that they claim belongs to the people, entitlements that state authorities and traditional leaders are no longer safeguarding for them. The success of the consonant NGO advocacy movements has amplified the collectivized casual labor power of the galamseys, and it empowered the earlier collective political work of the Ashanti Miners' Club.

Perhaps most illuminating are the ways in which these sovereignties and moral economies—all contestations over labor, values, and life itself—are imbued with complex spiritual dimensions. At times, the spiritual powers upend earthly legal, economic, or political formations. At other times, they underwrite or empower them. At yet other times, they are neutral. The spiritual aspects are inextricable from the legal, economic, and political spheres. They are all of a piece, subtly interwoven like the finest of golden cloths, where the stitching is invisible to the naked eye. Here, the most authentic sovereign power is spiritually sovereign. It is that which is just, true, and lasting.

Further, these spiritual figures furnish a vivid portrayal of the vitality of shadows—their potency, significance, potentiality. Shadow authority overrides the usual distinctions made between the sacred and the secular and extends far beyond the usual discussions about illicit "shadow" economies, states, and networks. The conception advanced here disclaims the notion of shadows as ersatz, substandard, or otherwise insufficient versions of more authentic forms—as in phrases like "only a pale shadow of." Here, shadow forms come to life, resurrect, undeaden, and enliven. They even may be said to have flesh and to have souls, as it were. Neither pure representations nor mere projections, these shadows are *figures*, incarnate in living social texts as with Roland Barthes's exemplary authorial spirits.[12] They dance on the graves of their near ruin, much in the way that Aimé Césaire wrote of vitality in the "red flesh of the soil" or the "blazing flesh of the sky."[13] There are echoes here, too, of the classic anthropological and theological works on various African ancestors, spirits, and deities as powerful "shadows" or "shades." We might also recall here the Akan notion of a "shadow soul," *sunsum*, that *part* of a personal soul that is truly mortal, that exists only so long as a person can cast a shadow as an incarnate being. The *sunsum* aspect of the soul is elemental of the earthly human, born and dying with the emergence and the dissipation of each this-worldly consciousness in discrete humans. The Twi word *sunsuma* means, fittingly, "shadow." Some shadows seem finite, ephemeral; others appear to be eternal.

Yet all of this talk of shadows should not eclipse the continuities of the light and lifeblood of the state in contemporary circumstances. The state has not truly receded; it has only shapeshifted. It has activated new points of its vertiginous potentialities.[14] Far from vanishing amid the throes of globalization since the decline of the welfare state and the opening of many formerly protectionist national economies, the sovereign state actually has assumed new ways of fashioning and distributing life and death that are far more variegated and more unevenly emboldened and weakened than the more reductive evisceration narratives suggest. It would be more accurate to say that the capacities of many formerly unified state functions have been disaggregated, with some capacities retrenched and others maintained or expanded.

At times, however, Ghana's neoliberal state appears in hollow forms, spectral screens upon which members of a variously enamored, attached, anxious, or furious populace project desires, fears, and ambivalences.[15] In Obuasi, many of these vexed attachments are transferred onto the more immediately powerful shadow forms of rule—the mine and the galamseys' association, but also to the akomfo, the imams and the mallams, and the pastor-prophets. In these instances, the nation-state itself lies in the background as a more distant, often seemingly fading figure of uncertain power, viscerality, tangibility, and authority.

The spiritual armatures of forms of shadow rule and of the moral economies of labor in Obuasi provide powerful reflections of broader global trends toward re-spiritualization, or re-enchantment, of sovereignty and of political life, formal and informal. This, it is often said, has unfolded particularly in the wake of the desiccation of state-centered programs and amid the flourishing of privatized forms of governance. The hailed re-enchantment is also said to have arisen alongside the decline of formal collectivized labor power and the receding of a hoped-for future of bureaucratic economic planning and population management. As Wendy Brown recently has observed, both neoliberal and neoconservative political logics now draw upon forms of pastoral legitimacy and emphasize an underlying armature of sovereign violence. Brown also argues that the particularly neoconservative variety of contemporary governance templates has become compelling within "a political culture shaped by the late modern decontainment of religion consequent to waning state sovereignty, a sovereignty originally designed in part precisely to contain and subtend both economic and religious power."[16]

Of course, the much-remarked process of late-modern "decontainment" of religion has entailed a *less* stark rupture with immediately prior political forms in Ghana than perhaps elsewhere in the world. In Ghana, spiritual backing of earthly power arguably has never waned or been systematically "contained" by the conceptual and rhetorical itineraries of rationalist political cultures, the projected disenchanted endpoint in the secularizing march of Weber's "spirit of capitalism"[17]— and in the teleology of much of modern social theory besides. In fact, in such settings, one cannot *and could never* convincingly disentangle religious from economic, political, or social life. Kwame Anthony Appiah has argued this powerfully for the Asante case and for African cultures, more broadly, as have others.[18] Yet spiritual authority—while never having been absent—has assumed a resurgence of prominence in novel forms of politics and publics in contemporary Ghana. In particular, spiritual authority has come to underwrite some of the most powerful forms of governance and terror that the newly proliferating forms of shadow authority deploy.

The legal theorist Robert Cover, in his poignant essay on the interpretive violence that imbues all legal orders, examines how defiant negotiations of any legal order are inevitably inscribed in word and in flesh. He draws upon the "miracle of suffering" that attends martyrdom, with its invocations of allegiance to a superordinate Law, honored to death. Here, fealty is realized in bloody script. As Cover writes, martyrdom "reminds us that the normative world-building which constitutes 'Law' is never just a mental or spiritual act. A legal world is built only to the extent that there are commitments that place bodies on the line. The torture of the martyr is an extreme and repulsive form of the organized violence of institutions. It reminds us that as long as that is so, the interpretive commitments of a community which resists official law must also be realized in the flesh, even if it be the flesh of its own adherents."[19]

Within the haunting, hazardous realms of the galamseys, which often result in untimely deaths of young laborers, laboring bodies—unruly yet disciplined— serve as privileged substances for the staging of redrafted symbolic investiture and ethical claims for the relations among the city, the soul, and the sacred. So, too, do the bodies of others rendered dispossessed, impoverished, or superfluous by contemporary processes. The galamseys have gained momentum alongside the broader advocacy movements and spiritual authorities, in order to claim compensation from the mine, the state, and traditional authorities for destructions of lands, environments, lives, and livelihoods. Rather than clamor defiantly for the abolition of "the city"—standing metonymically for the law and for the mine and its backing by the forces of state coercion—these advocacy and galamsey forces seek sustenance through collective shadow forms and spiritual sources, alongside seeking redress from the mine and the state. In so doing, they recalibrate the relation of the city to the sacred so that incarnate souls ultimately might reenter the political life of the city anew.

If the recent eruption of renewed galamsey violence attests to bodies on the line for the rule of the mine's Law—and, by extension, the law of the city, or the nation—then it also illuminates the fissures in the walls of the city, its aporetic openings. This embodied violence fuels a reconsideration of the imperfect alignment between the city and the sacred, law and justice, ethics and metaphysics, representation and desire.[20] To mobilize the social complexes of violence in Obuasi into a narrative that obscures such vacillations and deliberative considerations— in the pursuit of renouncing reason, determinacy, authority, domination—would seem to engage in an interpretive sleight-of-hand that Gillian Rose describes as the postmodern move in its most general—even, ironically, its most fundamental, dogmatic, or metaphysical—form. It would be to indulge, in her words, in "despairing rationalism without reason."[21]

The forceful renegotiation of the souls within the spaces that flow from the disconnections between law and justice, metaphysics and ethics, representation and desire, is what we might call the exercising of a contemporary condition of freedom. As the dispossessed communities, the retrenched miners, and the galamseys continue to gain collective force, despite recent setbacks, and to make ever more compelling claims from the mine—and, more broadly, from the nation and from the global community of onlookers—they are engaged in what could figure as a soulful wailing at the walls of the city. The blood of their sacrifices and the ambivalent tears of their rage run to either side of this broken wall, alternately to the city, and beyond its confines. And when they return to the city to make their claims anew, they enlist the continued realities of vertical rule in political and ethical life, in labor and livelihood. They seek to refashion these forms of rule in order to reclaim viable futures. This social transformation is born of the soulful mediations of their proverbial flesh and blood, deployed in the powerful reformulation of what it means to be free, within and through the Law, in its spirit of rebirth.

ACKNOWLEDGMENTS

The itinerary for this book has been long, and my thoughts have benefited from conversations with a great many people along the way. Some have offered wonderful insights through brief encounters, while other conversations have continued for almost a decade. First, I am deeply grateful to all of those in Ghana who spoke with me, who taught me, and who took me into their lives. In honor of their anonymity in this book, and by virtue of their great number, I cannot name all of them, but I will always harbor profound thanks.

The research for this book began years ago, while I was a doctoral student in anthropology at the University of Chicago. I am very grateful for the many enlightening conversations I enjoyed over those years—and, subsequently, in postdoctoral positions at Harvard and Princeton, and now as an assistant professor in anthropology at Princeton. Many thanks to my doctoral committee at Chicago—Ralph Austen, Jean Comaroff, John Comaroff, and François Richard. Each, in distinctive fashion, offered sage guidance and much illumination across the years, since this project first emerged. During law school and over the subsequent years, Christine Desan has been an invaluable mentor and source of inspiration.

My debts to others are deep and voluminous. I hope that the length of the list will not diminish my genuine expression of great gratitude. For fruitful conversations and exchanges, I wish to thank many, including: Kwame Prince Aboagye, Nadia Abu El-Haj, Deepa Das Acevedo, John Acevedo, Kwabena Oteng Acheampong, Lauren Adrover, Emmanuel Ababio Ofosu-Mensah, Hussein Ali Agrama, Emmanuel Akyeampong, William Alford, Jean Allman, Fernanda Almeida, Alfred Aman, David Amponsah, Andrew Apter, Adam Ashforth, Raymond Atuguba, Mark Auslander, Andrea Ballestero, J.M. Barreto, Shadi Bartsch-Zimmer, Yota Batsaki, Sven Beckert, Naor Ben-Yehoyada, Synnøve Kristine Nepstad Bendixsen, Peter Benson, Bjørn Bertelsen, David Bholat, Chris Bloechl, Laura Bloechl, Rob Blunt, Lawrence Bobo, Lady Booth Olson, Brian Brazeal, Keith Breckenridge, Vigdis Broch-Due, Vince Brown, Ella Butler, Annalisa Butticci, Lee Cabatingan, Filipe Calvão, Steve Caton, Anne

Ch'ien, Brenda Chalfin, Kerry Chance, Diane Ciekawy, M. Kamari Clarke, Jennifer Cole, Sue Cook, Natalja Czarnecki, Cindy Daase, Dennis Davis, Marisol de la Cadena, Zebulon York Dingley, Darja Djordjevic, Sean Dowdy, Bernard Dubbeld, Nate Ela, Carrie Elkins, Kojo Richard Ellimah, Holly Ellis, Harri Englund, Judy Farquhar, Paja Faudree, Ali Feiser, Jim Ferguson, Mariane Ferme, Elizabeth Ferry, Kim Fortun, Duana Fullwiley, Angela Garcia, Claudia Gastrow, Skip Gates, Peter Geschiere, Genevieve Godbout, Brian Goldstone, Casey Golomski, Alex Golub, Ørnulf T. Gulbrandsen, Jane Guyer, Rosalind Hackett, Janet Halley, Patricia Hania, William Hanks, Anita Hannig, Thomas Blom Hansen, Kristyn Hara, Bernard Harcourt, Michael Herzfeld, Yaqub Hilal, Gavin Hilson, Daniel Hoffman, Pablo Holmes, Britta Ingebretson, Rachel Jean-Baptiste, Peter Just, Jeffrey Kahn, Sohini Karr, Webb Keane, John Kelly, David Kennedy, Duncan Kennedy, David Kertzer, Stuart Kirsch, Matthew Knisley, Eduardo Kohn, Kwasi Konadu, Afiba Ruby Kumordzie, Brian Larkin, Frederick M. Lawrence, Kathy Lawrence, Hilary Leathem, Krishna Lewis, Sarah Lewis, Philip Liste, Julie Livingston, Kate Ludwig, Tanya Luhrmann, Sabine Lunig, Catherine Lutz, Anne-Maria Makhulu, Liisa Malkki, Anna Katharina Mangold, Jane Manners, Joseph Masco, Adeline Masquelier, Heidi Matthews, Jean-Christophe Maur, William Mazzarella, Achille Mbembe, Mike McGovern, Kate McHarry, Amy McLachlan, George Paul Meiu, Ben Mensah, Birgit Meyer, Patrice Michaels, Martha Minow, Ingrid Monson, Donald Moore, Erin Moore, Sally Falk Moore, Meghan Morris, Rosalind Morris, Valentina Napolitano, Jacob Olupona, Emily Osborn, Stephan Palmié, Peter Pels, Jeremy Perelman, Jemima Pierre, Charlie Piot, Moishe Postone, Elizabeth Povinelli, Michael Puett, Ato Quayson, Jothie Rajah, Kaushik Sunder Rajan, Michael Ralph, Kate Ramsey, William Reno, Justin Richland, Annelise Riles, Richard Roberts, Mary Robertson, Nick Robinson, Janet Roitman, Adam Sargent, Ellen Schattschneider, Caroline Schuster, Jay Schutte, Manuel Schwab, Rosalind Shaw, Chris Sheklian, Jesse Shipley, Parker Shipton, Michael Silverstein, Bhrigupati Singh, Olaf H. Smedal, Daniel Jordan Smith, Jim Smith, Jay Sosa, Michael Taussig, Brandon Terry, Deborah Thomas, Umut Turem, Gary Urton, Lydia Walker, Charlotte Walker-Said, Michael Watts, Britta Weiffen, Brad Weiss, Joey Weiss, Delia Wendel, Laura West, Hylton White, Lucie White, David C. Williams, Susan H. Williams, Abby Wolf, Eric Adjei Yaw, Shirley Yeung, Xiao-bo Yuan, Tyler Zoanni, and Peer Zumbansen.

My colleagues at Princeton have provided a most inspiring intellectual community and an ideal space for scholarly discourse. I am grateful to so many, including: Wendy Belcher, Aisha Beliso-de Jesús, Mark Beissinger, João Biehl, Wayne Bivens-Tatum, Jim Boon, John Borneman, Amy Borovoy, Isabelle Clark-Decès, Elizabeth Davis, Jacob Dlamini, Gabriela Drinovan, Juliana Dweck, Julia Elyachar, Hannah Essien, Didier Fassin, Carol Greenhouse, Abdellah Hammoudi, Mary Harper, Dirk Hartog, Jeff Himpele, Amy Krauss, Emmanuel Kreike, Jeremiah LaMontagne, Melissa Lane, Satyel Larson, Rena Lederman, Patty Lieb, Florian Lionnet, Janet Monge, Ryo Morimoto, Mahiri Mwita, Chika Okeke-Agulu, Serguei Oushakine, Bridget Purcell, Erin Raffety, Laurence Ralph, Lawrence Rosen, Carolyn Rouse, Perry Sherouse, Kim Lane Scheppele, Susan Stewart, Nomi Stone, Beate Witzler, Mo Lin Yee, and Carol Zanca. Before starting my professorship at Princeton, I learned a great deal during a year as a postdoctoral research fellow at the Princeton Institute for International and Regional Studies. Before this, I greatly benefited from a year as a lecturer in law at Harvard Law School and as a lecturer in social studies at Harvard College, as well as from an ongoing fellowship at the W. E. B. Du Bois Research Institute for African and African American Research in the Hutchins Center at Harvard. During my first year as an assistant professor at Princeton, I was enriched by my participation as a faculty fellow in the Fung Global Fellows Program. I also constantly learn from my faculty affiliations with the Program in African Studies and the Program in Law and Public Affairs (LAPA) at Princeton, as well as from my external faculty membership at the Stevanovich Institute on the Formation of Knowledge at the University of Chicago. I owe thanks to all of those involved in these communities, as well as to the undergraduate and graduate students I have taught at these institutions. These people are too numerous to name, but I have learned so much from so many of them.

I am very grateful to the reviewers and editors at the University of California Press. This book was enriched by deeply insightful reviews from Jesse Shipley and Jim Smith, as well as from an anonymous review from the faculty board. Editors from the press—Dore Brown, Kate Marshall, and Enrique Ochoa-Kaup—provided greatly clarifying and insightful advice at all turns. Gary J. Hamel provided a truly excellent copyedit of the book. I also am very grateful for the brilliant edits and advice of the Atelier series editor, Kevin O'Neill, who significantly enhanced the depth and clarity of the text. Likewise, I am very thankful to the other author participants in the series book workshop for Atelier in San Jose, California, in the fall of 2018—Namita Vijay Dharia, Marina Andrea Welker, and Laurie Denyer Willis.

My wonderful, dear family has been a great source of joy and inspiration in so many ways. I wish to thank all of them, including Mary Coyle, Mel Coyle, Ryan Coyle, Terry Coyle, Tom Coyle, Charles D. Hafner, Martha Hafner, Neal Katyal, Andrew Mistone, Bethany Mistone, Kenadie Mistone, Estelle Rosen, Hugo Rosen, Joanna Rosen, Sebastian Rosen, Sidney Rosen, and Shuo Zhang.

I also owe many thanks for the various sources of fellowship and grant support that I have received for this research over the years. These include: the US Environmental Protection Agency; Social Science Research Council; American Council of Learned Societies; American Philosophical Society; Wenner-Gren Foundation for Anthropological Research; the Some Institutes for Advanced Study; Lincoln Institute of Land Policy; West African Research Association; and Institute for Poverty, Land, and Agrarian Studies. At the University of Chicago, this research was generously supported through the Nicholson Center for British Studies; Human Rights Program; African Language Fund; Committee on African and African American Studies; and Division of the Social Sciences. At Harvard University, this research was generously supported by the W. E. B. Du Bois Research Institute for African and African American Research in the Hutchins Center; Program on the Study of Capitalism; Institute for Global Law and Policy; and the Committee on African Studies. At Princeton University, this research has been generously supported by the University Center for Human Values; David A. Gardner '69 Magic Innovation Fund; Humanities Council; University Committee on Research in the Humanities and Social Sciences; Program in African Studies; Fung Global Fellows Program; Office of the Dean of the Faculty; and Princeton Institute for International and Regional Studies.

Beyond all, I am grateful to Jeffrey Rosen, my beloved husband. He is interlaced throughout these pages. He read through the entire manuscript, offering abundant insights and reflections that clarified and enhanced the text. He also reads the world with me, helping to refine our ways of navigation through it. Ever since he entered my life at the start of 2017, he has transmuted my path and my being in countless ways that cannot be described. In continuous fashion, I am amazed and fortified by his immense grace, brilliance, kindness, and authenticity, as well as by his profound openness to encountering life in all of its mysteries and glories. My work, my thoughts, and my spirit are perpetual beneficiaries of his extraordinary light and wisdom.

NOTES

INTRODUCTION

1. George Ernest Asare, "Obuasi Residents Flee as Illegal Miners Go on a Rampage," *Daily Graphic*, March 21, 2013, available at http://graphic.com.gh/General-News/obuasi -residents-flee-as-illegal-miners-go-on-rampage.html.

2. By dint of IRB prohibitions for this study, I was not able to photograph the galamseys at work, as their work is mostly formally illegal in Obuasi. Photographer George Osodi has a beautiful and moving collection of images of galamseys available on his website, under an assemblage titled "De Money 'Ghana Gold'": https://georgeosodi.photoshelter.com/portfolio /Goooovg60HC6G7LQ (accessed April 15, 2019). The etymology of the word *galamsey* is ultimately unknown and unclear. It is sometimes used interchangeably with *galamseyer*. Both words are used in English and in Twi, the principal indigenous language spoken in the area of Obuasi and across much of southern Ghana. According to many oral historical accounts that I gathered during my field research, the word derived from a combination of the English phrase "gather them and sell" during British colonialism. In the early days, children and others could find nuggets on the ground in the gold fields, particularly after a rainfall that would grace the land to reveal them. Finders would then take such nuggets to a central market in town to be weighed and sold.

3. The gold mine lies in the Adanse state, which originally sat to the south of the Asante state and has been incorporated into it since the eighteenth century. Indigenous mining has occurred there for centuries. In 1897, three Fante businessmen from Cape Coast, Ghana—Joseph Biney, Joseph Ellis, and Joseph Brown—collaborated with British investor Sir Edwin Arthur Cade to formally incorporate Ashanti Goldfields Corporation (AGC), AGA's corporate predecessor, and list it on the London Stock Exchange. Through formal incorporation, the owners sought to attract capital to modernize the mining operations underground. AGA merged with AGC in 2004. For extensive histories of mining in Ghana, including in

Obuasi, see, for example: Raymond E. Dumett, *El Dorado in West Africa: The Gold-Mining Frontier, African Labor, and Colonial Capitalism in the Gold Coast, 1875–1900* (Athens: Ohio University Press, 1998); Donald Keith Robotham, *Moneystone: Consciousness and Kinship amongst Miners in Ghana* (PhD diss., University of Chicago, 1987); Donald Keith Robotham, *Militants or Proletarians? The Economic Culture of Underground Gold Miners in Southern Ghana, 1906–1976.* Cambridge, UK: African Studies Centre, 1989; Jeff Crisp, *The Story of an African Working Class: Ghanaian Miners' Struggles, 1870–1980* (London: Zed Books, 1984); Edward S. Ayensu, *Ashanti Gold: The African Legacy of the World's Most Precious Metal* (London: Marshall, 1997); Emmanuel Ababio Ofosu-Mensah, "Traditional Gold Mining in Adanse," *Nordic Journal of African Studies* 19 (2010): 124–47; Ofosu-Mensah, "Labour Migration during the Colonial Period to the Obuasi Mines in Ghana," *International Research Journal of Library Information and Archival Studies* 1, no. 1 (2011): 6–22; Ofosu-Mensah, "Gold Mining and the Socio-economic Development of Obuasi in Adanse," *African Journal of History and Culture* 3, no. 4 (2011): 54–64; Ofosu-Mensah, *Gold Mining in Adanse: Pre-colonial and Modern* (Saarbrücken, Germany: Lambert Academic Publishing, 2014).

4. Ghana recently has ranked as Africa's second-largest gold producer and ninth among gold-producing countries across the globe. Among global gold-producing mines, Obuasi recently was ranked tenth. Obuasi's rank on the continent has been measured by overall size of the gold resources within the deposits at gold-producing sites. South Deep (now owned by Gold Fields and containing 81,413,000 ounces of gold) and Mponeng (also owned by AngloGold Ashanti and containing 39,557,000 ounces of gold) are two separate mines near Johannesburg, both of which are larger than the deposit at Obuasi (containing 29,830,000 ounces of gold). Measured by independent mines, Obuasi ranks third for the African continent. Carlos Andres, "World's Top 10 Gold Deposits," *Gold Miners Investment Newsletter*, August 7, 2013, available at http://www.mining.com/web/worlds-top-10-gold-deposits/.

5. For short-order coverage in the local media, see, for example: XYZ News, "National Security Rescues 'Buried' Illegal Miners," March 22, 2013, available at http://vibeghana .com/2013/03/22/national-security-rescues-burried-illegal-miners/.

6. All foreign italicized words in this book are in Twi (Asante dialect)—Twi also being called, less commonly, Akan—unless otherwise noted. Twi is the indigenous lingua franca throughout much of southern Ghana, though a great many languages abound throughout the nation. English is the official language of the country, having been inculcated during British colonialism in the Gold Coast Colony. Schools throughout the country now routinely teach it. It is also the language of official government discourse, documents, state court proceedings, and the like. Most Ghanaians speak English, often fluently, particularly in the areas of towns and cities. This includes most interlocutors in my research. I used a mix of English; Twi (Asante dialect); and, where necessary, interpreters. In Obuasi, a subset of the miners and other town residents come from groups in the northern region of Ghana. These people speak many additional languages that are not mutually intelligible with each other or with Twi, and such languages are not understood by most from the southern part of Ghana. People from the North often use Hausa among each other, as Hausa is the lingua franca of much of northern Ghana. However, these people, when they live in southern Ghana, usually also speak Twi and English.

7. For extensive elaborations on the Akan cosmological systems, see, for example, Kwame Gyekye, *An Essay on African Philosophical Thought: The Akan Conceptual Scheme* (Philadelphia: Temple University Press, 1995); Nana Akua Kyerewaa Opokuwaa, *The Quest for Spiritual Transformation: Introduction to Traditional Akan Religion, Rituals, and Practices* (Lincoln, NE: iUniverse, 2005); Peter Kwasi Sarpong, *Libation* (Accra, Ghana: Anansesem); Ivor Wilks, *Forests of Gold: Essays on the Akan and the Kingdom of Asante* (Athens: Ohio University Press, 1993); J. B. Danquah, *The Akan Doctrine of God: A Fragment of Gold Coast Ethics and Religion* (London: Lutterworth Press, 1944). For a leading collection on Akan people, more generally, see: Kwasi Konadu, ed. *The Akan People: A Documentary History* (Princeton, NJ: Markus Wiener, 2013).

8. Of course, the innovation of this concept in the language of moral economy came with E. P. Thompson's work. See: Thompson, *The Making of the English Working Class* (New York: Vintage Books, 1963); Thompson, *Customs in Common: Studies in Traditional Popular Culture* (New York: New Press, 1993).

9. In the Akan system, gold at times acts as a microphone, amplifier, telephone, or other line of connection with the spiritual realm. However, not all of the *abosom* (Akan deities) are favorable toward gold or to their priests' proximity to gold in sacred shrines, with some preferring other metals or no metals at all. For powerful examinations of the channels of divining crystals—including as telephones—and much else in ritual spaces, see: William F. Hanks, "Counterparts: Co-presence and Ritual Intersubjectivity," *Language & Communication* 33 (2013): 263–77. Hanks writes of a Maya shaman at the heart of his study: "DC likened his crystals to a telephone with which he could converse with spirits" (271). See also, more generally: William F. Hanks, *Referential Practice: Language and Lived Space among the Maya* (Chicago: University of Chicago Press, 1990); Hanks, *Converting Words: Maya in the Age of the Cross* (Berkeley: University of California Press, 2010). For other intricate studies of co-presence, though sometimes coded with different language, see, for example: Aisha Beliso-de Jesús, *Electric Santería: Racial and Sexual Assemblages of Transnational Religion* (New York: Columbia University Press, 2015); Kate Ramsey, *The Spirits and the Law: Vodou and Power in Haiti* (Chicago: University of Chicago Press, 2011); Vincent Brown, *The Reaper's Garden: Death and Power in the World of Atlantic Slavery* (Cambridge, MA: Harvard University Press, 2008); Maya Deren, *Divine Horsemen: The Living Gods of Haiti* (Kingston, NY: McPherson, 1983); Stephan Palmié, *Wizards and Scientists: Explorations in Afro-Cuban Modernity and Tradition* (Durham, NC: Duke University Press, 2002); William James, *The Varieties of Religious Experience: A Study in Human Nature* (New York: Penguin, 1982 [1902–1910]); and Webb Keane, *Christian Moderns: Freedom and Fetish in the Mission Encounter* (Berkeley: University of California Press, 2006).

10. For discussions of ancient and contemporary texts and conundrums, I draw inspiration from, among many others, Gillian Rose's soul-stirring work, *Mourning Becomes the Law: Philosophy and Representation* (Cambridge: Cambridge University Press, 1996). See also Rose's shattering examinations of triadic conflicts in her memoir, penned as she was dying of cancer, *Love's Work* (New York: Penguin, 2011 [1995]). For classical statements from the so-called Western canon on considerations of the just city and the just soul, and their articulations with higher truth, higher law, and the divine, see, for example: Plato, *The Republic* (New York: Penguin, 2007 [380 BCE]); Aristotle, *De Anima (On the Soul)*, translated by

Hugh Lawson-Tancred (New York: Penguin, 1987 [350 BCE]); Aristotle, *The Politics*, translated by T. A. Sinclair (New York: Penguin, 1981 [350 BCE]). For a more recent, illuminating meditation, see, for example: Kwame Anthony Appiah, *In My Father's House: Africa in the Philosophy of Culture* (New York: Oxford University Press, 1993). Oludamini Ogunnaike recently published a brilliant article on the articulations and divergences among strands of African philosophical thought and the so-called Western philosophical orientations, which, of course, were never actually isolated—except in the ideology of self-conception—from broader conversations with and strong influences from thought in the rest of the world. In the piece, he quotes a powerful formulation by the famed Sufi sage and Malian mystic Tierno Bokar on knowledge in-and-of-itself, on the natures of inscribed versus lived versions of the same essential storehouse of the light of wisdom: "Writing is one thing and knowledge is another. Writing is the photographing of knowledge, but it is not knowledge itself. Knowledge is a light which is within man. It is the heritage all the ancestors knew and have transmitted to us as seed, just as the mature baobab is contained in its seed," quoted in Ogunnaike, "African Philosophy Reconsidered: Africa, Religion, Race, and Philosophy," *Journal of Africana Religions* 5 (2017): 181–216. See also: Emmanuel Chukwudi Eze, ed., *African Philosophy: An Anthology* (Cambridge, MA: Blackwell Publishers, 1997).

11. One important recent work that advances a notion of shadow sovereigns focuses on the realm of transnational corporations and critiques their ever-growing power, writ large, along with their evisceration of formal rule-of-law regimes: Susan George, *Shadow Sovereigns: How Global Corporations Are Seizing Power* (New York: Polity, 2015). See also: Joshua Barkan, *Corporate Sovereignty: Law and Government under Capitalism* (Minneapolis: University of Minnesota Press, 2013). For broader considerations, see, for example: Carolyn Nordstrom, *Shadows of War: Violence, Power, and International Profiteering in the Twenty-First Century* (Berkeley: University of California Press, 2004); Carolyn Nordstrom, "Shadows and Sovereigns," *Theory, Culture, & Society* 17, no. 4 (2000): 35–54; Alfred C. Aman and Carol Greenhouse, *Transnational Law: Cases and Problems in an Interconnected World* (Durham, NC: Carolina Academic Press, 2017).

12. A great deal has been written in recent times, in the anthropology of religion and in adjacent fields, exploring the various governance roles (shadow and otherwise) of spiritual forces and groups in conflict—outside of, alongside, against, and within state sovereignties. There are many extraordinary studies, too voluminous to list here in any exhaustive fashion. For the case of Africa, see, for example: Jean Comaroff and John L. Comaroff, eds., *Millennial Capitalism and the Culture of Neoliberalism* (Durham, NC: Duke University Press, 2001); James H. Smith and Rosalind I. J. Hackett, eds. *Displacing the State: Religion and Conflict in Neoliberal Africa* (Notre Dame, IN: University of Notre Dame Press, 2011); Jesse Weaver Shipley, "Comedians, Pastors, and the Miraculous Agency of Charisma in Ghana," *Cultural Anthropology* 24, no. 3 (2009): 523–52; Birgit Meyer, "The Power of Money: Politics, Occult Force, and Pentecostalism in Ghana," *African Studies Review* 41, no. 3 (1998): 15–37; Birgit Meyer and Peter Pels, eds., *Magic and Modernity: Interfaces of Revelation and Concealment* (Stanford, CA: Stanford University Press, 2003); Rosalind C. Morris and Daniel H. Leonard, *The Returns of Fetishism: Charles de Brosses and the Afterlives of an Idea* (Chicago: University of Chicago Press, 2017); Adeline Masquelier, *Prayer Has Spoiled Everything: Possession, Power, and Identity in an Islamic Town of Niger* (Durham, NC: Duke University

Press, 2001); Jacob Olupona, *The City of 201 Gods: Ile-Ife (Nigeria) in Time, Space and the Imagination* (Berkeley: University of California Press, 2011); James H. Smith, *Bewitching Development: Witchcraft and the Reinvention of Development in Neoliberal Kenya* (Chicago: University of Chicago Press, 2008); Brad Weiss, *The Making and Unmaking of the Haya Lived World: Consumption, Commoditization, and Everyday Practice* (Durham, NC: Duke University Press, 1996); Peter Geschiere, *The Modernity of Witchcraft: Politics and the Occult in Postcolonial Africa*, trans. Janet Roitman and Peter Geschiere (Charlottesville: University of Virginia Press); Harry West, *Kupilikula: Governance and the Invisible Realm in Mozambique* (Chicago: University of Chicago Press, 2005); Achille Mbembe, *On the Postcolony* (Berkeley: University of California Press, 2001); Charles Piot, *Nostalgia for the Future: West Africa after the Cold War* (Chicago: University of Chicago Press, 2010); Ruth Marshall, *Political Spiritualities: The Pentecostal Revolution in Nigeria* (Chicago: University of Chicago Press, 2009); and Florence Bernault, "Body, Power and Sacrifice in Equatorial Africa," *Journal of African History* 47 (2006): 207–39.

13. This public perception is not at all unfounded, given the structural economic dynamics as well as the law and governance issues in place. Since the onset of neoliberal reforms in 1986, which denationalized and heavily liberalized the gold mining industry, gold has been the nation's most profitable industry—its single largest contributor to foreign exchange earnings. Additionally, foreign direct investment in Ghana's gold-mining industry has increased by around sixfold since the reforms. However, as such profits skyrocketed, contributions from gold mining to the national GDP have remained virtually stable—currently at around 8 percent. This is due to dramatic tax-break allowances and holidays, as well as to other mechanisms that allow for heavy capital flight, leading to the offshoring of the vast majority of gains from large-scale corporate mining. Galamsey gold exports also contribute to the loss of state revenue, as they often travel through illegal or illicit distribution channels that bypass taxation and other public revenue mechanisms.

14. According to many popular and media accounts, the increased presence of foreigners, particularly Chinese, in the industry is dramatically enhancing the environmental footprint of galamsey mining on the lands. For example, in early 2015, an estimate surfaced that indicated that about 75 percent of the waterways had been polluted by artisanal mining across Ghana. See, e.g., Darci Stanger. "Galamsey: Environmental Impact of Illegal Gold Mining in Ghana." *Georgetown Environmental Law Review*, February 13, 2015, available at https://gelr.org/2015/02/13/galamsey-environmental-impact-of-illegal-gold-mining-in-ghana/. However, it is important to bear in mind that many Ghanaians allege that corporate industry spokespersons and some government officials tend to hyperbolize the galamseys' contributions to environmental problems associated with mining, and to downplay the significant contributions of the corporate mining sector to polluting or destroying waters and lands.

15. See, for example, a recent Ghana Chamber of Mines report: "Performance of the Mining Industry in 2017—GcoM Report," January 6, 2018, available at http://ghanacham berofmines.org/wp-content/uploads/2016/11/Performance-of-the-Industry-2017.pdf.

16. This book draws on and extends earlier work on the spirits of the mines. For example, Michael Taussig and June Nash document a critical point at which a former peasantry is being drawn into deeply ambivalent relations, spiritual and otherwise, with wage labor

and capitalism, in the cavernous vessels of the then recently arrived industrial mining. Faced with the harsh, unrelenting realities of this new form of labor, missionized local miners resignified the tutelary indigenous spirits of the mountain and its resources into the Devil (called *Tío*, or uncle in Spanish), to be alternately feared and propitiated for protection, wealth, mercy, and retribution. In contrast to those earlier works, this study of Obuasi offers a contemporary situation in which industrial labor has endured for a century but recently has been heavily casualized, and many fired or unemployed laborers flock to smaller galamsey groups, who enlist spiritual power to foster intragroup solidarity but also to vigorously compete with each other. Further, here, the African indigenous deities continue to coexist by name—sometimes peacefully, sometimes in tension—with Christian and Islamic spiritual forms, despite the heavy presences of the latter two faiths in the lands of present-day Ghana for centuries. Michael Taussig, *The Devil and Commodity Fetishism in South America* (Chapel Hill: University of North Carolina Press, 1980); June Nash, *We Eat the Mines and the Mines Eat Us: Dependency and Exploitation in Bolivian Tin Mines* (New York: Columbia University Press, 1993 [1979]).

17. There have been many powerful, illuminating studies in the anthropology of mining that have emerged in recent years. See, for example: Stuart Kirsch, *Mining Capitalism: The Relationship between Corporations and Their Critics* (Berkeley: University of California Press, 2014). Kirsch, *Reverse Anthropology: Indigenous Analysis of Social and Environmental Relations in New Guinea* (Stanford, CA: Stanford University Press, 2006); Rosalind C. Morris, "The Miner's Ear," *Transition* 98 (2008): 96–115; Morris, "The Mute and the Unspeakable: Political Subjectivity, Violent Crime, and the 'Sexual Thing' in a South African Mining Community," in *Law and Disorder in the Postcolony*, edited by Jean Comaroff and John Comaroff (Chicago: University of Chicago Press, 2006), 57–101; Morris, "Shadows in the Cave: Deindustrialization and the Afterlives of Gold in South Africa," talk delivered in the Department of Anthropology at Princeton University, paper on file with author, 2017; Morris, "Shadow and Impress: Ethnography, Film, and the Task of Writing History in the Space of South Africa's Deindustrialization," *History & Theory* 57, no. 4 (2018): 102–25; Morris, *Unstable Ground: The Lives, Deaths, and Afterlives of Gold in South Africa*, manuscript on file with author; James H. Smith, "Tantalus in the Digital Age: Coltan Ore, Temporal Dispossession, and 'Movement' in the Eastern Democratic Republic of the Congo," *American Ethnologist* 38, no. 1 (2011): 17–35; William Kentridge and Rosalind C. Morris, *Accounts and Drawings from Underground: The East Rand Proprietary Mines Cash Book, 1906* (Chicago.: Seagull, University of Chicago Press, 2015); James H. Smith, "Colonizing Banro: Kingship, Temporality, and Mining of Futures in the Goldfields of South Kivu, DRC," in *The Politics of Custom: Chiefship, Capital, and the State*, edited by John L. Comaroff and Jean Comaroff (Chicago: University of Chicago Press, 2018), 279–304; James Smith, "May It Never End: Price Wars, Networks and Temporality in the '3Ts' Mining Trade of the Eastern DR Congo," *HAU: Journal of Ethnographic Theory* 5, no. 1 (2015): 1–35; Elizabeth Ferry, "Fetishism and Hauism in Central Mexico: Using Marx and Mauss to Understand Commodity Production in a Cooperative Setting," in *Anthropological Perspectives on Economic Development and Integration*, edited by Norbert Dannhaeuser and Cynthia Werner (Bingley, UK: Emerald Group Publishing, 2003), 261–81; Ferry, "Geologies of Power: Value Transformations of Mineral Specimens from Guanajuato, Mexico," *American Ethnologist* 32, no. 3 (2005): 420–

36; Ferry, *Minerals, Collecting, and Value Across the US-Mexico Border* (Bloomington: Indiana University Press, 2013); Ferry, "On Not Being a Sign: Gold's Semiotic Claims," *Signs and Society* 4, no. 1 (2016): 57–79; Ferry, "Gold Prices as Material-Social Actors: The Case of the London Gold Fix," *Extractive Industries and Society* 3 (2016): 82–85; Ferry, "Royal Roads and Entangled Webs: Mining Metals and Making Value in El Cubo, Guanajuato, Mexico," *Journal of Anthropological Research* 75, no. 1 (2019): 6–20; Alex Golub, *Leviathans at the Gold Mine: Creating Indigenous and Corporate Actors in Papua New Guinea* (Durham, NC: Duke University Press, 2014); James Ferguson, *Expectations of Modernity: Myths and Meanings of Urban Life on the Zambian Copperbelt* (Berkeley: University of California Press, 1999); Ferguson, *Global Shadows: Africa in the Neoliberal World Order* (Durham, NC: Duke University Press, 2006); Danny Hoffman, "Yellow Woman: Suspicion and Cooperation on Liberia's Gold Mines," *American Anthropologist* 121, no. 1 (2019): 138–48; Danny Hoffman, "Corpus: Mining the Border," *Cultural Anthropology* (2012), available at https://culanth.org/photo_essays/; Dinah Rajak, *In Good Company: An Anatomy of Corporate Social Responsibility* (Stanford, CA: Stanford University Press, 2011); Filipe Calvão, "The Company Oracle: Corporate Security and Diviner-Detectives in Angola's Diamond Mines," *Comparative Studies in Society and History* 59, no. 3 (2017): 574–99; Marina Welker, *Enacting the Corporation: An American Mining Firm in Postauthoritarian Indonesia* (Berkeley: University of California Press, 2014); Brian Brazeal, "The Fetish and the Stone: A Moral Economy of Charlatans and Thieves," in *The Work of "Possession" in Afro-Atlantic Religions*, edited by Paul Johnson (Chicago: University of Chicago Press, 2014); Brazeal, "Austerity, Luxury, and Uncertainty in the Indian Emerald Trade," *Journal of Material Culture* 22, no. 4 (2017): 437–52; Mareike Winchell, "Economies of Obligation: Patronage as Relational Wealth in Bolivian Gold Mining," *HAU: Journal of Ethnographic Theory* 7, no. 3 (2017): 159–83; Cristiano Lanzano, "Gold Digging and the Politics of Time: Changing Timescapes of Artisanal Mining in West Africa," *Extractive Industries and Society* 5, no. 2 (2018): 253–59; Lorenzo D'Angelo, "Who Owns the Diamonds? The Occult Economy of Diamond Mining in Sierra Leone," *Africa* 84, no. 2 (2014): 269–93; Robert Jan Pijpers and Thomas Hylland Eriksen, eds., *Mining Encounters: Extractive Industries in an Overheated World* (London: Pluto Press, 2019); Sabine Lunig and Robert Jan Pijpers, "Governing Access to Gold in Ghana: In-depth Geopolitics on Mining Concessions," *Africa* 87, no. 4 (2017): 758–79; Sabine Lunig, "The Future of Artisanal Miners from a Large-Scale Perspective: From Valued Pathfinders to Disposable Illegals?" *Futures* 62 (2014): 67–74; Sabine Lunig, "Mining Temporalities: Future Perspectives," *Extractive Industries and Society* 5, no. 2 (2018): 281–86; Robyn D'Avignon, "Primitive Techniques: From 'Customary' to 'Artisanal' Mining in French West Africa," *Journal of African History* 59, no. 2 (2018): 179–97; Filip De Boeck, "Domesticating Diamonds and Dollars: Expenditure, Identity, and Sharing in Southwestern Zaire," *Development and Change* 29 (1998): 777–810. My approach here resonates with Chris Ballard and Glenn Banks's important guidance to resist the tidy allure of monolithic treatments of bodies such as "the mining company," "the state," or "resisting indigenous groups," which often are scripted identities that gloss over infinitely more complex social and cultural realities on the ground in mine settings. Members of these groups often work in unobvious modes of alliance and contestation, shifting allegiances and strategic navigations in ways that ethnography, with its fine-grained and long-durational mode of observation and analysis, is uniquely positioned to document, interpret, and reveal. See, Ballard and Banks, "Resource Wars: The Anthropology of Mining," *Annual Review of Anthropology* 32 (2003): 287–313. See also: Catherine Coumans, "Occupying Spaces Created by Conflict: Anthropologists, Development NGOs, Responsible Investment, and Mining," *Current Anthropology* 52, supp. 3(2011): S29–S43. For an earlier authoritative review, which focused much more on industrial labor settings and contests between states and mining corporations prior to what Ballard and Banks, in their 2003 piece, dubbed the "minerals boom of the 1980s" and the widening field of social impacts on local communities (politically represented as such), see Ricardo Godoy, "Mining: Anthropological Perspectives," *Annual Review of Anthropology* 14 (1985): 199–217.

18. These so-called traditional (or customary) authorities are both territorial and descent based. Ghana has a dual system of parallel jurisdictions—customary and liberal state regimes—that govern property, contracts, and other domains of legal life. The traditional authorities are seated within ethnicity-based lineages of rulers of customary jurisdictions, but the range of rule is now spatial, with people from other groups residing among those of the primary ethnic group with customary jurisdiction in the territory. Further, there is fluidity of exact ethnic group and office, such that, at times, any suitable member of the broader Akan ethnic group can serve in a royal office of lower order in a sub-Akan group. For example, there are Fante sub-chiefs in the higher Adanse paramountcy division of the still higher, more encompassing Asante kingdom—the Fante, Adanse, and Asante, along with many other groups, all being Akan.

19. This enterprise, my striving to account for ways in which the so-called nonhuman world works in perpetual co-creation with the human world to fashion the latter as such, partakes of a classical anthropological sensibility. Yet this endeavor recently has been revitalized in several modalities that seek to examine and interpret how the world beyond the human interfaces, co-constitutes, and otherwise interacts with the "world of the human," per se. As Eduardo Kohn puts part of his version of such an endeavor, which seeks to decenter the conventional sign and to reveal what he calls "the very different nonsymbolic properties of those other [unfamiliar, often hidden] semiotic forms" that help to generate "context": "An anthropology beyond the human is in large part about learning to appreciate how the human is also the product of that which lies beyond human contexts." *How Forests Think: Toward an Anthropology Beyond the Human* (Berkeley: University of California Press, 2013), 14–15. Marisol de la Cadena has advanced another recent, powerful call to attend to incommensurability and alternate modes of translating worlds that both register and exceed the standard categories and concepts of what she calls modern and non-modern modes of understanding. She investigates the perpetual entanglements of worlds that are politically marked as indigenous and nonindigenous, including (seemingly) non-spirited and spirited habits of perception and being. This is central for understanding both modern political struggles and modes of effective ethnographic craft. De la Cadena, *Earth Beings: Ecologies of Practice across Andean Worlds* (Durham, NC: Duke University Press, 2015). See also: Elizabeth Povinelli, *Labor's Lot: The Power, History, and Culture of Aboriginal Action* (Chicago: University of Chicago Press, 1993). In a different though related critical vein, Povinelli also has issued a powerful call for a look into a fundamental distinction, always alive and unusually unremarked, between ontologies of Life and Nonlife, which she calls "geontopower." In her argument, this ontological distinction, this assertion, subtends the

prevalent analytics of modern (and, for her, what she calls late liberal) formations: sovereign power, disciplinary power, and biopower. *Geontologies: A Requiem to Late Liberalism* (Durham, NC: Duke University Press), (especially) 8–10. As Povinelli elaborates deeper in the text, "The sovereign people of geontopower are those who abide by the fundamental separation of Life and Nonlife with all the subsequent implications of this separation on intentionality, vulnerability, and ethical implication. That is, what is sovereign is the division of Life and Nonlife as the fundamental ground of the governance of difference and markets. Where Indigenous people agree to participate as an animist voice in the governmental order of the people they are included as part of this sovereign people. Where they do not, they are cast out" (37–38). In the gold fields of Ghana, the various distinctions of Life and Nonlife—including, in no small part, the vitalities and spiritualities that suffuse all things and that vie (or collaborate) to govern them—are fundamental to the functioning of power, sovereignty, politics, law, ethics, and claims to basic entitlements to humanity.

20. As Otumfuo Nana Agyeman Prempeh I, king of Asante, asserted in his 1907 essay on the history of the Asante nation, written while in colonial exile in Seychelles, "In essence, the Gold Coast administration, supported by mining and other commercial interests, had carried out a coup in Asante," Agyeman Prempeh, *"The History of Ashanti Kings and the Whole Country Itself" and Other Writings*, edited by Emmanuel Akyeampong, A. Adu Boahen, N. Lawler, T.C. McCaskie, and Ivor Wilks (Oxford: Oxford University Press, 2008 [1907]); Raymond E. Dumett, *El Dorado in West Africa: The Gold-Mining Frontier, African Labor, and Colonial Capitalism in the Gold Coast, 1875–1900* (Athens: Ohio University Press, 1998); Jeff Crisp, *The Story of an African Working Class: Ghanaian Miners' Struggles, 1870–1980* (London: Zed Books, 1984); Kwamina B. Dickson, *A Historical Geography of Ghana* (London: Cambridge University Press, 1969); G.O. Kesse, *Mineral and Rock Resources of Ghana* (Rotterdam, Netherlands: A.A. Balkema, 1985); Allan McPhee, *The Economic Revolution in British West Africa* (London: Frank Cass (1971 [1926]); Adu Boahen, *Ghana: Evolution and Change in the Nineteenth and Twentieth Centuries* (London: Longman, 1975).; Ivor Wilks, *Asante in the Nineteenth Century: The Structure and Evolution of a Political Order* (Cambridge: Cambridge University Press, 1975); Carl C. Reindorf, *History of the Gold Coast and Asante, Based on Tradition and Historical Facts* (Accra: Ghana Universities Press, 2007 [1895]); Ivor Wilks, *Forests of Gold: Essays on the Akan and the Kingdom of Asante* (Athens: Ohio University Press, 1993); Thomas C. McCaskie, *State and Society in Pre-colonial Asante* (Cambridge: Cambridge University Press, 1995).

21. Throughout *Fires of Gold*, I use spellings such as "Ashanti Region," "Adansi," or "Obuasi," when these refer to official designations that the current government of Ghana uses. These are Anglicized versions of "Asante," "Adanse," and "Obuase." I use Asante, Adanse, and other such spellings when I am referring to the ethnic group—or their lands, spirits, or other resources—in line with common usages in Ghana and in scholarship on the country.

22. For detailed descriptions of mine labor recruitment during British colonialism, see Dumett, *El Dorado in West Africa*; Crisp, *Story of an African Working Class*; Robotham, *Militants or Proletarians?* For examinations of the "South African model" for forced labor recruitment under apartheid, see, for example: T. Dunbar Moodie and Vivienne Ndatshe, *Going for Gold: Men, Mines, and Migration* (Berkeley: University of California Press, 1994);

William Worger, *South Africa's City of Diamonds: Mine Workers and Monopoly Capitalism in Kimberley, 1867–1895* (New Haven, CT: Yale University Press, 1987).

23. Mining sectors often have served as the first sites for the shift to neoliberal political economies, from the first neoliberal reform experiment in Chile in 1973 onward, across the globe. For an important, systematic anthropological study that foregrounds mining transformations and notes the start of neoliberalism in Chile, see Stuart Kirsch, *Mining Capitalism*. For more general treatment of the phenomenon of neoliberalism, see, for example, David Harvey, *A Brief History of Neoliberalism* (New York: Oxford University Press, 2005).

24. George Ernest Asare, "Calm Returns to Obuasi," *Daily Graphic*, March 22, 2013, available at http://graphic.com.gh/General-News/calm-returns-to-obuasi.html.

25. George Ernest Asare, "Obuasi Residents Flee as Illegal Miners Go on a Rampage," *Daily Graphic*, March 21, 2013, available at http://graphic.com.gh/General-News/obuasi-residents-flee-as-illegal-miners-go-on-rampage.html.

26. In the late 1990s, AGA's labor force of about fourteen thousand was slashed to about six thousand. During my long stretch of fieldwork in 2012, the employed figure hovered around three thousand. In fall of 2014, the total descended to a miniscule number of around two hundred employees, as AGA shut down most of its Obuasi mine—temporarily, the company announced, in order to update and mechanize much of the underground operations. AGA also complained of declining profits and productivity, citing the economic and security threats of the invading galamseys as a chief problem for the mine's viability. AGA's workforce is now only a pale shadow of what it was throughout much of the twentieth century, when the totals generally hovered in the several tens of thousands. The Obuasi mine remains shut down, at least as of the completion of this book, though AGA has announced that it has renegotiated its contract with the government and that it plans to reopen and pour the first gold again by the end of 2019. This echoes a seemingly endless pendulum swing, a boom-and-bust cycle that hammers the social worlds of extractive theaters.

27. An ethnography of the campaigns leading up to AGA's "Public Eye Award" for the Obuasi operations—and of the multiple scales of activism, evidence, and "rendering visible"—can be found in a recent essay, Lauren Coyle, "Tender Is the Mine: Law, Shadow Rule, and the Public Gaze in Ghana," in *Corporate Social Responsibility? Human Rights in the New Global Economy*, edited by Charlotte Walker-Said and John Kelly (Chicago: University of Chicago Press, 2015).

28. Ibid.

29. Wacam, as an NGO, began in Wassa territory in the Western Region of Ghana, in a town called Tarkwa, where the other principal deep underground mine of Ghana is located. A local couple from the Tarwka area originally took up the cause of organizing local community people who had grievances against Gold Fields, the major transnational mining company that runs the mine in Tarkwa. As in Obuasi, surface-mining operations over the course of the 1990s had destroyed many farmlands and streams and had left many communities displaced. Likewise, mine security often brutalized the galamsey forces in the area. Thus, there are many direct parallels between the circumstances in Wassa and Obuasi.

30. Yet, of course, AGA has a troubled recent past on the African continent. For example, AngloGold has suffered former allegations of controversial secret mining contracts and alleged collaboration with violent groups in the northeastern region of the Democratic

Republic of Congo. Human Rights Watch, *The Curse of Gold* (New York: Human Rights Watch, June 1, 2005), available at https://www.hrw.org/sites/default/files/reports/drc0505_0 .pdf. See also: Michael Deibert, "A Glittering Demon: Mining, Poverty and Politics in the Democratic Republic of Congo," *CorpWatch*, June 26, 2008, available at: https://corpwatch .org/article/glittering-demon-mining-poverty-and-politics-democratic-republic-congo.

31. There has been much coverage of these patterns of environmental destruction, dispossession, and displacement, as well as of human rights abuses at the hands of mining companies, by civil society actors, lawyers, and some scholars. See, for example: Thomas M. Akabzaa, J.S. Seyire, and K. Afriyie, *The Glittering Façade: Effects of Mining Activities on Obuasi and Its Surrounding Communities* (Accra, Ghana: Third World Network-Africa, 2008); Emmanuel Ababio Ofosu-Mensah, "Gold Mining and the Socio-economic Development of Obuasi in Adanse"; Thomas Akabzaa, *Boom and Dislocation: The Environmental and Social Impacts of Mining in the Wassa West District of Ghana* (Accra, Ghana: Third World Network—Africa, 2000); Thomas Akabzaa, "The Challenges of Development: Mining Codes in Africa and Corporate Responsibility," in *International and Comparative Mineral Law and Policy: Trends and Prospects*, edited by Elizabeth Bastida, Thomas Walde, and Janeth Warden- Fernández (The Hague, Netherlands: Kluwer Law International, 2005); P.K. Agbesinyale, *Ghana's Gold Rush and Regional Development: The Case of Wassa West District* (Dortmund, Germany: SPRING Centre, University of Dortmund, 2003); Emmanuel Ababio Ofosu-Mensah, "Mining as a Factor of Social Conflict in Ghana," *Global Journal of History and Culture* 1, no. 1 (2011): 7–21.

32. Max Weber, *The Vocation Lectures*, translated by Rodney Livingstone, edited by David Owen and Tracy Strong (Indianapolis: Hackett Books, 2004 [1919]). See also: Weber, *Economy and Society: An Outline of Interpretive Sociology*, 2 vols. (Berkeley: University of California Press, 1978 [1922]). As Pierre Bourdieu put the matter, in felicitous formulation and focusing on the performative power of language: "Those who, like Max Weber, have set the magical or charismatic law of the collective oath or the ordeal in opposition to a rational law based on calculability and predictability, forget that the most rigorously rationalized law is never anything more than an act of social magic which works. Legal discourse is a creative speech which brings into existence that which it utters. It is the limit aimed at by all performative utterances—blessings, curses, orders, wishes or insults. In other words, it is the divine word, the word of divine right, which, like the *intuitus originarius* which Kant ascribed to God, creates what it states, in contrast to all derived, observational statements, which simply record a preexistent given. One should never forget that language, by virtue of the infinite generative but also *originative* capacity—in the Kantian sense—which it derives from its power to produce existence by producing the collectively recognized, and thus realized, representation of existence, is no doubt the principal support of the dream of absolute power." *Language and Symbolic Power*, edited by Gino Raymond and Matthew Adamson, translated by Gino Raymond and Matthew Adamson (Cambridge, UK: Polity Press, 1991), 42.

33. See, for example: Saskia Sassen, *Territory, Authority, Rights: From Medieval to Global Assemblages* (Princeton, NJ: Princeton University Press, 2006); Arjun Appadurai, "Sovereignty without Territoriality: Notes for a Postnational Geography," in *The Anthropology of Space and Place—Locating Culture* (Oxford: Blackwell, 2003), 337–49; Antony Anghie,

Imperialism, Sovereignty, and the Making of International Law (Cambridge, UK: Cambridge University Press, 2007); Michael Dillon, "Correlating Sovereign and Biopower," in *Sovereign Lives: Power in Global Politics* (London: Routledge, 2005); Mariane Ferme, "Deterritorialized Citizenship and the Resonances of the Sierra Leonean State," in *Anthropology in the Margins of the State*, edited by Veena Das and Deborah Poole (Santa Fe, NM: School of American Research Press, 2004); Mariane Ferme, "Flexible Sovereignty? Paramount Chiefs, Deterritorialization, and Political Mediations in Sierra Leone," *Cambridge Anthropology* 23, no. 2 (2003): 21–35; Mark Goodale and Sally Engle Merry, eds. *The Practice of Human Rights: Tracking Law between the Global and the Local* (New York: Cambridge University Press, 2007); Charles Piot, *Nostalgia for the Future: West Africa after the Cold War* (Chicago: University of Chicago Press, 2010); Michael Hardt and Antonio Negri, *Empire* (Cambridge, MA: Harvard University Press, 2000); Hardt and Negri, *Multitude: War and Democracy in the Age of Empire* (New York: Penguin Press, 2004); John Agnew, "Mapping Political Power beyond State Boundaries: Territory, Identity, and Movement in World Politics," *Millennium* 28 (1999): 499–521.

34. Donald Moore, *Suffering for Territory: Race, Place, and Power in Zimbabwe* (Durham, NC: Duke University Press, 2005), 233. See also: Michael Watts, "Resource Curse? Governmentality, Oil and Power in the Niger Delta, Nigeria," *Geopolitics* 9, no. 1 (2004): 50–80; Brenda Chalfin, *Neoliberal Frontiers: An Ethnography of Sovereignty in West Africa* (Chicago: University of Chicago Press, 2010); Janet Roitman, *Fiscal Disobedience: An Anthropology of Economic Regulation in Central Africa* (Princeton, NJ: Princeton University Press, 2005); James Ferguson, "Seeing Like an Oil Company: Space, Security, and Global Capital in Neoliberal Africa," *American Anthropologist* 107, no. 3 (2005): 377–82; James Ferguson, *Global Shadows: Africa in the Neoliberal World Order* (Durham, NC: Duke University Press, 2006). For more general, deep explorations of vitality, improvisation, creativity, and endurance among laborers and others in cosmopolitan urban Africa, see, for example: Ato Quayson, *Oxford Street, Accra: City Life and the Itineraries of Transnationalism* (Durham, NC: Duke University Press, 2014); Brian Larkin, *Signal and Noise: Media, Infrastructure, and Urban Culture in Nigeria* (Durham, NC: Duke University Press, 2008); Julia Elyachar, *Markets of Dispossession: NGOs, Economic Development, and the State in Cairo* (Durham, NC: Duke University Press, 2005); and AbdouMaliq Simone, *Improvised Lives: Rhythms of Endurance in an Urban South* (Hoboken, NJ: John Wiley & Sons, 2018). See, more generally: Thomas Hylland Eriksen, *Boomtown: Runaway Globalisation on the Queensland Coast* (London: Pluto Press, 2018); Philip Liste, "Geographical Knowledge at Work: Human Rights Litigation and Transnational Territoriality," *European Journal of International Relations* 22, no. 1 (2016): 217–39; Liste, "Colliding Geographies: Space at Work in Global Governance," *Journal of International Relations and Development* 19, no. 2 (2016): 199–221; Thomas L. Ilgen, "Reconfigured Sovereignty in the Age of Globalization," in *Reconfigured Sovereignty: Multi-Layered Governance in the Global Age*, edited by Thomas L. Ilgen, 6–35 (Farnham, UK: Ashgate, 2003).

35. Michel Foucault, *Power/Knowledge: Selected Interviews and Other Writings, 1972–1977*, edited by C. Gordon (New York: Pantheon Books, 1980), 121.

36. Thomas Blom Hansen and Finn Stepputat, "Sovereignty Revisited," *Annual Review of Anthropology* 35 (2006): 295–315. See also: Hansen and Stepputat, eds., *Sovereign Bodies: Citizens, Migrants, and States in the Postcolonial World* (Princeton, NJ: Princeton University

Press, 2005); Deborah A. Thomas, *Exceptional Violence: Embodied Citizenship in Transnational Jamaica* (Durham, NC: Duke University Press, 2011); Thomas, "The Problem with Violence: Exceptionality and Sovereignty in the New World," *Journal of Transnational American Studies* 5 (2013), no. 1.

37. Hansen and Stepputat, "Sovereignty Revisited," 297. Their proposed approach foregrounds what they term "de facto sovereignty, i.e., the ability to kill, punish, and discipline with impunity wherever it is found and practiced," as opposed to sovereignty as a matter of "formal ideologies of rule and legality," 296.

38. Carl Schmitt. *The Concept of the Political*, translated by George Schwab (Chicago: University of Chicago Press, 1995 [1932]). See also: Schmitt, *Political Theology: Four Chapters on the Concept of Sovereignty*, translated by G. Schwab (Chicago: University of Chicago Press, 2005 [1922]); Schmitt, *Legality and Legitimacy*, translated by J. Seitzer (Durham, NC: Duke University Press, 2004 [1932]); Schmitt, *Political Theology II: The Myth of the Closure of Any Political Theology*, translated by M. Hoelzl and G. Ward (Chicago: University of Chicago Press, 2008 [1970]).

39. The allusion here is to a classic study on divine kingship, Ernst Kantorowicz's *The King's Two Bodies: A Study in Medieval Political Theology* (Princeton, NJ: Princeton University Press, 1957).

40. Hansen and Stepputat, "Sovereignty Revisited," 296–97. See: Giorgio Agamben, *Homo Sacer: Sovereign Power and Bare Life (Homo Sacer I)*, translated by Daniel Heller-Roazen (Stanford, CA: Stanford University Press, 1998); Agamben, *State of Exception (Homo Sacer II, 1)*, translated by Kevin Attell (Chicago: University of Chicago Press, 2005); Agamben, *The Kingdom and the Glory: For a Theological Genealogy of Economy and Government (Homo Sacer II, 2)* (Stanford, CA: Stanford University Press, 2007). See also, Eric Santner, *The Royal Remains: The People's Two Bodies and the Endgames of Sovereignty* (Chicago: University of Chicago Press, 2011). As Santner argues, renegotiating the terms of proper symbolic enrollment and investiture is not merely a matter of locating and evaluating sources of legitimacy for political authority, but also, "more profoundly, [a matter of] our capacity to feel represented in the social field, to experience those representations as *viable facilitations of our vitality*," xiv.

41. See, e.g., Ferguson, *Global Shadows*; Comaroff and Comaroff, *Theory from the South*; Jean Comaroff and John L. Comaroff, eds., *Law and Disorder in the Postcolony* (Chicago: University of Chicago Press, 2006); Anna Tsing, *Friction: An Ethnography of Global Connection* (Princeton, NJ: Princeton University Press, 2005); Piot, *Nostalgia for the Future*; James Ferguson and Akhil Gupta, "Spatializing States: Toward an Ethnography of Neoliberal Governmentality," *American Ethnologist* 29, no. 4 (2002): 981–1002; Hansen and Stepputat, "Sovereignty Revisited"; Bjørn Enge Bertelsen, *Violent Becomings: State Formation, Sociality, and Power in Mozambique* (New York: Berghahn); Jeffrey Kahn, *Islands of Sovereignty: Haitian Migration and the Borders of Empire* (Chicago: University of Chicago Press, 2018); Yarimar Bonilla, "Unsettling Sovereignty," *Cultural Anthropology* 32, no. 3 (2017): 330–39; Aiwa Ong, *Neoliberalism as Exception: Mutations in Citizenship and Sovereignty* (Durham, NC: Duke University Press, 2006).

42. We also witness something other than a decisive shift from a vertical model of sacred political authority premised on the archetype of the king's sublime dual body—Body Natural

and Body Politic—to a horizontal figuration of "the People's" or the population's sacred flesh, and something other than purely exceptional states that entail the complete stripping of symbolic or political entitlement and the relegating of such (here, galamsey or other dispossessed) bodies to an unqualified state of "bare life," without signification in the prevailing constitutional order or without the capacity even to be meaningfully sacrificed. See, for example: Agamben, *Homo Sacer*; Agamben, *State of Exception*. Of course, the lateralizing dynamics are only amplified by the attendant outsourcing of the performance of many traditional sovereign functions—policing, intelligence, military operations, prisons, health care, and so on. See, for example: Jean Comaroff and John Comaroff, *Theory from the South; or, How Euro-America Is Evolving toward Africa* (Boulder, CO: Paradigm, 2012), 97; Piot, *Nostalgia for the Future*.

43. This argument aligns with a central contention in critical legal studies. Legal regimes create the contours of economic life through ways both prohibitive *and* permissive. The permissive forms of legal systems—particularly the often tacit privilege to injure (for example, through exclusion, displacement, or dispossession of property or claims to it)—often remain hidden beneath the surface of legal consciousness. This serves to naturalize the economic and social processes that legal constellations help to produce, though always through dialectical interplays with other dimensions of life. Such interpretive sleights of hand also tend to localize violence in particular actors or in "economic winds," rather than analyzing the ways in which the violence is generated and sometimes incentivized by the legal rules (including background ones) at play. Law permits, performs, and produces certain versions of the world at the same time as it disallows, prohibits, disincentivizes, and represses others. See, for example: Duncan Kennedy, *A Critique of Adjudication (fin de siècle)* (Cambridge, MA: Harvard University Press, 1997); Duncan Kennedy, "The Critique of Rights in Critical Legal Studies," in *Left Legalism, Left Critique*, edited by Janet Halley and Wendy Brown (Durham, NC: Duke University Press, 2002), 178–228; Duncan Kennedy, "Three Globalizations of Law and Legal Thought: 1850–2000," in *The New Law and Economic Development*, edited by David M. Trubek and Alvaro Santos (New York: Cambridge University Press, 2006); Christine Desan, *Making Money: Coin, Currency, and the Coming of Capitalism* (Oxford: Oxford University Press, 2015); Wendy Brown and Janet Halley, "Introduction," in *Left Legalism/Left Critique*, edited by Wendy Brown and Janet Halley (Durham, NC: Duke University Press, 2002), 1–37; Robert Hale, "Coercion and Distribution in a Supposedly Non-Coercive State," *Political Science Quarterly* 38 (1923): 470–78; David Kennedy, *The Dark Sides of Virtue: Reassessing International Humanitarianism* (Princeton, NJ: Princeton University Press, 2005); Bernard Harcourt, *Illusion of Free Markets* (Cambridge, MA: Harvard University Press, 2011); Jeremy Perelman and Lucie White, "Stones of Hope: Experience and Theory in African Economic and Social Rights Activism," in *Stones of Hope: How African Activists Reclaim Human Rights to Challenge Global Poverty*, edited by Lucie E. White and Jeremy Perelman (Stanford, CA: Stanford University Press, 2010), 149–71; Orly Lobel, "The Paradox of Extralegal Activism: Critical Legal Consciousness and Transformative Politics," *Harvard Law Review* 120 (2007): 937–88. For powerful interweaving of anthropological research with similar considerations from critical legal studies, see: Meghan Morris, "Speculative Fields: Property in the Shadow of Post-Conflict Colombia," *Cultural Anthropology* (forthcoming, 2019); Morris, *Property in the Shadow of Post-Conflict Colombia*, book manuscript on file with author.

44. As the Comaroffs noted in 2006, around 105 new constitutions had arisen since 1989, the majority of them in postcolonies. Comaroff and Comaroff, *Law and Disorder in the Postcolony*.

45. Kirsch, *Mining Capitalism*; Welker, *Enacting the Corporation*; Marina Welker, "'Corporate Security Begins in the Community': Mining, the Corporate Social Responsibility Industry, and Environmental Advocacy in Indonesia," *Cultural Anthropology* 24, no. 1 (2009):142–79; William Reno, *Warlord Politics and African States* (Boulder, CO: Lynne Rienner, 1998); Smith, "Tantalus in the Digital Age"; Golub, *Leviathans at the Gold Mine*; Nico Schrijver, *Sovereignty over Natural Resources: Balancing Rights and Duties* (New York: Cambridge University Press, 1997); de Boeck, "Domesticating Diamonds and Dollars."

46. In contrast, as Ferguson notes, James Scott has argued that these features apply not only to the more robust developmental modernist states, but also to downsized neoliberal states and to the state-like characteristics of largely unconstrained global corporations. James Ferguson, "Seeing Like an Oil Company: Space, Security, and Global Capital in Neoliberal Africa," *American Anthropologist* 107, no. 3 (2005): 377–82; Ferguson, *Global Shadows*; James C. Scott, *Seeing Like a State: How Certain Schemes to Improve the Human Condition Have Failed* (New Haven, CT: Yale University Press, 1998).

47. Ferguson, *Global Shadows*; William Reno, *Warlord Politics*; James Ferguson and Akhil Gupta, "Spatializing States: Toward an Ethnography of Neoliberal Governmentality," *American Ethnologist* 29, no. 4 (2002): 981–1002; Morris, "The Mute and the Unspeakable"; Morris, "Shadow and Impress: Ethnography, Film, and the Task of Writing History in the Space of South Africa's Deindustrialization," *History & Theory* 57, no. 4 (2018): 102–25; James H. Smith, "Tantalus in the Digital Age"; Kirsch, *Mining Capitalism*; Golub, *Leviathans at the Gold Mine*.

48. For the case of Ghana, see: Dumett, *El Dorado in West Africa*; Crisp, *Story of an African Working Class*; Ayensu, *Ashanti Gold*; Gareth Austin, *Labour, Land and Capital in Ghana: From Slavery to Free Labour in Asante, 1807–1956* (Rochester, NY: University of Rochester Press, 2005); Chalfin, *Neoliberal Frontiers*; Christian Lund, ed., *Twilight Institutions: Public Authority and Local Politics in Africa* (Hoboken, NJ: Wiley-Blackwell, 2007). See, more generally: Achille Mbembe, *On the Postcolony* (Berkeley: University of California Press, 2001); Jean-Francois Bayart, Stephen Ellis, and Beatrice Hibou, *The Criminalization of the State in Africa*, translated by Stephen Ellis (Bloomington: Indiana University Press, 1999); Jean-Francois Bayart, *The State in Africa: The Politics of the Belly* (London: Longman, 1993); Comaroff and Comaroff, *Law and Disorder*; John Kelly, "The Other Leviathans: Corporate Investment and the Construction of a Sugar Company," in *White and Deadly: Sugar and Colonialism*, edited by Pal Ahluwadia, Bill Ashcroft, and Roger Knight (Commack, NY: Nova Science, 1999), 95–134.

49. Relatedly, Brenda Chalfin's important book, *Neoliberal Frontiers*, furnishes a recent analysis of Ghana's re-centering of fiscal authority as a primary modality of sovereignty in the neoliberal moment. She argues that the customs authority is now central to Ghana's international sovereignty, typifying its neoliberal incarnation in the role it plays in acceding on behalf of Ghana to international influences regarding the shape of Ghana's trade, border, crime, and fiscal regulations. Neoliberal customs activities also undergird much of Ghana's domestic sovereign functioning, enhancing effective policing and extraction of revenue.

Theoretically, Chalfin locates customs regimes in general, throughout modern sovereign formations, at the interchange of self-regulating, bureaucratic governmentality *and* top-down, coercive sovereign sanctions, extraction, and general rule. This involves a theoretical approach to neoliberal sovereignty as not so much a breaking *down* but a breaking *apart* of sovereign functions. Chalfin, *Neoliberal Frontiers*, 25–27. For a compelling account of the fashioning of national capacities and reputations, in the case of Senegal, through international relations that are forged at key historical moments, see: Michael Ralph, *Forensics of Capital* (Chicago: University of Chicago Press, 2015).

50. Here, I draw inspiration from the critical theories of political sacrifice that "will have been worth it," at least ostensibly, from the projected standpoint of some redeemed future, in Elizabeth Povinelli's *Economies of Abandonment: Social Belonging and Endurance in Late Liberalism* (Durham, NC: Duke University Press, 2011).

51. Rosalind Morris, "Returning the Body without Haunting: Mourning 'Nai Phi' and the End of Revolution in Thailand," in *Loss*, edited by David L. Eng and David Kazanjian (Berkeley: University of California Press, 2003), 29–58.

52. Many recent works document how newly diffused states fervently deploy efforts to secure a persuasive mirage of presence, coherence, and efficacy—either through straightforward artifice or through overstatement, and often through participating in the manufacturing of fear and its subsequent containment or assuagement in mass-mediated public imaginaries. In some cases, certain neoliberal states are theorized as having become not much more than simulacral political orders. Here, orchestrated fears and their amelioration anchor sovereign presence through the artful production of sovereign power. It is not that such spectral appearances are *mere* artifice; they rework the world, purporting to merely signify what they in fact produce. See, for example: Mbembe, *On the Postcolony*; Piot, *Nostalgia for the Future*; Comaroff and Comaroff, *Law and Disorder in the Postcolony*.

53. Thomas Hobbes, *Leviathan: Or the Matter, Forme, and Power of a Commonwealth Ecclesiastical and Civil* (New York: Simon & Schuster, 1964 [1651]). Danilyn Rutherford's *Laughing at Leviathan* is a major recent work in anthropology that addresses the expansive discursivity and performative power of the fashioned (and fashioning) audiences of sovereigns. Danilyn Rutherford, *Laughing at Leviathan: Sovereignty and Audience in West Papua* (Chicago: University of Chicago Press, 2012). In Achille Mbembe's powerful essay, "Necropolitics," he also expressly complicates a developmentalist origins myth with what he calls "multiple concepts of sovereignty," which he places at the birth of modernity rather than as a strictly recent phenomenon. Likewise, he debunks the normative, universalist, developmentalist idea of sovereignty as the culmination of reasoned discourse among an increasingly free and deliberative body politic, buttressed by consensus-building and shared—or, at least, more or less consonant—normative orders; all of this, with individualistic, spasmodic, antisocial, irrational passions and impulses supposedly held at bay. His treatment of sovereignty draws upon and contributes to the trend of scholarship that reincorporates elements of fantasy, passion, and even cruel whim and arbitrary exactions of death or injury into the realm of the constitutive sovereign in the strict sense. Mbembe, "Necropolitics," *Public Culture* 15, no. 1 (2003): 11–40.

54. In this enterprise, forms of the subject are perpetually and reiteratively constituted not only through foreclosures and subsequent prohibitions, but also through the productive

effects of symbolic allegiances or of disciplinary injunctions to self-police and self-care. Here, I draw inspiration from Judith Butler's generative approach to power and subjectivity, combining psychoanalytic notions with Foucauldian theories of subjectivation, in *The Psychic Life of Power: Theories in Subjection* (Stanford, CA: Stanford University Press, 1997). The selves in the field, I have found, perpetually undergo a process that John Borneman and Abdellah Hammoudi have felicitously dubbed "dialectical objectification," for the fieldwork observation process and for the emergence of knowledge writ large. John Borneman and Abdellah Hammoudi, "The Fieldwork Encounter, Experience, and the Making of Truth: An Introduction," in *Being There: The Fieldwork Encounter and the Making of Truth*, edited by John Borneman and Abdellah Hammoudi (Berkeley: University of California Press, 2009), 1–25. I make a case for the necessity of philosophical concepts, including ever-provisional apprehensions of subjectivity itself, to become more anthropological in an essay on Hegel, Adorno, and the negative dialectical project: Lauren Coyle (Rosen), "The Spiritless Rose in the Cross of the Present: Retracing Hegel in Adorno's *Negative Dialectics* and Related Lectures," *Telos* 155: 39–61.

1. ARTISANAL MINERS AND SACRIFICIAL LAWS

1. In 2011, AGA personnel flew this man to South Africa for a special surgical procedure that would restore normal urinary functioning—a medical procedure that he could not afford over the intervening eight years after the attack.

2. According to Emmanuel Akyeampong, the rise of this locally produced gin as a popular cultural drink throughout Ghana dates only to about 1930, following the passages of the Gin and Geneva Ordinance of 1930, which restricted importation and "threatened to nip in the bud the emergent lifestyle of commoners in colonial towns and peri-urban villages." Emmanuel Akyeampong, "*Ahenfo Nsa* (the 'Drink of Kings'): Dutch Schnapps and Ritual in Ghanaian History," in *Merchants, Missionaries, and Migrants: 300 Years of Dutch-Ghanaian Relations*, edited by I. van Kessel (KIT Publishers, 2002), 51–61, 56; see also, Akyeampong, *Drink, Power, and Cultural Change: A Social History of Alcohol in Ghana, c. 1800 to Recent Times* (Portsmouth, NH: Heinemann, 1996). Akpeteshie now flourishes throughout much of Ghana as a locally and popularly distilled gin that often claims the very cheapest of selling prices (at times, the equivalent of about ten cents (USD) per shot). Thus, the working and underemployed classes may regularly enjoy it in generous quantities, and it is regularly for sale at the smallest "drinking spots"—sometimes, little more than a small, makeshift booth, or an open-air stand. Such drinking spots are strewn throughout Obuasi.

3. Eva Meyerowitz describes the underground world as Nyame's aspect as the Goddess of Death, though Nyame is often considered masculine. *The Sacred State of the Akan* (London: Faber and Faber, 1953). See also: Meyerowitz, *The Divine Kingship in Ghana and Ancient Egypt* (London: Faber and Faber, 1960).

4. National Coalition on Mining (NCOM), Ghana, "NCOM Condemns AngloGold-Ashanti (AGA) for Allegedly Burying Alive 40 Small-Scale Miners at Blackis Pit Near Obuasi." *TWN Africa*, September 14, 2009, available at http://apps.twnafrica.org/blog/index.cfm?c=ncom&p=2.

5. Commission on Human Rights and Administrative Justice, "The State of Human Rights in Mining Communities in Ghana," 2008, available at: https://chraj.gov.gh/.

2. SPIRITUAL SOVEREIGNS IN THE SHADOWS

1. Many accounts of the elusive and ultimately punitive nature of ill-gotten riches run throughout the literature. Wealth, oftentimes and almost by divine dictate, will come to consume the spirit of the holder if his or her spirit is not strong. At the very least, the initial beneficiary eventually will lose all he or she has acquired by means of an unethical ritual. See, for example: Andrew Walsh, "'Hot Money' and Daring Consumption in a Northern Malagasy Sapphire-Mining Town," *American Ethnologist* 30, no. 2 (2003): 290–305; Golub, *Leviathans at the Gold Mine*; Smith, *Bewitching Development*; Nash, *We Eat the Mines*; Taussig, *The Devil and Commodity Fetishism*; Mircea Eliade, *The Forge and the Crucible: The Origins and Structures of Alchemy*, trans. Stephen Corrin (Chicago: University of Chicago Press, 1978); Jane Parish, "The Dynamics of Witchcraft and Indigenous Shrines Among the Akan," *Africa* 69, no. 3 (1999): 426–48; Jane Parish, "Beyond Occult Economies: Akan Spirits, New York Idols, and Detroit Automobiles," *HAU: Journal of Ethnographic Theory* 5, no. 2 (2015):101–20; Rena Lederman, "Sorcery and Social Change in Mendi," *Social Analysis* 8 (1981): 15–26; Harri Englund, "Witchcraft, Modernity and the Person: The Morality of Accumulation in Central Malawi," *Critique of Anthropology* 16, no. 3 (1996): 257–79; Peter Geschiere, *Witchcraft, Intimacy, and Trust: Africa in Comparison* (Chicago: University of Chicago Press, 2013); Geschiere, "Globalization and the Power of Indeterminate Meaning: Witchcraft and Spirit Cults in Africa and East Asia," in *Globalization and Identity: Dialectics of Flow and Closure*, edited by Birgit Meyer and Peter Geschiere (Oxford, UK: Oxford University Press, 1999), 211–38; Geschiere, "Witchcraft and the Limits of the Law: Cameroon and South Africa," in *Law and Disorder in the Postcolony*, edited by Jean Comaroff and John L. Comaroff (Chicago: University of Chicago Press, 2006), 219–46. For significant recent studies of the cultural, genealogical, and psychical fashioning and experientiality of madness, in particular, see, for example: Elizabeth Davis, *Bad Souls: Madness and Responsibility in Modern Greece* (Durham, NC: Duke University Press, 2012); Stefania Pandolfo, *Knot of the Soul: Madness, Psychoanalysis, Islam* (Chicago: University of Chicago Press, 2018).

2. Abdellah Hammoudi, who grew up in Morocco, shared with me that it is common knowledge across North Africa that jinn can be commissioned or contracted to prospect and to call forth the gold. However, there is not much written about this in Western languages (Hammoudi, personal communication). For Hammoudi's signal work on sacrifice, more generally, see: Abdellah Hammoudi, *The Victim and Its Masks: An Essay on Sacrifice and Masquerade in the Maghreb* (Chicago: University of Chicago Press, 1993).

3. In Obuasi, the akomfo and others do not tend to refer to the general spirit thought to back the gold and to the other spirits that interact with the gold—often shorthanded as "the gold spirit"—by a name, other than saying *sika kra* (soul's gold). If a presiding deity backing the gold in the territory is named, it is Bona. Elsewhere in the literature, Nana Adade Kofi is named as the Akan deity (*obosom*) of iron and metals in general. He is a warrior god, "an Obrafo but is better known as an impatient messenger who is quite fiery. . . . [He] wears an iron chain around his neck, leg, and arm. . . . [He] likes raw rice, gin, palm wine, and all that Nana Panyin [his mother, a very powerful deity of justice] eats." Nana Akua Kyerewaa Opokuwaa, *The Quest for Spiritual Transformation: Introduction to Traditional Akan Religion, Rituals, and Practices* (Lincoln, NE: iUniverse, 2005). In some lands of Asante, ancestors (*nsamanfo*) may own the territories, though many scholars have noted that this is a

more recent phenomenon. See, for example: Ofosu-Mensah, "Traditional Gold Mining in Adanse"; Meyerowitz, *The Sacred State of the Akan*, 35n4; R. S. Rattray, *Ashanti Law and Constitution* (Oxford: Clarendon Press, 1929), 346; R. S. Rattray, *Religion and Art in Ashanti* (Oxford: Clarendon Press, 1927); Thomas C. McCaskie, "People and Animals: Constru(ct)ing the Asante Experience," *Africa* 62, no. 2 (1992): 221–47; Sandra Greene, *Sacred Sites and the Colonial Encounter: A History of Meaning and Memory in Ghana* (Bloomington: Indiana University Press, 2002).

4. For elaborate discussions of spiritual alchemy and the ascension of human consciousness across much history and in many cultures, see, for example: Titus Burckhardt, *The Mirror of the Intellect: Essays on Traditional Science and Sacred Art* (Albany: State University of New York Press, 1987); Burckhardt, *Alchemy: Science of the Cosmos, Science of the Soul* (Louisville, KY: Fons Vitae, 1997); Mircea Eliade, *Myths, Dreams, and Mysteries*, trans. Philip Mairet (New York: Harper & Brothers, 1960); Eliade, *The Forge and the Crucible*; Ioan P. Couliano, *Eros and Magic in the Renaissance*, translated by Margaret Cook (Chicago: University of Chicago Press, 1987). For an extensive cataloging of kindred beliefs—as well as representations in modalities such as dreams, drawings, and other representations of internal and external worlds—throughout the world, see: Carl Jung, *Alchemical Studies* (Princeton, NJ: Princeton University Press, 1967). See also, in its entirety, including Jung's commentary about the linkages of what he calls Eastern understandings with his own innovations in psychological theory, Richard Wilhelm's translation of the anonymous ancient Taoist text, *The Secret of the Golden Flower: A Chinese Book of Life* (San Diego, CA: Harcourt, 1962 [1929]). For a lucid treatment of Jung's working through the parallels of alchemical transmutation and processes of personal individuation and transformation, see: Marie-Louis von Franz, *Alchemy: An Introduction to the Symbolism and the Psychology* (Toronto, ON: Inner City Books, 1980). For a panoramic of alchemical imagery, symbolism, and coded knowledge across many artistic and esoteric traditions from medieval times to the present, see: Alexander Roob, *Alchemy and Mysticism* (Los Angeles: Taschen, 2019). In gold's mystical capacities, which facilitate and bear witness to spiritual transmutation of matter, we might locate resonance with Hegel's statement: "The *being of spirit is a bone*." Georg Wilhelm Friedrich Hegel, *The Phenomenology of Spirit*, translated and edited by Terry Pinkard (New York: Cambridge University Press, 2017 [1807]), 191 (emphasis in the original).

5. Thomas C. McCaskie, "Accumulation, Wealth, and Belief in Asante History. I. To the Close of the Nineteenth Century," *Africa* 53 (1983): 23–43, 26. William Pietz analyzed the ways in which, historically, the Akan goldweights rendered commensurable economic and metaphysical values among the Akan and those European and Arab traders who arrived to seek gold and other objects: "The goldweights, then, functioned precisely to relate incommensurable social values, those from traditional Akan culture as expressed in proverbs or traditional healing, with the newer market values introduced from outside. The brass figures constituted a new cultural territory embodying the possibility of movement across diverse value codes: the weights were singular productions of Akan artists (students of these objects often remark on the seeming infinity of different forms given to these figures) that could function in the market activity of gold weighing, communicate the traditional wisdom of some native proverb, or be endowed with power to protect or to heal sick

individuals when worn upon the body." "The Problem of the Fetish, I," *RES: Journal of Anthropology and Aesthetics* 9 (1985): 5–17, 16. See also, Kwame Arhin, "Gold-Mining and Trading among the Ashanti of Ghana," *Journal des Africanistes* 48 (1978): 89–100. In a separate vein, though related to gold's appearance of almost self-executing power, Elizabeth Ferry has put forth a fascinating analysis of the common convention of gold's inherent value and worth, arguing that it is a particularly pronounced instance of the "naturalization of convention": "This vociferous iteration of value in nature over value by convention makes gold especially apt for the kinds of meaning making and contestation so prevalent in debates over commodity money and 'fiat currency,' the 'realness' of gold and the perceived similarities of gold and Bitcoin." "On Not Being a Sign: Gold's Semiotic Claims," *Signs and Society* 4, no. 1 (2016): 57–79, 77–78.

6. For extensive contemplations regarding the Akan concepts of the soul, the sacred nature of gold, and the complex relations among divine rule, ancestors, and deities, see, for example: Kwame Gyekye, *An Essay on African Philosophical Thought: The Akan Conceptual Scheme* (Philadelphia: Temple University Press, 1995); Peter Kwasi Sarpong, *The Sacred Stools of the Akan* (Accra: Ghana Publishing Corporation, 1971); Ivor Wilks, *Forests of Gold: Essays on the Akan and the Kingdom of Asante* (Athens: Ohio University Press, 1993); Agyeman Prempeh, *"The History of Ashanti Kings and the Whole Country Itself" and Other Writings*, ed. Emmanuel Akyeampong, A. Adu Boahen, N. Lawler, T. C. McCaskie, and Ivor Wilks (Oxford: Oxford University Press, 2008 [1907]); Emmanuel Akyeampong, "Christianity, Modernity, and the Weight of Tradition in the Life of Asantehene Agyeman Prempeh I., c. 1888–1931," *Africa* 69 (1999): 279–311; J. B. Danquah, *The Akan Doctrine of God: A Fragment of Gold Coast Ethics and Religion* (London: Lutterworth Press, 1944); Johann Gottlieb Christaller, *A Collection of Three Thousand and Six Hundred Tshi Proverbs* (Basel: Basel Missionary Society, 1879); Eva L. R. Meyerowitz, "Concepts of the Soul among the Akan of the Gold Coast," *Africa* 21 (1951): 24–31; Lauren Coyle (Rosen), "Fallen Chiefs and Sacrificial Mining in Ghana," in *The Politics of Custom*, edited by John L. Comaroff and Jean Comaroff (Chicago: University of Chicago Press, 2018), 247–78; Kofi A. Busia, "The Ashanti of the Gold Coast," in *African Worlds: Studies in the Cosmological Ideas and Social Values of African Peoples*, edited by D. Forde (London: Oxford University Press, 1954).

7. Here, I enlist Valerio Valeri's neologism of *sacrifier* for the person or the collective on whose behalf a sacrifice is being performed, in his English approximation of the French "sacrificateur," which Hubert and Mauss use in their seminal 1898 essay on sacrifice. I also follow Valeri's usage of Hubert and Mauss's "sacrificer" for the person—oftentimes a ritual authority—who actually performs the sacrifice. Valeri, *Kingship and Sacrifice: Ritual and Society in Ancient Hawaii*, translated by Paula Wissing (Chicago: University of Chicago Press, 1985); Henri Hubert and Marcel Mauss, *Sacrifice: Its Nature and Functions* (Chicago: University of Chicago Press, 1991 [1898]).

8. Emmanuel Akyeampong, *"Ahenfo Nsa* (the 'Drink of Kings'): Dutch Schnapps and Ritual in Ghanaian History," in *Merchants, Missionaries, and Migrants: 300 Years of Dutch-Ghanaian Relations*, edited by I. van Kessel (Karlsruhe, Germany: KIT Publishers, 2002), 51–61, 53.

9. Akyeampong, *"Ahenfo Nsa"*; also citing, for discussion of the god Brofo in Larteh, who rules over rain and harvests and refuses alcohol, David Brokensha, *Social Change at*

Larteh, Ghana (Oxford: Oxford University Press, 1966), 160. See also: Jean Allman and John Parker, *Tongnaab: The History of a West African God* (Bloomington: Indiana University Press, 2005); Peter Kwasi Sarpong, *Libation* (Accra: Anansesem Publications, 1996); J. B. Danquah, *The Akan Doctrine of God: A Fragment of Gold Coast Ethics and Religion* (London: Lutterworth Press, 1944); Rattray, *Religion and Art in Ashanti*; Meyer Fortes, *Oedipus and Job in West African Religion* (Cambridge: Cambridge University Press, 1959); Birgit Meyer, *Translating the Devil: Religion and Modernity among the Ewe of Ghana* (Trenton, NJ: Africa World Press, 1999); David Amponsah, "Desirable Customs: A History of Indigenous Religion and the Making of Modern Ghana, c. 1800–1966," PhD diss., Harvard University, 2015; Greene, *Sacred Sites*; Jane Parish, "Black Market, Free Market: Anti-Witchcraft Shrines and Fetishes among the Akan," in *Magical Interpretations, Material Realities: Modernity, Witchcraft and the Occult in Postcolonial Africa*, edited by Henrietta L. Moore and Todd Sanders (London: Routledge, 2001), 118–35.

   10. Ofosu-Mensah, "Traditional Gold Mining in Adanse," 132. Adae festivals take place in six-week cycles, each with two constituent ceremonies—an Akwasidae, held on a Sunday, and Awukudae, held on a Wednesday. There are nine cycles of the Adae in the Akan calendar, of which the ninth marks the new year; these festivals are thought to be critically important for strengthening, renewing, and honoring ties among the living and between the incarnate humans and the ancestors. The ancestors are fed in the rooms housing the blackened stools that serve as the seats for their spirits. The Akwasidae celebrations generally involve a large pubic feast, though the central ritual feast in the Stool-house— where the ancestral stools are kept and venerated—is closed to all but authorized participants. Ofosu-Mensah, "Traditional Gold Mining in Adanse," 131n38. As Emmanuel Akyeampong observes, "The *adae* celebrates one's genealogy. To abrogate it is the equivalent of genealogical erasure or social death." "Christianity, Modernity, and the Weight of Tradition in the Life of Asantehene Agyeman Prempeh I., c. 1888–1931," *Africa* 69 (1999): 279–311, 295. See also: Anthony Ephirim-Donkor, *African Spirituality: On Becoming Ancestors* (Lanham, MD: University Press of America, 2011); Kofi A. Opoku, *West African Traditional Religion* (Accra, Ghana: FEP Int., 1978).

   11. Victor Turner, "Images of Anti-Temporality: An Essay in the Anthropology of Experience," *Harvard Theological Review* 75, no. 2 (1982): 243–65.

   12. See, for example, Taussig, *Devil and Commodity Fetishism*; Nash, *We Eat the Mines*; Kirsch, *Reverse Anthropology*; Ferry, "Geologies of Power"; Smith, "Tantalus in the Digital Age"; Kirsch, *Mining Capitalism*.

   13. Crisp, *The Story of an African Working Class*. Jean Allman and Richard Parker draw upon Roger Thomas, who established that men were coming in rather large numbers from the north to the mines in the south before the full-fledged recruitment campaigns were launched, "but they objected to any form of contract, wishing to be free to come and go as they pleased." Roger Thomas, "Forced Labour in British West Africa: The Case of the Northern Territories of the Gold Coast, 1906–1927," *Journal of African History* 14 (1973): 79–103, 99, quoted in Allman and Parker, *Tongnaab*, 254–55n79. See also, Gareth Austin, *Labour, Land and Capital in Ghana: From Slavery to Free Labour in Asante, 1807–1956* (Rochester, NY: University of Rochester Press (2005); Dumett, *El Dorado in West Africa*. For work on the forced mine labor recruitment and its violent afterlives, see, for example, Morris, "The Miner's Ear"; William

Worger, *South Africa's City of Diamonds: Mine Workers and Monopoly Capitalism in Kimberley, 1867–1895* (New Haven, CT: Yale University Press, 1987); Keith Breckenridge, "'Money with Dignity': Migrants, Minelords and the Cultural Politics of the South African Gold Standard Crisis, 1920–33," *Journal of African History* 36, no. 2 (1995): 271–304.

14. As Allman and Parker noted, in their rich history of the northern god Tongnaab—from a shrine that rests with the Tallensi, the subjects of Meyer Fortes's famous and extensive ethnographic monographs—the fact that southerners often viewed northerners as less "developed" and as more intimately connected to nature also gave them a comparative power. The northerners were seen to be much more adept at working synergistically with the elements, summoning and deploying magical proprieties and the spirits of so many things in their environments. Allman and Parker show how the increased traffic during the inter-war period of Tallensi laborers from the north to mines, trading centers, and cocoa farms in the south of Ghana also furnished new spaces for spiritual interchange and market places. As they explain, in the south, "Nana Tongo" became a healing cult primarily geared toward addressing witchcraft, and "[b]y 1930, it had emerged as the most prominent of a whole constellation of anti-witchcraft movements that were consciously marketed—very like the rising number of Christian denominations—as potent new 'exotic' imports." Allman and Parker, *Tongnaab*, 143–44.

15. Keith Hart. "Informal Income Opportunities and Urban Employment in Ghana." *Journal of Modern African Studies* 11, no. 1 (1973): 61–89; Hart, "Market and State after the Cold War: The Informal Economy Reconsidered," in *Contesting Markets: Analyses of Ideology, Discourse and Practice*, edited by R. Dilley (Edinburgh: Edinburgh University Press, 1992). For important studies of artisanal miners and informal economies in Ghana and elsewhere, see, for example: Gavin Hilson, "A Contextual Review of the Ghanaian Small-Scale Mining Industry." *Mining, Minerals and Sustainable Development, No. 76* (London: International Institute for Environment and Development, 2001); Hilson, ed., *The Socioeconomic Impacts of Artisanal and Small-Scale Mining in Developing Countries* (Rotterdam, Netherlands: A.A. Balkema, 2003); Hilson, ed., *Small-Scale Mining, Rural Subsistence and Poverty in West Africa* (Warwickshire, UK: Practical Action Publishing, 2006).

16. For a most insightful exploration of mass commodification in contemporary society, including objects that signify, embody, or conduct *mana*, that all-pervasive and all-permeating lifeforce so well-known to the anthropological literature, see William Mazzarella, *The Mana of Mass Society* (Chicago: University of Chicago Press, 2017). For a deeply powerful study of the mass mediation and commodification of Thai spirit mediums and spiritual circulations, see: Rosalind C. Morris, *In the Place of Origins: Modernity and Its Mediums in Northern Thailand* (Durham, NC: Duke University Press, 2000).

17. Jesse Weaver Shipley, "Comedians, Pastors, and the Miraculous Agency of Charisma in Ghana." *Cultural Anthropology* 24, no. 3 (2009): 523–52; Birgit Meyer, "The Power of Money: Politics, Occult Force, and Pentecostalism in Ghana," *African Studies Review* 41, no. 3 (1998): 15–37; Meyer, "Commodities and the Power of Prayer: Pentecostalist Attitudes towards Consumption in Contemporary Ghana," in *Globalization and Identity: Dialectics of Flow and Closure*, edited by Birgit Meyer and Peter Geschiere (Oxford: Oxford University Press, 1999), 151–76; Meyer, *Translating the Devil: Religion and Modernity among the Ewe of Ghana* (Trenton, NJ: Africa World Press, 1999).

18. Anthony Ephirim-Donkor has argued that it is much more correct to say that deities and spirits "mount" or "alight upon" an okomfo, rather than possess him or her. "Possession" implies a coercive usurpation of will, whereas the okomfo engages in a much more complex process of calling, training, and learning to negotiate and control the spirit that works through the medium, most often at the medium's acceptance and election. "Akom: The Ultimate Mediumship Experience among the Akan," *Journal of the American Academy of Religion* 76 (2008): 54–81. See, more generally: Michael Lambek, "Spirits and Spouses: Possession as a System of Communication among the Malagasy Speakers of Mayotte," *American Ethnologist* 7, no. 2 (1980): 318–31; Lambek, *Human Spirits: A Cultural Account of Trance in Mayotte* (New York: Cambridge University Press, 1981); David Lan, *Guns and Rain: Guerillas and Spirit Mediums in Zimbabwe* (Berkeley: University of California Press, 1985).

3. PRAY FOR THE MINE

1. Of course, a great deal has been written about the prohibition on sacrifice across Christian denominations. For one lucid and extensive discussion, which leans heavily on biblical exegesis, see: Daniel C. Ullucci, *The Christian Rejection of Animal Sacrifice* (Oxford: Oxford University Press, 2012).

2. For broader comparative discussions of such sacrifices and related sacrifices, see, for example: Florence Bernault, "Body, Power and Sacrifice in Equatorial Africa," *Journal of African History* 47 (2006): 207–39; Luc De Heusch, *Sacrifice in Africa: A Structuralist Approach* (Manchester, UK: Manchester University Press, 1986); Pierre Bourdieu, *The Logic of Practice*, translated by Richard Nice (Stanford, CA: Stanford University Press, 1990), 234–48; Abdellah Hammoudi. *The Victim and Its Masks: An Essay on Sacrifice and Masquerade in the Maghreb* (Chicago: University of Chicago Press, 1993); Filip De Boeck, "Beyond the Grave: History, Memory, and Death in Postcolonial Congo/Zaire," in *Memory and the Postcolony: African Anthropology and the Critique of Power,* edited by Richard Werbner (New York: Zed Books, 1998); Michael Jackson, *Minima Ethnographica: Intersubjectivity and the Anthropological Project* (Chicago.: University of Chicago Press, 1998); Peter Geschiere, *The Modernity of Witchcraft: Politics and the Occult in Postcolonial Africa* (Berkeley: University of California Press, 1997); Birgit Meyer, "The Power of Money: Politics, Occult Force, and Pentecostalism in Ghana," *African Studies Review* 41, no. 3 (1998): 15–37; Birgit Meyer, *Translating the Devil: Religion and Modernity among the Ewe of Ghana* (Trenton, NJ: Africa World Press, 1999); Jane Parish, "The Dynamics of Witchcraft and Indigenous Shrines among the Akan," *Africa* 69, no. 3 (1999): 426–48; Michael Lambek, "Sacrifice and the Problem of Beginning: Mediations from Sakalava Mythopraxis," *Journal of the Royal Anthropological Institute* 13, no. 1 (2007): 19–38; William Pietz, "The Problem of the Fetish I"; Smith, *Bewitching Development*; Godfrey Lienhardt, *Divinity and Experience: The Religion of the Dinka* (London: Oxford University Press, 1961); E. E. Evans-Pritchard, *Witchcraft, Oracles, and Magic among the Azande* (Oxford: Clarendon Press, 1968 [1937]); Evans-Pritchard, "The Meaning of Sacrifice among the Nuer," *Journal of the Royal Anthropological Institute of Great Britain and Ireland* 84 (1954): 21–33.

3. For more general discussions of this flourishing, see, for example: Birgit Meyer, "The Power of Money: Politics, Occult Force, and Pentecostalism in Ghana," *African Studies*

Review 41, no. 3 (1998): 15–37; Jesse Weaver Shipley, "Comedians, Pastors, and the Miraculous Agency of Charisma in Ghana," *Cultural Anthropology* 24, no. 3 (2009): 523–52; Shipley, *Trickster Theatre: The Poetics of Freedom in Urban Africa* (Bloomington: Indiana University Press, 2015); Kevin Lewis O'Neill, *City of God: Christian Citizenship in Postwar Guatemala* (Berkeley: University of California Press, 2010); Kevin Lewis O'Neill, *Secure the Soul: Christian Piety and Gang Prevention in Guatemala* (Berkeley: University of California Press, 2015); Annalisa Butticci, *African Pentecostals in Catholic Europe: The Politics of Presence in the Twenty-First Century* (Cambridge, MA: Harvard University Press, 2016); Jane E. Soothill, *Gender, Social Change, and Spiritual Power: Charismatic Christianity in Ghana* (Leiden, Netherlands: Brill, 2007); Ruth Marshall, *Political Spiritualities: The Pentecostal Revolution in Nigeria* (Chicago: University of Chicago Press, 2009); Harri Englund, ed., *Christianity and Public Culture in Africa* (Athens: Ohio University Press, 2011); Jane Guyer, "Prophecy and the Near Future: Thoughts on Macroeconomic, Evangelical, and Punctuated Time," *American Ethnologist* 34, no. 3 (2007): 409–21; David Martin, *Pentecostalism: The World Their Parish* (New York: Wiley-Blackwell, 2001); Ogbu Kalu, *African Pentecostalism: An Introduction* (Oxford: Oxford University Press, 2008); Thomas J. Csordas, *The Sacred Self: A Cultural Phenomenology of Charismatic Healing* (Berkeley: University of California Press, 1994); Thomas J. Csordas, "Introduction: Modalities of Transnational Transcendence," in *Transnational Transcendence: Essays on Religion and Globalization*, edited by Thomas J. Csordas (Berkeley: University of California Press, 2009), 1–30. For studies of Christian Zionist movements in cultural resistance and healing, see: Jean Comaroff, *Body of Power, Spirit of Resistance: The Culture and History of a South African People* (Chicago: University of Chicago Press, 1985); Rune Flikke, "Healing in Polluted Places: Mountains, Air, and Weather in Zulu Zionist Ritual Practice," *Journal for the Study of Religion, Nature, and Culture* 12, no. 1 (2018): 76–95.

4. For a deeply compelling study of social transformations in sonic phenomena, focused on a Muslim city, Kano, in the north of Nigeria, see Brian Larkin, *Signal and Noise: Media, Infrastructure, and Urban Culture in Nigeria* (Durham, NC: Duke University Press, 2008).

4. FALLEN CHIEFS AND DIVINE VIOLENCE

1. Peter Geschiere, *The Perils of Belonging: Autochthony, Citizenship, and Exclusion in Africa and Europe* (Chicago: University of Chicago Press, 2009), 20–21.

2. Increasingly, galamseys also are said to enter shadow deals with chiefs, displacing farmers and destroying water sources. See: Coyle (Rosen), "Tender Is the Mine"; Coyle (Rosen), "Fallen Chiefs and Sacrificial Mining." Tania Li has recently published a fascinating study of the effects of a cash-crop boom of cacao in highland Indonesia. She charts how a group's decision to privatize land previously held in common has differentially enriched some and impoverished others, leaving them landless as well as often jobless. As opposed to a state or a corporation arriving to displace people, kin and neighbors helped to produce these deepening inequalities, with multiple transformative effects, especially for the many who were not enriched and who cannot find other work. *Land's End: Capitalist Relations on an Indigenous Frontier* (Durham, NC: Duke University Press, 2014).

3. Also at play is the rising prominence of Pentecostal and charismatic Christianity in Obuasi and, of course, across Africa, more generally, as described in chapter 3.

4. See, more broadly: Susan E. Cook, "The Business of Being Bafokeng: The Corporatization of a Tribal Authority in South Africa," *Current Anthropology* 52, no. s3: 151–59; John L. Comaroff and Jean Comaroff, *Ethnicity, Inc.* (Chicago: University of Chicago Press, 2009); Rebecca Hardin, "Concessionary Politics: Property, Patronage, and Political Rivalry in Central African Forest Management," *Current Anthropology* 52, no. 3 (2011): S113–S125; Rebecca Hardin, "Contradictions of Corporate Conservation," in "Corporate Social Responsibility," edited by Catherine Dolan and Dinah Rajak, special issue, *Focaal: Journal of European Anthropology* 60 (2011).

5. Paul Nugent, "States and Social Contracts in Africa," *New Left Review* 63 (2010): 35–68. See also: Sara Berry, *Chiefs Know Their Boundaries: Essays on Property, Power, and the Past in Asante, 1896–1996* (Portsmouth, NH: Heinemann, 2001).

6. Richard Rathbone, *Nkrumah and the Chiefs: The Politics of Chieftaincy in Ghana, 1951–1960* (Athens: Ohio University Press, 2000); Rathbone, "From Kingdom to Nation: Changing African Constructions of Identity," in *Chieftaincy in Ghana: Culture, Governance and Development*, edited by Irene K. Odotei and Albert K. Awedoba (Accra, Ghana: Sub-Saharan Publishers, 2006), 43–54; Irene K. Odotei and Albert K. Awedoba, eds., *Chieftancy in Ghana: Culture, Governance and Development* (Accra, Ghana: Sub-Saharan Publishers, 2006); Kofi A. Busia, *The Position of the Chief in the Modern Political System of Ashanti* (Oxford: Oxford University Press, 1951).

7. See, for example: Terence Ranger, "Invention of Tradition in Colonial Africa," in *The Invention of Tradition*, edited by Eric Hobsbawm and Terence Ranger (Cambridge: Cambridge University Press, 1983), 211–62; Martin Chanock, *Law, Custom, and Social Order: The Colonial Experience in Malawi and Zambia* (Cambridge: Cambridge University Press, 1985); Francis G. Snyder, *Capitalism and Legal Change: An African Transformation* (New York: Academic Press, 1981); Bernard Cohn, *Colonialism and Its Forms of Knowledge* (Princeton, NJ: Princeton University Press, 1996); John L. Comaroff, "Colonialism, Culture, and the Law: A Foreword," *Law and Social Inquiry* 26, no. 2 (2001): 305–14; John L. Comaroff, "Reflections on the Colonial State, in South Africa and Elsewhere: Fragments, Factions, Facts and Fictions," *Social Identities* 4, no. 3 (1998): 321–61; Elizabeth Colson, "The Impact of the Colonial Period on the Definition of Land Rights," in *Colonialism in Africa, Vol. 4: Profiles of Change: African Society and Colonial Rule*, edited by Victor Turner (London: Cambridge University Press, 1971), 221–51; Donald I. Ray, "Divided Sovereign: Traditional Authority and the State in Ghana," *Journal of Legal Pluralism and Unofficial Law* 28 (1996): 181–202.

8. The effects of the "invention of tradition" in the parts of the colony that lacked centralized political authority differed markedly from those with kingdoms, of which Akan groups were a part. In the resource-scarce savannah regions (present-day Upper East and Upper West Regions, in the north of the country) and also in the present-day Volta Region (in the east of the country), there had been no continuous centralized authority, and social order was maintained generally by communal consensus. The British, however, created administrative offices in which they installed "chiefs." The authorities bestowed these chiefs with the authority enjoyed by rulers in the other regions of Ghana—namely, present-day Northern, Brong-Ahafo, Ashanti, Western, Central, Eastern, and Southern Volta Regions. See, for example: Kwame Arhin, *The Political Systems of Ghana: Background to Transformations in*

Traditional Authority in the Colonial and Post-Colonial Periods (Accra, Ghana: Historical Society of Ghana, 2002).

9. See, for example: Kojo Sebastian Amanor, "Sustainable Development, Corporate Accumulation and Community Expropriation: Land and Natural Resources in West Africa," in *Land and Sustainable Development in Africa*, edited by Kojo Sebastian Amanor and Sam Moyo (London: Zed Books, 2008), 127–58.

10. Extensive descriptions of the techniques and economies of precolonial "artisanal" mining in Asante can be found, for example, in Dumett, *El Dorado*; Kwame Arhin, "Gold-Mining and Trading among the Ashanti of Ghana," *Journal des Africanistes* 48, no. 1 (1978): 89–100.

11. Jim Silver, "The Failure of European Mining Companies in the Nineteenth-Century Gold Coast," *Journal of African History* 22 (1981): 511–29, 513; Dumett, *El Dorado*; Meyerowitz, *The Sacred State of the Akan*. Although gender and sex are not the central focus of this work, the dynamics of gender and sex, of course, are deeply complex, culturally fashioned, and socially significant in historical and contemporary societies in present-day Ghana. See, for example: Victoria B. Tashjian and Jean Allman, *"I Will Not Eat Stone": A Women's History of Colonial Asante* (Portsmouth, NH: Heinemann, 2000). For broader treatment across colonial Africa and for excellent reviews of the terrain of the literature, see, for example: Jean Allman, Susan Geiger, and Nakanyike Musisi, eds., *Women in African Colonial Histories* (Bloomington: Indiana University Press, 2002); Iris Berger, "African Women's History: Themes and Perspectives," *Journal of Colonialism and Colonial History* 4, no. 1 (2003); Jean Allman and Antoinette Burton, "Destination Globalization? Women, Gender, and Comparative Colonial Histories in the New Millennium," *Journal of Colonialism and Colonial History* 4, no. 1 (2003); Ben Talton and Quincy Mills, eds., *Black Subjects in Africa and Its Diasporas: Race and Gender in Research and Writing* (New York: Palgrave Macmillan, 2011).

12. Dumett, *El Dorado*; Ivor Wilks, *Asante in the Nineteenth Century*; Crisp, *The Story of an African Working Class*.

13. Ofosu-Mensah documented the centrality of artisanal gold mining from the Adanse area (annexed by the Asante Empire), where Obuasi sits, to European gold exports from the thirteenth though the nineteenth centuries, in "Traditional Gold Mining in Adanse"; see also, Dumett, *El Dorado*; Timothy F. Garrard, *Akan Weights and the Gold Trade* (New York: Longman, 1980); Arhin, "Gold-Mining and Trading." Ofosu-Mensah also noted how Akan cosmology holds that the Adanse state, which probably took form in the twelfth century CE, was the site of Nyame's creation of the world, "Traditional Gold Mining in Adanse," 126n10.

14. Kwame Arhin, "Trade, Accumulation and the State in Asante in the Nineteenth Century," *Africa* 60 (1990): 524–37; Wilks, *Asante in the Nineteenth Century*; Edward Reynolds, *Trade and Economic Change on the Gold Coast, 1807–1874* (London: Longman, 1974); Walter Rodney, "Gold and Slaves on the Gold Coast," *Transactions of the Historical Society of Ghana* 10 (1969): 13–28; Richard Bean, "A Note on the Relative Importance of Slaves and Gold in West African Exports," *Journal of African History* 14 (1977): 351–56; Robin Law, ed., *From Slave Trade to "Legitimate" Commerce: The Commercial Transition in Nineteenth-Century West Africa* (Cambridge: Cambridge University Press, 1995).

15. Nugent, "States and Social Contracts in Africa"; David Kimble, *A Political History of Ghana: The Rise of Gold Coast Nationalism, 1850–1928* (Oxford: Oxford University Press, 1963).

16. Austin, *Labour, Land and Capital in Ghana*; Björn Beckman, *Organising the Farmers: Cocoa Politics and National Development in Ghana* (Uppsala, Sweden: Scandinavian Institute of African Studies, 1976); Polly Hill, *The Migrant Cocoa-Farmers of Southern Ghana: A Study in Rural Capitalism* (London: Cambridge University Press, 1963).

17. Nugent, "States and Social Contracts in Africa," 46.

18. As gold was central to British colonial interests and invasions, it was also central as a galvanizing force for anticolonial campaigns. Protecting gold and other natural resources from foreign predations was a key prerogative of strong anticolonial movements and post-Independence state governments to keep the vital resources (historically, cocoa, timber, palm oil, shea butter, and gold) as primary sources of national wealth, for the people of Ghana. These endeavors, of course, were also racialized contests over keeping the natural resources and the fruits of the economy for Ghanaians, not for (often white) colonial or neocolonial interests. Kwame Nkrumah, who led the United Gold Coast Convention (UGCC, est. 1947) in the anticolonial movement and later became Ghana's first president and prime minister (1957–1966), founding the socialist Convention People's Party (CPP, est. 1966), was centrally preoccupied with endeavors to shield gold and other resources from the depredations of global markets, which so often violently privileged foreign ventures and disinherited Ghanaians. Nkrumah joined his efforts with leaders across Africa to unite in this front, envisioning pan-African political and protectionist economic blocs. For deep histories of these movements, see, for example: Kwame Arhin, *The Life and Work of Kwame Nkrumah* (Trenton, NJ: Africa World Press, 1993); Basil Davidson, *Black Star: A View of the Life and Times of Kwame Nkrumah* (Oxford, UK: James Currey, 2007 [1973]); Jeffrey Ahlman, *Living with Nkrumahism: Nation, State, and Pan-Africanism in Ghana* (Athens: Ohio University Press, 2017). For a deeply illuminating examination of the roles and the fashioning of race in the formation of Ghana and of the local, national, and transnational formations of black consciousness and white privilege in continuous play, see: Jemima Pierre, *The Predicament of Blackness: Postcolonial Ghana and the Politics of Race* (Chicago: University of Chicago Press, 2012). As Pierre beautifully argues, "A modern, postcolonial space is invariably a racialized one; it is a space where racial and cultural logics continue to be constituted and reconstituted in the images, institutions, and relationships of the structuring colonial moment," xii. While the social constructions of race and ethnicity in Ghana are not the main focus of this book, their central importance in studies of historical and contemporary Ghana (and Africa, and the rest of the world) cannot be understated. For landmark histories and ethnographies of key commodities, see, for example: Brenda Chalfin, *Shea Butter Republic: State Power, Global Markets, and the Making of an Indigenous Commodity* (New York: Routledge, 2004); Austin, *Labour, Land and Capital in Ghana*; Dumett, *El Dorado in West Africa*.

19. The AGA concession itself spans five traditional stool territories, which are administered by their respective traditional councils and paramount chiefs. The most prominent of these, for Obuasi, is the Adansi Traditional Council. It is made up of seven divisional councils, four of which cover areas in Obuasi Municipality: Edubiase, Akrokerri, Ayease, and Dompoase. The *ohemaa* (queen mother) of Akrokerri presides over the vast majority of the customary surface land within which much of Obuasi sits. She is the most powerful traditional ruler in the town, answerable to paramount chiefs and, ultimately, to the

Asantehene, the king of Asante. The other traditional councils that cover areas of AGA's concession, each with their own divisions, are the Bekwai, Adankraja, Manso Nkwanta, and Manso Mem councils.

20. These facets of a virtual company town echo those of similar extractive sites throughout colonial and postcolonial Africa—and elsewhere.

21. See, for example: Lindsay Whitfield, "Trustees of Development from Conditionality to Governance: Poverty Reduction Strategy Papers in Ghana," *Journal of Modern African Studies* 43, no. 4 (2005): 641–64; A. I. Abdulai, "The Ghanaian Chief as a Manager: Between Tradition and Modernity," in *Chieftaincy in Ghana: Culture, Governance and Development*, edited by Irene K. Odotei and Albert K. Awedoba, 27–42 (Accra, Ghana: Sub-Saharan Publishers, 2006).

22. Government of Ghana, Minerals and Mining Act 1986; Minerals and Mining Act 2006.

23. Kwame Nkrumah, *Dark Days in Ghana* (London: Zed Books, 1968).

24. For "standardized nightmare," see Monica Wilson, "Witch Beliefs and Social Structure," *American Journal of Sociology* 56, no. 4 (1951): 307–13. For powerful analyses of the interplays among valences of violence, memory, despair, and revitalized politics, see: Rosalind Shaw, *Memories of the Slave Trade: Ritual and the Historical Imagination in Sierra Leone* (Chicago: University of Chicago Press, 2002); Jennifer Cole, *Forget Colonialism?: Sacrifice and the Art of Memory in Madagascar* (Berkeley: University of California Press, 2001); Katherine Verdery, *The Political Lives of Dead Bodies: Reburial and Postsocialist Change* (New York: Columbia University Press, 1999); Serguei Oushakine, *The Patriotism of Despair: Nation, War, and Loss in Russia* (Ithaca, NY: Cornell University Press, 2009); Jothie Rajah, *Authoritarian Rule of Law: Legislation, Discourse and Legitimacy in Singapore* (Cambridge: Cambridge University Press, 2012).

25. Janet Roitman, "The Ethics of Illegality in the Chad Basin," in *Law and Disorder in the Postcolony*, edited by Jean Comaroff and John Comaroff, 247–72 (Chicago: University of Chicago Press, 2006); Roitman, *Fiscal Disobedience: An Anthropology of Economic Regulation in Central Africa* (Princeton, NJ: Princeton University Press, 2005). For very nuanced and important analyses of ethical realms and social obligations in formally illegal spaces, see, for example: Daniel Jordan Smith, *A Culture of Corruption: Everyday Deception and Popular Discontent in Nigeria* (Princeton, NJ: Princeton University Press, 2007); James Smith, "Tantalus in the Digital Age"; Reno, *Warlord Politics and African States*; Sasha Newell, "Estranged Belongings: A Moral Economy of Theft in Abidjan, Côte d'Ivoire," *Anthropological Theory* 6, no. 2 (2006): 179–203; Angela Garcia, "The Promise: On the Morality of the Marginal and the Illicit," *Ethos* 42, no. 1 (2014): 51–64; Laurence Ralph, *Renegade Dreams: Living through Injury in Gangland Chicago* (Chicago: University of Chicago Press, 2014).

26. Ofosu-Mensah, "Traditional Gold Mining in Adanse," 132.

27. R. Sutherland Rattray, ed. and trans., *Ashanti Proverbs* (Oxford: Clarendon Press, 1916), 163.

28. Meyerowitz, *The Sacred State of the Akan*, 199.

29. Meyerowitz, *The Sacred State of the Akan*, 197.

30. M. McLeod, "On the Spread of Anti-Witchcraft Cults in Modern Asante." In *Changing Social Structure in Ghana*, edited by Jack Goody, 117 (London: International African Institute, 1975).

31. Ofosu-Mensah, "Traditional Gold Mining in Adanse," 131n38.

32. Emmanuel Akyeampong, "Christianity, Modernity and the Weight of Tradition in the Life of Asantehene Agyeman Prempeh I., c. 1888–1931," *Africa* 69, no. 2 (1999): 295.

33. Walter Benjamin, "Critique of Violence," in *Reflections: Essays, Aphorisms, Autobiographical Writings*, translated by Edmund Jephcott (New York: Schocken Books, 1921 [1978]), 277–300.

34. Benjamin distinguished between mythical and divine violence, equating the former with lawmaking violence. He specifies the mythical nature of lawmaking violence in what he calls the executive and the administrative domains. Benjamin, "Critique of Violence," 295, 300.

5. EFFIGIES, STRIKES, AND COURTS

1. See, for example: "AGC Says Obuasi Strike Costing 2,500 Ounces of Gold Daily," *Ghana Business News*, May 20, 1999, available at: http://www.ghanaweb.com/Ghana HomePage/economy/artikel.php?ID=6864; "AGC Says Ghana Losing 700,000 Dollars a Day in Obuasi Strike," *Ghana Business News*, May 21, 1999, available at: http://www .ghanaweb.com/GhanaHomePage/NewsArchive/artikel.php?ID=6860; "Ashanti Goldfields Company Limited Announces a Temporary Unofficial Stoppage at Its Obuasi Mines," *Business Wire*, May 17, 1999, available at: https://www.ghanaweb.com/GhanaHomePage/News Archive/Ashanti-Goldfields-Company-Limited-Announces-a-Temporary-Unofficial -Stoppage-At-Its-Obuasi-Mines-6533; "Wildcat Strike at Obuasi," *Africa Energy Intelligence*, no. 253, June 2, 1999, available at: http://www.africaintelligence.com/AEM/mining/1999/06 /02/wildcat-strike-at-obuasi,55998-BRE.

2. "AGC Says Ghana Losing."

3. In the 1999 strike, AGC, for its part, defended its position in the package negotiated with the Union, maintaining that the benefits—including a lump-sum payment (equal to about $131 at the time) that was close to the average laborer's wages for one month; a life insurance scheme funded by AGC that the mine claimed amounted to a 3 percent increase in payment; and "an aggressive bonus scheme that rewards productivity." At the same time, the global price of gold had plummeted from $376 per ounce on January 1, 1997, to $275 per ounce in May 1999, owing to IMF and central banks' large sales of gold alongside the financial crisis in Asia, the region with the largest demand for the ore. AGC trumpeted the fact that, despite these inhospitable global market conditions, it had not laid off any of its nine thousand mineworkers, as had mines elsewhere. In addition to this, AGC continued, many employees enjoyed subsidized mine housing, access to school scholarships for their children, and medical benefits. "AGC Says Ghana Losing."

4. Also, while AGC claimed that wages, indexed to the dollar, had increased by 25 percent in local currency terms over the two years prior to the strike, others countered that general inflation and cost-of-living increases had proceeded at least apace. Further, many miners claimed that they had not received any wage increase in four years; they became particularly agitated when they discovered that miners at AGC's mine in Siguiri, Guinea, were receiving higher wages. "Ashanti Gold Miners Strike for Higher Pay," *Ghana News Agency*, May 16, 1999, available at: http://ghanaweb.net/GhanaHomePage//economy

/artikel.php?ID=6532; Trevor Johnson, "Ghana's Ashanti Goldfields Going for a Song," World Socialist Web Site, October 30, 1999, available at: http://www.wsws.org/en/arti cles/1999/10/gold-o30.html.

5. This judgment partakes of a wider culture of mistrust and skepticism of union officials. Miners have long distrusted the Union representatives, viewing them as ordinarily aligned with mine management interests and seeking the comparatively favorable terms of an appointment in the mine's Human Resources Department upon the expiration of Union leadership positions. Miners frequently lamented to me that their Union representatives rarely concern themselves with pleasing their "constituency," or with adequately represent-ing their interests. By and large, Union officials do not seek reelection to their Union offices. Rather, they take a comfortable appointment in one of the mine's management offices. Here, in the 1999 strike, the Union officials appear to have collaborated with government officials against the mine, for political reasons.

6. "NDC Sacks Obuasi Independent Candidate," *Ghanaian Chronicle*, November 30, 2004, available at: http://www.modernghana.com/news/67595/1/ndc-sacks-obuasi-inde pendent-candidate.html.

7. In addition, there was a huge railway strike in the Gold Coast in the same year. As Fredrick Cooper argues, this strike activity dovetailed with mounting nationalist, anticolo-nial political mobilization in the Gold Coast, setting the stage for the onset of the popular urban uprisings during the famous Accra Riots of 1948. As Cooper has shown, these were the first significant, mass political demonstrations in the Gold Coast that extended beyond protests or strikes anchored in industry sectors, trade groups, or guilds. As such, the Accra Riots also have been celebrated as the onset of a broader "political consciousness," a turning point in the politicization of popular discontent that ultimately would culminate in success-ful Independence movements. In contrast to standard political histories concerning the Accra Riots and the rise of nationalist movements, Cooper argues that the conditions were ripe for such broad-based political mobilization on account of the large-scale workers' strikes that had rocked the Gold Coast—and that also were erupting in industrial centers across Africa around the same time. Cooper explains, "The strikes of the late 1940s were significant not just in number or in man-days lost, but in the quality of the strike process itself: they included general strikes or other such events which transcended the boundaries of a particular industry or location, and they took place in vulnerable nodes of the colonial economies, particularly in transportation." He also notes that a central labor organization took shape in the Gold Coast, which, colonial authorities thought, threatened to emerge at the front of a popular anticolonial resistance. Frederick Cooper, *Decolonization and African Society: The Labor Question in French and British Africa* (New York: Cambridge University Press, 1996), 226–27.

8. For British Africa, in addition to the Gold Coast, Cooper invokes the central events of several general port city strikes—in Mombasa in 1947, in Dar es Salaam in 1947, and in Zanzibar in 1948—along with a general strike in 1948 in Bulawayo in Rhodesia, a large gov-ernment and railway strike in Nigeria in 1945, and a wave of forty-six strikes across Nigeria from 1949 to 1950. Cooper, *Decolonization*, 226.

9. Peter had actually been appointed to a district court as a judge, but he resigned in protest over what he perceived to be the compromised natures of the judiciary. He provided

me with a copy of his resignation letter, which cited, among other things, dissatisfaction with how often judges were drunk, or otherwise were concerned primarily with collecting informal payments from litigants or from others with stakes in court cases over which they were presiding.

CONCLUSION: OUT OF THE GOLDEN TWILIGHT?

1. "Obuasi Mine to Shut Down," *Daily Graphic*, April 14, 2014, available at: https://www.graphic.com.gh/business/business-news/obuasi-mine-to-shut-down.html.

2. For a breathtaking examination of fire symbolism and its links to insight and to the soul throughout literature and the other arts, as well as across cultures, see: Gaston Bachelard, *The Psychoanalysis of Fire*, translated by Alan C. M. Ross (Boston: Beacon Press, 1964 [1938]).

3. However, the same write-up also criticizes the alleged mishandlings of Assembly funds over the years: "For instance, the Obuasi Municipal Assembly in 2007 constructed the Obuasi Entrance Arch at a cost of Gh¢89,000 whilst local people yearn for a good road network, potable water, quality healthcare and education." The amount of Gh¢89,000 now equals around $18,388 (in October 2018), though the cedi was much stronger against the dollar in 2007, the year of the arch expenditure. Kofi Adu Domfeh, "Ghana EITI to Explore Impact of Mining on Local Economy—Obuasi under Spotlight," MAC: Mines and Communities, July 23, 2014, available at: http://www.minesandcommunities.org/article.php?a=12716.

4. Mark Morcombe, "Renewing the Obuasi Mine: Managing Challenges through Innovation and Best Practices," quoted in "Obuasi Mine Faces Closure; Over 1,000 Workers to Be Laid-Off," *Ghanaian Chronicle*, January 18, 2014, available at: http://www.ghanaweb.com/GhanaHomePage/NewsArchive/artikel.php?ID=298173.

5. Obuasi CSOs Platform, "Obuasi CSOs Platform Condemn Abrogation of Contract between Mining and Building Contractors (MBC) and AngloGold Ashanti (AGA)," *Modern Ghana*, April 22, 2014, available at: http://www.modernghana.com/news/536744/1/obuasi-csos-platform-condemn-abrogation-of.html. The Obuasi CSOs Platform is a loose association of related NGOs speaking out on behalf of retrenched workers and mining-affected community members. Kofi writes many of their statements. The platform describes its mission thus: "The Obuasi Concerned Civil Society Platform is a coalition of civil society groups that campaigns to ensure Obuasi and its people get a fair benefit of the wealth that nature has endowed the people with." The Platform was assembled at the end of 2013, and its members include prominent NGOs with presences in Obuasi: Centre for Social Impact Studies (CeSIS), Alliance for Obuasi Development (AfOD), Green Ghana Initiative (GGI), Extractive Engagement Group (EEG), and Youth Alliance for Development (YAD). The leading NGO presence is CeSIS, which involves most of the key mining activists who formerly represented Wacam's presence in Obuasi.

6. Obuasi CSOs Platform, "Obuasi CSOs Platform Condemn Abrogation."

7. Karl Marx, *Capital, Vol. I* (New York: New World Paperbacks, 1867 [1967]). See also, for example: Moishe Postone, *Time, Labor, and Social Domination: A Reinterpretation of Marxist Critical Theory* (New York: Cambridge University Press, 1993).

8. The stability agreements stipulate royalty payments, which are production-based, at around 3 percent (of the then prevailing range of 3–6 percent). The agreements also locked in a very generous capital allowance regime, by which the companies can write off investments or expenditures for the mines in Ghana to diminish tax liability; this allows great circumnavigation of tax liability, such that the large companies pay little to no taxes to the government. Corporate taxes are applied to the category of "profits," which companies can ordinarily diminish or eliminate through capital allowances, deducting from their liability. For example, the parent company of, say, the Ghanaian arm of AGA ultimately garners much of the financial gains by "lending to" (at above-market rates) or "investing in" (sometimes, with greatly overpriced machinery, materials, or labor costs) the subsidiary of AGA that operates in Ghana. The parent company can do this either directly or, usually, through one of its affiliated subsidiaries, often incorporated in a tax haven (often Caribbean). Another way in which the subsidiary in Ghana can evade taxes is through a mechanism called "transfer pricing"—that is, through selling the raw material (here, unrefined gold) at below-market rates, so the profit gains to the point source mine in Ghana are not great and, therefore, generate less tax revenue. Much of this happens in a zone of international law that is highly ambiguous, another "gray" zone in which sovereign power is unclear or absent, and such practices are not subject to clear jurisdictional dictates or political governance. Further, this is an oft-hidden feature of the global economy; most people do not understand that these means and ends are in place, and they blame corrupt government officials more than the more significant structural economic dynamics. Transnational corporations arguably *must* operate in these ways in order to stay competitive vis-à-vis other corporations who are behaving in the same way. This is a critical frontier in global law and governance— and one that seems to elude, at this time, the firm grasp of any particular sovereign power. As these processes are further demystified and come into ever greater public consciousness around the world, they promise to be a signal domain for the global contestation of sovereignty and political economy.

9. By all appearances, such players were able to entirely forestall the actual renegotiations. In fact, Parliament never even passed the implementing legislation that was called for when the finance minister in November 2011 announced that the government, as part of "upward adjustment," would implement a windfall profit tax of 10 percent on all mining companies. During the huge surge in mining prices in the early 2000s—from $400 per ounce in 2004 to the peak of around $1,600 per ounce in late 2011—the Ghanaian government's revenues from mining increased only marginally. The public coffers barely gained from these soaring global mineral prices, while transnational mining giants, of course, benefitted handsomely. The lack of a windfall tax by itself cannot explain this failure of the government to capture mining rents in national revenue; with an almost fourfold increase in gold price, one would expect revenue to be dramatically enhanced through other mechanisms, such as royalties and corporate taxes paid. However, various capital allowance structures and ring-fencing mechanisms allow for significant write-offs for domestic point-source operations, allowing for hardly any tax ordinarily to be paid to the Ghanaian government.

10. When the renegotiations were first announced, I was in Ghana. I responded to some friends with enthusiasm, thinking that this was a good-faith sign that the government was serious about enhancing state revenues from mining, to try to help reverse at least part of

the resource curse. A longtime mining advocate returned my optimism with well-placed caution: "This is a tall order, the issues they plan to address, and it is missing the key element of a *timetable*. If things proceed as 'business as usual,' we can expect nothing to ever really happen with these meetings." With this sort of arrangement, with the savviest of legal representatives and consultants on the side of the companies (and with the ever-possible informal payments to key players from the government), endless deferral of substantive action may well ensue.

11. For details on the anatomies of some of these corporate strategies, which can cost nations in the Global South billions in national revenue, see a very lucid summary in Natural Resource Watch, *Report on Ghana*, from February 2012, available from Oxfam Ibis: https://oxfamibis.dk. This report shows that, despite the recent surge in gold prices, Ghana's governmental revenue from mining in 2009 was only around $155 million, while total mineral revenue generated out of the country reached $2.38 billion. Most concerning is the fact that, in 2009, mining only constituted about 6.5 percent of governmental revenue, which is not much higher than the percentage claimed before the global price surge. While there are no current long-term estimates for total revenue lost to illicit capital flight in Ghana, at least to my knowledge, there is a recent study on Zambia that estimates that the country lost $17.3 billion to illicit capital flight from 1970 to 2010. Anthony Simpasa, Degol Hailu, Sebastian Levine, and Roberto Julio Tibana, "Capturing Mineral Revenues in Zambia: Past Trends and Future Prospects," United Nations Development Programme, Discussion Paper, August 2013, 8, available at: http://www.un.org/en/land-natural-resources-conflict/pdfs/capturing-mineral-revenues-zambia.pdf.

12. Roland Barthes, *The Pleasure of the Text*, trans. Richard Miller (New York: Hill and Wang, 1975).

13. Aimé Césaire, *Notebook of a Return to My Native Land*, ed. and trans. Clayton Eshleman and Annete Smith (Middleton, CT: Wesleyan University Press, 2001 [1947]); 1947 version quoted in Frantz Fanon, *Black Skin, White Masks*, translated by Charles Lam Markmann (New York: Grove Press, 1952), 102.

14. For a very nuanced recent take on the ever-unfolding, vital fields of potentialities and emergent being-ness inherent in all worlds, see the essays in João Biehl and Peter Locke, eds., *Unfinished: The Anthropology of Becoming* (Durham, NC: Duke University Press, 2017).

15. Begoña Aretxaga, "Maddening States," *Annual Review of Anthropology* 32 (2003): 393–410, especially 394–95.

16. Wendy Brown, "American Nightmare: Neoliberalism, Neoconservatism, and Dedemocratization," *Political Theory* 34, no. 6 (2006): 690–714, quote at 706.

17. Max Weber, *The Protestant Ethic and the Spirit of Capitalism*, trans. Stephen Kalberg (New York: Oxford University Press, 2011 [1905]).

18. Kwame Anthony Appiah, *In My Father's House: Africa in the Philosophy of Culture* (New York: Oxford University Press, 1992).

19. Robert Cover, "Violence and the Word," *Yale Law Journal* 95 (1986): 1601–29, quote at 1605. See also: Robert Cover, *Narrative, Violence, and the Law: The Essays of Robert Cover*, ed. Martha Minow, Michael Ryan, and Austin Sarat (Ann Arbor: University of Michigan Press, 1992).

20. I use *justice* here with trepidation, and in a resolutely post-foundational sense, very well aware of the important critiques of its ideological freight and of the obfuscating veneer of determinacy it furnishes in multiple domains—law, politics, and social life, more broadly. "In the name of justice" often operates, of course, as an ersatz or feigned divine imprimatur for earthly atrocities, Walter Benjamin's notion of the divine's being "the sign and seal but never the means of sacred execution," adding that this is "what we call sovereign violence." Benjamin, "Critique of Violence," 300. As a symbolic dictate or injunction, and as an ethical measure—often religiously mobilized as a powerful justificatory phantasm that circles around and stands behind prominent *signata* (in Victor Turner's sense)—"justice" is always historically specific and socially constituted, never the transhistorical, universally transcendental category that—however elusive—remains only to be rationally deduced from a bounded set of *a priori* concepts and ontological principles, according to evermore perfected rational procedures. See also: Victor Turner, "Symbolic Studies," *Annual Review of Anthropology* 4 (1975): 145–61.

21. Rose, *Mourning Becomes the Law*, 7, 11.

BIBLIOGRAPHY

Abdulai, A.I. "The Ghanaian Chief as a Manager: Between Tradition and Modernity." In *Chieftaincy in Ghana: Culture, Governance and Development*, edited by Irene K. Odotei and Albert K. Awedoba, 27–42. Accra, Ghana: Sub-Saharan Publishers, 2006.

Abotchie, Chris. "Has the Position of the Chief Become Anachronistic in Contemporary Ghanaian Politics?" In *Chieftaincy in Ghana: Culture, Governance and Development*, edited by Y. Irene K. Odotei and Albert K. Awedoba, 169–82. Accra, Ghana: Sub-Saharan Publishers, 2006.

Abram, David. *The Spell of the Sensuous: Perception and Language in a More-Than-Human World*. New York: Vintage, 2012.

Abynn, Anthony Kwesi. "'Live and Let Live': The Relationship between Artisanal/Small-Scale and Large-Scale Miners at Abosso Goldfields, Ghana." In *Small-Scale Mining, Rural Subsistence, and Poverty in West Africa*, edited by Gavin Hilson, 227–40. Rugby, UK: Practical Action Publishing, 2006.

Acquah, Justice G.K. "The Judicial Role of the Chief in Democratic Governance." In *Chieftaincy in Ghana: Culture, Governance and Development*, edited by Irene K. Odotei and Albert K. Awedoba, 27–42. Accra, Ghana: Sub-Saharan Publishers, 2006.

ActionAid. "Condemned without Trial: Women and Witchcraft in Ghana." Available at: https://www.actionaid.org.uk/sites/default/files/doc_lib/ghana_report_single_pages.pdf. 2012.

Adjaye, Awulae Annor III. "Local Government vis-à-vis Chieftaincy in Ghana: Interplay of Authority, Power and Responsibilities." In *Akan Worlds: Identity and Power in West Africa*, edited by Pierluigi Valsecchi and Fabio Viti, 81–94. Paris: L'Harmattan, 1999.

Adorno, Theodor. *Negative Dialectics*. Translated by E. B. Ashton. New York: Continuum, 1973 [1966].

Africa Energy Intelligence. "Wildcat Strike at Obuasi." June 2, no. 253. Available at: http://www.africaintelligence.com/AEM/mining/1999/06/02/wildcat-strike-at-obuasi,55998-BRE.

Agamben, Giorgio. *Homo Sacer: Sovereign Power and Bare Life (Homo Sacer I)*. Translated by Daniel Heller-Roazen. Stanford, CA: Stanford University Press, 1998.

———. *State of Exception (Homo Sacer II, 1)*. Translated by Kevin Attell. Chicago: University of Chicago Press, 2005.

———. *The Kingdom and the Glory: For a Theological Genealogy of Economy and Government (Homo Sacer II, 2)*. Stanford, CA: Stanford University Press, 2007.

———. *The Sacrament of Language: An Archaeology of the Oath (Homo Sacer II, 3)*. Translated by Adam Kotsko. Stanford, CA: Stanford University Press, 2008.

———. *Opus Dei: An Archeology of Duty (Homo Sacer II, 5)*. Translated by Adam Kotsko. Stanford, CA: Stanford University Press, 2013.

Agbesinyale, P. K. *Ghana's Gold Rush and Regional Development: The Case of Wassa West District* (Dortmund, Germany: SPRING Centre, University of Dortmund, 2003).

Agnew, John. "Mapping Political Power beyond State Boundaries: Territory, Identity, and Movement in World Politics." *Millennium* 28 (1999): 499–521.

Agrawal, Arun. "The Politics of Development and Conservation: Legacies of Colonialism." *Peace and Change* 22, no. 4 (1997): 463–82.

———. *Environmentality: Technologies of Government and the Making of Subjects*. Durham, NC: Duke University Press, 2005.

Agrawal, Arun, and Jesse Ribot. "Accountability in Decentralization: A Framework with South Asian and West African Cases." *Journal of Developing Areas* 33, no. 4 (1999): 473–502.

Agyekum-Gyasi, Collins. "Tension at AGC. *Modern Ghana*, January 22." Available at: http://www.modernghana.com/news/12011/1/tension-at-agc.html, 2001.

Ahlman, Jeffrey, *Living with Nkrumahism: Nation, State, and Pan-Africanism in Ghana*. Athens, OH: Ohio University Press, 2017.

Akabzaa, Thomas. *Boom and Dislocation: The Environmental and Social Impacts of Mining in the Wassa West District of Ghana*. Accra, Ghana: Third World Network—Africa, 2000.

———. "The Challenges of Development: Mining Codes in Africa and Corporate Responsibility." In *International and Comparative Mineral Law and Policy: Trends and Prospects*, edited by Elizabeth Bastida, Thomas Walde, and Janeth Warden-Fernández. The Hague, Netherlands: Kluwer Law International, 2005.

Akabzaa, Thomas, and A. Darimani. "Impact of Mining Sector Investment in Ghana: A Study of the Tarkwa Mining Region." Draft report for Structural Adjustment Participatory Review International Network (SAPRIN). Washington, DC, 2001.

Akabzaa, Thomas M., J. S. Seyire, and K. Afriyie. *The Glittering Façade: Effects of Mining Activities on Obuasi and Its Surrounding Communities*. Accra, Ghana: Third World Network-Africa, 2008.

Akita, Shigeru. "Introduction: From Imperial History to Global History." In *Gentlemanly Capitalism, Imperialism, and Global History*, edited by Shigeru Akita. New York: Palgrave Macmillan, 2002.

Akyeampong, Emmanuel. "What's in a Drink: Class Struggle, Popular Culture, and the Politics of Akpeteshie (Local Gin) in Ghana, 1930–1967." *Journal of African History* 37, no. 2 (1996): 215–36.

———. *Drink, Power, and Cultural Change: A Social History of Alcohol in Ghana, c. 1800 to Recent Times*. Portsmouth, NH: Heinemann, 1996.

———. "Christianity, Modernity and the Weight of Tradition in the Life of Asantehene Agyeman Prempeh I., c. 1888–1931." *Africa* 69, no. 2 (1999): 279–311.

———. *Between the Sea and the Lagoon: An Eco-social History of the Anlo of Southeastern Ghana c. 1850 to Recent Times*. Athens: Ohio University Press, 2001.

———. "Folk Environmental Wisdom versus Scientific Knowledge: Producing and Contesting Knowledge in Anlo, Southeastern Ghana." In *Ghana in Africa and the World: Essays in Honor of Adu Boahen*, edited by Toyin Falola. Trenton, NJ: Africa World Press, 2002.

———. "*Ahenfo Nsa* (the 'Drink of Kings'): Dutch Schnapps and Ritual in Ghanaian History." In *Merchants, Missionaries, and Migrants: 300 Years of Dutch-Ghanaian Relations*, edited by I. van Kessel, 51–61. Karlsruhe, Germany: KIT Publishers, 2002.

———. "For Prayer and Profit: West Africa's Religious and Economic Ties to the Gulf 1960s to the Present." *Journal of African Development* 12, no. 1 (2010): 7–20.

Akyeampong, Emmanuel, and Pashington Obeng. "Spirituality, Gender and Power in Asante History." *International Journal of African Historical Studies* 28, no. 3 (1995): 481–508.

Aleinikoff, T. Alexander. "Transnational Spaces: Norms and Legitimacy." *Yale Journal of International Law* 33 (2008): 479–90.

Ali, Saleem, and Larissa Behrendt. "Mining and Indigenous Rights: The Emergence of a Global Social Movement." *Cultural Survival Quarterly* 25 (2001): 6–8.

Allman, Jean. *The Quills of the Porcupine: Asante Nationalism in an Emergent Ghana, 1954–1957*. Madison: University of Wisconsin Press, 1993.

Allman, Jean, and Antoinette Burton. "Destination Globalization? Women, Gender, and Comparative Colonial Histories in the New Millennium." *Journal of Colonialism and Colonial History* 4, no. 1 (2003).

Allman, Jean, and John Parker. *Tongnaab: The History of a West African God*. Bloomington: Indiana University Press, 2005.

Allman, Jean, Susan Geiger, and Nakanyike Musisi, eds. *Women in African Colonial Histories*. Bloomington: Indiana University Press, 2002.

Ally, Russell. *Gold and Empire: The Bank of England and South Africa's Gold Producers, 1886–1926*. Johannesburg, South Africa: Witwatersrand University Press, 1994.

Althusser, Louis. "The Social Contract (The Discrepancies)." In *Jean-Jacques Rousseau*, edited by Harold Bloom. New York: Chelsea House, 1988.

Aman, Alfred C., and Carol Greenhouse. *Transnational Law: Cases and Problems in an Interconnected World*. Durham, NC: Carolina Academic Press, 2017.

Amanor, Kojo Sebastian. *Global Restructuring and Land Rights in Ghana: Forest Food Chains, Timber and Rural Livelihoods*. Nordiska Afrikainstitutet Research Report No. 108. Uppsala, Sweden: Motala Grafiska, 1999.

———. "Sustainable Development, Corporate Accumulation and Community Expropriation: Land and Natural Resources in West Africa." In *Land and Sustainable Development in Africa*, edited by Kojo Sebastian Amanor and Sam Moyo, 127–58. London: Zed Books, 2008.

———. "Family Values, Land Sales and Agricultural Commodification in South-East Ghana." *Africa* 80, no. 1 (2010): 104–25.

Amanor, Kojo Sebastian, and Janine Ubink. "Contesting Land and Custom in Ghana: Introduction." In *Contesting Land and Custom in Ghana*, edited by Janine M. Ubink and Kojo S. Amanor, 9–26. Leiden, Netherlands: Leiden University Press, 2008.

Amin, Samir. *Accumulation on a World Scale: A Critique of the Theory of Underdevelopment.* Translated by Brian Pearce. New York: Monthly Review Press, 1974.

———. *Unequal Development: An Essay on the Social Formations of Peripheral Capitalism.* Translated by Brian Pearce. New York: Monthly Review Press, 1976.

Amponsah, David. *Desirable Customs: A History of Indigenous Religion and the Making of Modern Ghana, c. 1800–1966.* PhD diss., Harvard University, 2015.

Anderson, Benedict. *Imagined Communities: Reflections on the Origin and Spread of Nationalism.* London: Verso, 2006 [1983].

Andres, Carlos. "World's Top 10 Gold Deposits." *Gold Miners Investment Newsletter*, August 7, 2013. Available at http://www.mining.com/web/worlds-top-10-gold-deposits/.

Anghie, Antony. *Imperialism, Sovereignty, and the Making of International Law.* Cambridge, UK: Cambridge University Press, 2007.

Anonymous. *The Secret of the Golden Flower: A Chinese Book of Life.* Translated by Richard Wilhelm, with commentary by Carl Jung. San Diego: Harcourt, 1962 [1929, first published in German]).

Appadurai, Arjun. "Sovereignty without Territoriality: Notes for a Postnational Geography." In *The Anthropology of Space and Place—Locating Culture*, 337–49. Oxford: Blackwell, 2003.

———. "Grassroots Globalization and the Research Imagination." In *Anthropology in Theory: Issues in Epistemology*, translated by Henrietta L. Moore and Todd Sanders, 622–33. Malden, MA: Blackwell, 2006.

Appiah, Kwame Anthony. *In My Father's House: Africa in the Philosophy of Culture.* New York: Oxford University Press, 1992.

Appiah-Kubi, Kofi. "The Akan Concept of Human Personality." In *Traditional Religion in West Africa*, edited by E. A. Ade Adegbola, 259–64. Ibadan, Nigeria: Daystar, 1987.

Apter, Andrew. "Africa, Empire, and Anthropology: A Philological Exploration of Anthropology's Heart of Darkness." *Annual Review of Anthropology* 28 (1999): 577–98.

———. *The Pan-African Nation: Oil and the Spectacle of Culture in Nigeria.* Chicago: University of Chicago Press, 2005.

Apter, Emily, and William Pietz, eds. *Fetishism as Cultural Discourse.* Ithaca, NY: Cornell University Press, 1993.

Arendt, Hannah. *The Human Condition.* Chicago: University of Chicago Press, 1992 [1958].

Aretxaga, Begoña. "Maddening States." *Annual Review of Anthropology* 32 (2003): 393–410.

Arhin, Kwame. "The Pressure of Cash and Its Political Consequences in Asante in the Colonial Period." *Journal of African Studies* 3, no. 4 (1976–1977): 453–68.

———. "Gold-Mining and Trading among the Ashanti of Ghana." *Journal des Africanistes* 48, no. 1 (1978): 89–100.

———. "Peasants in 19th-century Asante." *Current Anthropology* 24, no. 4 (1983): 471–75.

———. "Trade, Accumulation and the State in Asante in the Nineteenth Century." *Africa* 60 (1990): 524–37.

———. *The Life and Work of Kwame Nkrumah*. Trenton, NJ: Africa World Press, 1993.

———. *Political Systems of Ghana: Traditional Rule in Colonial and Postcolonial Ghana*. Accra, Ghana: University of Ghana, 1994.

———. *The Political Systems of Ghana: Background to Transformations in Traditional Authority in the Colonial and Post-Colonial Periods*. Accra, Ghana: Historical Society of Ghana, 2002.

Aristotle. *The Politics*. Translated by T. A. Sinclair. New York: Penguin, 1981 [350 BCE]

———. *De Anima (On the Soul)*. Translated by Hugh Lawson-Tancred. New York: Penguin, 1987 [350 BCE].

Arthur, Kofi. "Ghana: Branch Secretary Interdiction Is Constitutional—GMWU." *Public Agenda*, February 19, 2001. Available at: http://allafrica.com/stories/200102190427.html.

Aryee, B. "Ghana's Mining Sector: Its Contribution to the National Economy." *Resources Policy* 27, no. 2 (2001): 61–75.

———. "Small-Scale Mining in Ghana as a Sustainable Development Activity: Its Development and a Review of the Contemporary Issues and Challenges." In *The Socioeconomic Impacts of Artisanal and Small-Scale Mining in Developing Countries*, 379–418. Rotterdam, Netherlands: A. A. Balkema, 2003.

Asad, Talal. *Genealogies of Religion: Disciplines and Reasons of Power in Christianity and Islam*. Baltimore: Johns Hopkins University Press, 1993.

Asare, George Ernest. "Obuasi Residents Flee as Illegal Miners Go on a Rampage." *Daily Graphic*, March 21, 2013. Available at: http://graphic.com.gh/General-News/obuasi-residents-flee-as-illegal-miners-go-on-rampage.html.

———. "Calm Returns to Obuasi." *Daily Graphic*, March 22, 2013. Available at: http://graphic.com.gh/General-News/calm-returns-to-obuasi.html.

Ashforth, Adam. *The Politics of Official Discourse in Twentieth-Century South Africa*. Oxford: Oxford University Press, 1990.

———. *Witchcraft, Violence, and Democracy in South Africa*. Chicago: University of Chicago Press, 2005.

Atta-Quayson, Alhassan. "Statement by National Coalition on Mining on 2012 Budget: Proceed with Further Reforms in the Mining Sector." *Modern Ghana*, November 21, 2011. Available at: https://www.modernghana.com/news/362239/statement-by-national-coalition-on-mining-on-2012-budget-pr.html.

Atuguba, Raymond. "An African Redefinition of Popular Democratic and Development Nomenclature." *International Journal of Innovative Research & Development* 5, no. 10 (2016): 58–65.

Aubynn, Anthony Kwesi. "'Live and Let Live': The Relationship between Artisanal/Small-Scale and Large-Scale Miners at Abosso Goldfields, Ghana." In *Small-Scale Mining, Rural Subsistence, and Poverty in West Africa*, edited by Gavin M. Hilson, 227–40. Warwickshire, UK: Practical Action Publishing, 2006.

Austen, Ralph. *African Economic History: Internal Development and External Dependency*. London: J. Currey, 1987.

———. "The Moral Economy of Witchcraft." In *Modernity and Its Malcontents*, edited by Jean Comaroff and John Comaroff, 89–110. Chicago: University of Chicago Press, 1993.

———. "Africa and Globalization: Colonialism, Decolonization and the Postcolonial Malaise." *Journal of Global History* 1, no. 3 (2006): 403–8.

Austin, Gareth. *Labour, Land and Capital in Ghana: From Slavery to Free Labour in Asante, 1807–1956*. Rochester, NY: University of Rochester Press, 2005.

Ayensu, Edward S. *Ashanti Gold: The African Legacy of the World's Most Precious Metal*. London: Marshall, 1997.

Bachelard, Gaston. *The Psychoanalysis of Fire*. Translated by Alan C. M. Ross. Boston: Beacon Press, 1964 [1938].

Ballard, Chris, and Glenn Banks. "Resource Wars: The Anthropology of Mining." *Annual Review of Anthropology* 32 (2003): 287–313.

Ballestero, Andrea. "The Ethics of a Formula: Calculating a Financial-Humanitarian Price for Water." *American Ethnologist* 42, no. 2 (2015): 262–78.

Barkan, Joshua. *Corporate Sovereignty: Law and Government under Capitalism*. Minneapolis: University of Minnesota Press, 2013.

Barnes, J. A. "The Village Headman in British Central Africa: The Fort Jameson Ngoni." *Africa* 19, no. 2 (1949): 100–106.

Barnes, Sandra. *Patrons and Power: Creating a Political Community in Metropolitan Lagos*. Bloomington: Indiana University Press, 1986.

Barry, Andrew, Thomas Osborne, and Nikolas S. Rose. *Foucault and Political Reason: Liberalism, Neo-Liberalism, and Rationalities of Government*. Chicago: University of Chicago Press, 1996.

Bartelson, Jens. *A Genealogy of Sovereignty*. Cambridge, UK: Cambridge University Press, 1995.

———. "The Concept of Sovereignty Revisited." *European Journal of International Law* 17, no. 2 (2006): 463–74.

Barthes, Roland. *The Pleasure of the Text*. Translated by Richard Miller. New York: Hill and Wang, 1975.

Bastida, Elizabeth, Thomas Walde, and Janeth Warden-Fernández. "Introduction and Overview: International and Comparative Perspectives of Mineral Law and Policy." In *International and Comparative Mineral Law and Policy: Trends and Prospects*, edited by Elizabeth Bastida, Thomas Walde, and Janeth Warden-Fernández. The Hague, Netherlands: Kluwer Law International, 2005.

Bataille, Georges. *The Accursed Share: An Essay on General Economy, Vols. 1–3*. Translated by Robert Hurley. New York: Zone Books, 1991 [1949].

Bates, Robert H. *Input Structure, Output Functions, and Systems Capacity: A Study of the Mineworkers' Union of Zambia*. Cambridge, MA: Center for International Studies, MIT, 1969.

Bayart, Jean-Francois. *The State in Africa: The Politics of the Belly*. London: Longman, 1993.

Bayart, Jean-Francois, Stephen Ellis, and Beatrice Hibou. *The Criminalization of the State in Africa*. Translated by Stephen Ellis. Bloomington: Indiana University Press, 1999.

Bean, Richard. "A Note on the Relative Importance of Slaves and Gold in West African Exports." *Journal of African History* 14 (1977): 351–56.

Beaulac, Stéphane. *The Power of Language in the Making of International Law: The Word Sovereignty in Bodin and Vattel and the Myth of Westphalia*. Leiden: Martinus Nijhoff, 2004.

Beckert, Sven. "From Tuskegee to Togo." *Journal of American History* 92, no. 2 (2005): 498–526.

Beckman, Björn. *Organising the Farmers: Cocoa Politics and National Development in Ghana*. Uppsala, Sweden: Scandinavian Institute of African Studies, 1976.

Beinart, W., and L. Hughes. *Environment and Empire*. Cambridge: Cambridge University Press, 2007.

Beliso-de Jesús, Aisha. *Electric Santería: Racial and Sexual Assemblages of Transnational Religion*. New York: Columbia University Press, 2015.

Benjamin, Walter. "Critique of Violence." In *Reflections: Essays, Aphorisms, Autobiographical Writings*, translated by Edmund Jephcott, 277–300. New York: Schocken Books, 1921 [1978].

———. *Illuminations*. New York: Schocken Books, 1969.

———. *Reflections*. New York: Schocken Books, 1969.

Benson, Peter. *Tobacco Capitalism: Growers, Migrant Workers, and the Changing Face of a Global History*. Princeton, NJ: Princeton University Press, 2012.

Benton, Lauren. *Law and Colonial Cultures: Legal Regimes in World History, 1400–1900*. Cambridge, UK: Cambridge University Press, 2002.

———. "Constitutions and Empires." *Law and Social Inquiry* 31 (2006): 177–98.

———. *A Search for Sovereignty: Law and Geography in European Empires, 1400–1900*. Cambridge: Cambridge University Press, 2006.

Berger, Iris. "African Women's History: Themes and Perspectives." *Journal of Colonialism and Colonial History* 4, no. 1 (2003).

Berlant, Lauren. *Cruel Optimism*. Durham, NC: Duke University Press, 2011.

Bernault, Florence. "Body, Power and Sacrifice in Equatorial Africa." *Journal of African History* 47 (2006): 207–39.

Bernstein, Anya. "More Alive Than All the Living: Sovereign Bodies and Cosmic Politics in Buddhist Siberia." *Cultural Anthropology* 27, no. 2 (2012): 261–85.

———. *Religious Bodies Politic: Rituals of Sovereignty in Buryat Buddhism*. Chicago: University of Chicago Press, 2013.

Bernstein, Peter L. *The Power of Gold: The History of an Obsession*. London: Wiley, 2000.

Berry, Sara. *No Condition Is Permanent: The Social Dynamics of Agrarian Change in Sub-Saharan Africa*. Madison: University of Wisconsin Press, 1993.

———. "Tomatoes, Land, and Hearsay: Property and History in Asante in the Time of Structural Adjustment." *World Development* 25, no. 8 (1997): 1225–41.

———. "Unsettled Accounts: Stool Debts, Chieftaincy Disputes and the Question of Asante Constitutionalism." *Journal of African History* 39, no. 1 (1998): 1–24.

———. *Chiefs Know Their Boundaries: Essays on Property, Power, and the Past in Asante, 1896–1996*. Portsmouth, NH: Heinemann, 2001.

———. "Privatization and the Politics of Belonging in West Africa." In *Property Rights and the Politics of Belonging*, edited by Richard Kuba and Carola Lentz. Leiden: E. J. Brill, 2005.

———. "Property, Authority and Citizenship: Land Claims, Politics and the Dynamics of Social Division in West Africa." 23–45. *Development and Change*, 2009.

Bertelsen, Bjørn Enge. *Violent Becomings: State Formation, Sociality, and Power in Mozambique*. New York: Berghahn.

Besson, Samantha, and John Tasioulas. "Introduction." In *The Philosophy of International Law*, edited by Samantha Besson and John Tasioulas, 1–32. New York: Oxford University Press, 2010.

Biehl, João, and Peter Locke, eds. *Unfinished: The Anthropology of Becoming*. Durham, NC: Duke University Press, 2017.

Binsbergen, Wim M. J. van, and Peter L. Geschiere, eds. *Commodification: Things, Agency, and Identities: The Social Life of Things Revisited*. Münster, Germany: Lit Verlag, 2005.

Bishara, Amahl. "Sovereignty and Popular Sovereignty for Palestinians and Beyond." *Cultural Anthropology* 32, no. 3 (2017): 349–58.

Boahen, Adu. *Ghana: Evolution and Change in the Nineteenth and Twentieth Centuries*. London: Longman, 1975.

Bodin, Jean. *On Sovereignty*. Edited by Julian Franklin. Cambridge: Cambridge University Press, 1992.

Bohannan, Paul. *Justice and Judgment among the Tiv*. Oxford: Oxford University Press, 1957.

———. "Ethnography and Comparison in Legal Anthropology." In *Law in Culture and Society*, edited by Laura Nader. Chicago: Aldine, 1969.

Boissevain, Jeremy. *Friends of Friends: Networks, Manipulators and Coalitions*. Oxford: Oxford University Press, 1974.

Bonilla, Yarimar. "Unsettling Sovereignty." *Cultural Anthropology* 32, no. 3 (2017): 330–39.

Borneman, John, and Abdellah Hammoudi. "The Fieldwork Encounter, Experience, and the Making of Truth: An Introduction." In *Being There: The Fieldwork Encounter and the Making of Truth*, edited by John Borneman and Abdellah Hammoudi, 1–25. Berkeley: University of California Press, 2009.

Borras, Saturnino M. Jr., Ruth Hall, Ian Scoones, Ben White, and Wendy Wolford. "Towards a Better Understanding of Global Land Grabbing: An Editorial Introduction." *Journal of Peasant Studies* 38, no. 2 (2011): 209–16.

Bourdieu, Pierre. *The Logic of Practice*. Translated by Richard Nice. Stanford, CA: Stanford University Press, 1990.

———. *Language and Symbolic Power*. Edited and translated by Gino Raymond and Matthew Adamson. Malden, MA: Polity Press, 1991.

Bowen, H. V. "Gentlemanly Capitalism and the Making of a Global British Empire: Some Connections and Contexts, 1688–1815." In *Gentlemanly Capitalism, Imperialism, and Global History*, edited by Shigeru Akita, 19–42. New York: Palgrave Macmillan, 2002.

Braudel, Fernand. *Civilization and Capitalism, 15th–18th Centuries*. 3 vols. Translated by Siân Reynolds. New York: Harper & Row, 1979 [1982–1984].

Brazeal, Brian. "The Fetish and the Stone: A Moral Economy of Charlatans and Thieves." In *Spirited Things: The Work of "Possession" in Afro-Atlantic Religions*, edited by Paul Christopher Johnson, 131–54. Chicago: University of Chicago Press, 2014.

———. "Austerity, Luxury, and Uncertainty in the Indian Emerald Trade." *Journal of Material Culture* 22, no. 4 (2017): 437–52.

Breckenridge, Keith. "'Money with Dignity': Migrants, Minelords and the Cultural Politics of the South African Gold Standard Crisis, 1920–33." *Journal of African History* 36, no. 2 (1995): 271–304.

Bridge, Gavin. "Contested Terrain: Mining and the Environment." *Annual Review of Environmental Resources* 29 (2004): 205–59.

———. "The Hole World: Scales and Spaces of Extraction." *Scenario* 5 (2015).

Brokensha, David W. *Social Change at Larteh, Ghana.* Oxford: Oxford University Press, 1966.

Brown, Vincent. "Spiritual Terror and Sacred Authority in Jamaican Slave Society." *Slavery and Abolition* 24, no. 1 (2003): 24–53.

———. *The Reaper's Garden: Death and Power in the World of Atlantic Slavery.* Cambridge, MA: Harvard University Press, 2008.

Brown, Wendy. *States of Injury: Power and Freedom in Late Modernity.* Princeton, NJ: Princeton University Press, 1995.

———. "American Nightmare: Neoliberalism, Neoconservatism, and De-democratization." *Political Theory* 34, no. 6 (2006): 690–714.

———. *Walled States, Waning Sovereignty.* New York: Zone Books, 2010.

Brown, Wendy, and Janet Halley. "Introduction." In *Left Legalism/Left Critique*, edited by Wendy Brown and Janet Halley, 1–37. Durham, NC: Duke University Press, 2002.

Brubaker, Rogers, and Frederick Cooper. "Beyond 'Identity.'" *Theory and Society* 29, no. 1 (2000): 1–47.

Buchanan, Nicholas, and Eve Darian-Smith. "Introduction: Law and the Problematics of Indigenous Authenticities." *Law and Social Inquiry* 36, no. 1 (2011): 115–24.

Burawoy, Michael. "The Anthropology of Industrial Work." *Annual Review of Anthropology* 8 (1979): 231–66.

Burckhardt, Titus. *The Mirror of the Intellect: Essays on Traditional Science and Sacred Art.* New York: SUNY Press, 1987.

———. *Alchemy: Science of the Cosmos, Science of the Soul.* Louisville, KY: Fons Vitae, 1997.

Burke, Timothy. *Lifebuoy Man, Lux Women: Commodification, Consumption and Cleanliness in Modern Zimbabwe.* Durham, NC: Duke University Press, 1996.

Busia, Kofi A. *The Position of the Chief in the Modern Political System of Ashanti.* Oxford: Oxford University Press, 1951.

———. "The Ashanti of the Gold Coast." In *African Worlds: Studies in the Cosmological Ideas and Social Values of African Peoples*, edited by D. Forde. Oxford: Oxford University Press, 1954.

Business Wire. "Ashanti Goldfields Company Limited Announces a Temporary Unofficial Stoppage at Its Obuasi Mines." Ghana Web, May 17, 1999. Available at: https://www.ghanaweb.com/GhanaHomePage/NewsArchive/Ashanti-Goldfields-Company-Limited-Announces-a-Temporary-Unofficial-Stoppage-At-Its-Obuasi-Mines-6533.

Butler, Judith. *The Psychic Life of Power: Theories in Subjection.* Stanford, CA: Stanford University Press, 1997.

———. *Precarious Life: The Powers of Mourning and Violence.* London: Verso, 2006.

Butler, Judith, and Athena Athanasiou. *Dispossession: The Performative in the Political.* Malden, MA: Polity Press, 2013.

Butticci, Annalisa. *African Pentecostals in Catholic Europe: The Politics of Presence in the Twenty-First Century.* Cambridge, MA: Harvard University Press, 2016.

Buur, Lars, and Helene Maria Kyed. "Contested Sources of Authority: Re-claiming State Sovereignty by Formalizing Traditional Authority in Mozambique." In *Twilight*

Institutions: Public Authority and Local Politics in Africa, edited by Christian Lund. Hoboken, NJ: Wiley-Blackwell, 2007.

Cadena, Marisol de la. "Indigenous Cosmopolitics in the Andes: Conceptual Reflections Beyond 'Politics.'" *Cultural Anthropology* 25, no. 2 (2010): 334–70.

———. *Earth Beings: Ecologies of Practice across Andean Worlds.* Durham, NC: Duke University Press, 2015.

Cain, P. J., and A. G. Hopkins. *British Imperialism, 1688–2000.* New York: Longman, 2002.

———. "The Peculiarities of British Capitalism: Imperialism and World Development." In *Gentlemanly Capitalism, Imperialism, and Global History*, edited by Shigeru Akita. New York: Palgrave Macmillan, 2002.

Calvão, Filipe. "Unfree Labor." *Annual Review of Anthropology* 45 (2016): 451–67.

———. "The Company Oracle: Corporate Security and Diviner-Detectives in Angola's Diamond Mines." *Comparative Studies in Society and History* 59, no. 3 (2017): 574–99.

Carmichael, John. *African Eldorado: Gold Coast to Ghana.* London: Duckworth, 1993.

Casanova, José. *Public Religions in the Modern World.* Chicago: University of Chicago Press, 1993.

Caton, Steven C., and Bernardo Zacka. "Abu Ghraib, the Security Apparatus, and the Performativity of Power." *American Ethnologist* 37, no. 2 (2010): 203–11.

Cavanaugh, William T. *Theopolitical Imagination.* London: T&T Clark, 2002.

Cerny, Philip. "Globalization and the Changing Logic of Collective Action." *International Organization* 49, no. 4 (1995): 595–25.

Césaire, Aimé. *Notebook of a Return to My Native Land.* Edited by Mireille Rosello. Translated by Mireille Rosello and Annie Pritchard. Hexham, UK: Bloodaxe, 1995 [1947].

———. *Discourse on Colonialism.* Translated by Joan Pinkham. New York: Monthly Review Press, 2000 [1955].

Chakrabarty, Dipesh. *Provincializing Europe: Postcolonial Thought and Historical Difference.* Princeton, NJ: Princeton University Press, 2000.

Chalfin, Brenda. *Shea Butter Republic: State Power, Global Markets, and the Making of an Indigenous Commodity.* New York: Routledge, 2004.

———. "Sovereigns and Citizens in Close Encounter: Airport Anthropology and Customs Regimes in Neoliberal Ghana." *American Ethnologist* 35, no. 4 (2008): 519–38.

———. *Neoliberal Frontiers: An Ethnography of Sovereignty in West Africa.* Chicago: University of Chicago Press, 2010.

Chance, Kerry Ryan. "'Where There Is Fire, There Is Politics': Ungovernability and Material Life in Urban South Africa." *Cultural Anthropology* 30, no. 3 (2015): 394–423.

Chanock, Martin. *Law, Custom, and Social Order: The Colonial Experience in Malawi and Zambia.* Cambridge: Cambridge University Press, 1985.

———. "A Peculiar Sharpness: An Essay on Property in the History of Customary Law in Colonial Africa." *Journal of African History* 32, no. 1 (1991): 65–88.

Chatterjee, Partha. *The Nation and Its Fragments: Colonial and Postcolonial Histories.* Princeton, NJ: Princeton University Press, 1993.

———. "Sovereign Violence and the Domain of the Political." In *Sovereign Bodies: Citizens, Migrants, and States in the Postcolonial World*, edited by Thomas Blom Hansen and Finn Stepputat, 82–102. Princeton, NJ: Princeton University Press, 2005.

Christaller, Johann Gottlieb. *A Collection of Three Thousand and Six Hundred Tshi Proverbs.* Basel, Germany: Basel Missionary Society, 1879.

Christiansë, Yvette. "Passing Away: The Unspeakable (Losses) of Postapartheid South Africa." In *Loss*, edited by David L. Eng and David Kazanjian, 372–95. Berkeley: University of California Press, 2003.

Ciekawy, Diane. "Witchcraft in Statecraft: Five Technologies of Power in Colonial and Postcolonial Coastal Kenya." *African Studies Review* 41, no. 3 (1998): 119–41.

Citi FM Online. "Windfall Tax Dropped—Prez Mahama." January 24, 2014. Available at: http://www.ghanatrade.gov.gh/Latest-News/windfall-tax-dropped-prez-mahama.html.

Clark, Ian. "Beyond the Great Divide: Globalization and the Theory of International Relations." *Review of International Studies* 24, no. 4 (1998): 479–98.

Clarke, Kamari Maxine. *Fictions of Justice: The International Criminal Court and the Challenges of Legal Pluralism in Sub-Saharan Africa.* New York: Cambridge University Press, 2009.

———. "Rethinking Sovereignty through Hashtag Publics: The New Body Politics." *Cultural Anthropology* 32, no. 3 (2017): 359–66.

Cohen, Jean L. "Whose Sovereignty? Empire Versus International Law." *Ethics & International Affairs* 18, no. 3 (2004): 1–24.

Cohn, Bernard. *Colonialism and Its Forms of Knowledge.* Princeton, NJ: Princeton University Press, 1996.

Cole, Catherine M. *Ghana's Concert Party Theatre.* Bloomington: Indiana University Press, 2001.

Cole, Jennifer. *Forget Colonialism? Sacrifice and the Art of Memory in Madagascar.* Berkeley: University of California Press, 2001.

Colson, Elizabeth. "Social Control and Vengeance in Plateau Tonga Society." *Africa* 23 (1953): 199–212.

———. "The Impact of the Colonial Period on the Definition of Land Rights." In *Colonialism in Africa, Vol. 4: Profiles of Change: African Society and Colonial Rule*, edited by Victor Turner, 221–51. Cambridge: Cambridge University Press, 1971.

Comaroff, Jean. *Body of Power, Spirit of Resistance: The Culture and History of a South African People.* Chicago: University of Chicago Press, 1985.

———. "Beyond Bare Life: AIDS, (Bio)Politics, and the Neo World Order." *Public Culture* 19 (2007): 197–219.

Comaroff, Jean, and John Comaroff. "The Madman and the Migrant: Work and Labor in the Historical Consciousness of a South African People." *American Ethnologist* 14, no. 2 (1987): 191–209.

———. "Occult Economies and the Violence of Abstraction: Notes from the South African Postcolony." *American Ethnologist* 26, no. 2 (1999): 279–303.

———, eds. *Millennial Capitalism and the Culture of Neoliberalism.* Durham, NC: Duke University Press, 2001.

———. *Theory from the South; or, How Euro-America Is Evolving toward Africa.* Boulder, CO: Paradigm, 2012.

Comaroff, John L. "Reflections on the Colonial State, in South Africa and Elsewhere: Fragments, Factions, Facts and Fictions." *Social Identities* 4, no. 3 (1998): 321–61.

———. "Colonialism, Culture, and the Law: A Foreword." *Law and Social Inquiry* 26, no. 2 (2001): 305–14.

———. "Reflections on the Rise of Legal Theology: Law and Religion in the Twenty-First Century." *Social Analysis* 53, no. 1 (2009): 193–216.

Comaroff, John L., and Jean Comaroff. *Ethnography and the Historical Imagination*. Boulder, CO: Westview Press, 1992.

———. *Of Revolution and Revelation, Vol. II, The Dialectics of Modernity on a South African Frontier*. Chicago.: University of Chicago Press, 1997.

———. "Policing Culture, Cultural Policing: Law and Social Order in Postcolonial South Africa." *Law and Social Inquiry* 29, no. 3 (2004): 513–46.

———. "Introduction." In *Law and Disorder in the Postcolony*, edited by Jean Comaroff and John L. Comaroff, 1–56. Chicago: University of Chicago Press, 2006.

———. *Ethnicity, Inc*. Chicago: University of Chicago Press, 2009.

Comaroff, John L., and Simon A. Roberts. *Rules and Processes: The Cultural Logic of Dispute in an African Context*. Chicago: University of Chicago Press, 1981.

Commission on Human Rights and Administrative Justice (CHRAJ, Ghana). "The State of Human Rights in Mining Communities in Ghana." 2008. Available at https://chraj.gov.gh/.

Connolly, William E. "The Complexity of Sovereignty." In *Sovereign Lives: Power in Global Politics*. London: Routledge, 2005.

Cook, Susan E. "The Business of Being Bafokeng: The Corporatization of a Tribal Authority in South Africa." *Current Anthropology* 52, no. S3: 151–59.

Cooke, Bill, and Uma Kothari, eds. *Participation: The New Tyranny?* London: Zed, 2001.

Cooper, Frederick. *Decolonization and African Society: The Labor Question in French and British Africa*. New York: Cambridge University Press, 1996.

Coronil, Fernando, and Julie Skurski, eds. *States of Violence*. Ann Arbor: University of Michigan Press, 2006.

Couliano, Ioan P. *Eros and Magic in the Renaissance*. Translated by Margaret Cook. Chicago: University of Chicago Press, 1987.

Coumans, Catherine. "Occupying Spaces Created by Conflict: Anthropologists, Development NGOs, Responsible Investment, and Mining." *Current Anthropology* 52 no. S3 (2011): 29–43.

Cover, Robert. "Violence and the Word." *Yale Law Journal* 95 (1986): 1601–9.

———. *Narrative, Violence, and the Law: The Essays of Robert Cover*. Edited by Martha Minow, Michael Ryan, and Austin Sarat. Ann Arbor: University of Michigan Press, 1992.

Coyle, Geoff. *The Riches Beneath Our Feet: How Mining Shaped Britain*. New York: Oxford University Press, 2010.

Coyle Rosen, Lauren. "The Birth of the Labor Bureau: Surveillance, Pacification, and the Statistical Objectivity Metanarrative." *Rethinking Marxism* 22, no. 4 (2010): 544–68.

———. "The Spiritless Rose in the Cross of the Present: Retracing Hegel in Adorno's *Negative Dialectics* and Related Lectures." *Telos* 155 (2011): 39–61.

———. "Tender Is the Mine: Law, Shadow Rule, and the Public Gaze in Ghana." In *Corporate Social Responsibility? Human Rights in the New Global Economy*, edited by John Kelly and Charlotte Walker-Said, 297–317. Chicago: University of Chicago Press, 2015.

———. "Fallen Chiefs and Sacrificial Mining in Ghana." In *The Politics of Custom: Chiefship, Capital, and the State*, edited by John L. Comaroff and Jean Comaroff, 247–78. Chicago: University of Chicago Press, 2018.

Crapanzano, Vincent. "Introduction." In *Case Studies in Spirit Possession*, edited by Vincent Crapanzano and V. Garrison. New York: Wiley, 1977.

Crisp, Jeff. *The Story of an African Working Class: Ghanaian Miners' Struggles, 1870–1980*. London: Zed Books, 1984.

Crush, Jonathan, Alan Jeeves, and David Yudelman. *South Africa's Labor Empire: A History of Black Migrancy to the Gold Mines*. Boulder, CO: Westview Press, 1991.

Crush, Jonathan. "Power and Surveillance on the South African Gold Mines." *Journal of Southern African Studies* 18 (1992): 825–44.

Csordas, Thomas J. *The Sacred Self: A Cultural Phenomenology of Charismatic Healing*. Berkeley: University of California Press, 1994.

———. "Introduction: Modalities of Transnational Transcendence." In *Transnational Transcendence: Essays on Religion and Globalization*, edited by Thomas J. Csordas, 1–30. Berkeley: University of California Press, 2009.

———. "Elements of Charismatic Persuasion and Healing." In *A Reader in Medical Anthropology: Theoretical Trajectories, Emergent Realities*, edited by Byron J. Good, Michael M. J. Fischer, Sarah S. Willen, and Mary-Jo DelVecchio Good, 91–107. Malden, MA: Wiley Blackwell, 2010.

Daily Graphic. "Stamping Out Illegal Mining. Editorial." April 30, 2013. Available at: http://graphic.com.gh/Editorial/stamping-out-illegal-mining.html.

———. "Obuasi Mine to Shut Down." April 14, 2014. Available at: https://www.graphic.com.gh/business/business-news/obuasi-mine-to-shut-down.html.

D'Angelo, Lorenzo. "Who Owns the Diamonds? The Occult Economy of Diamond Mining in Sierra Leone." *Africa* 84, no. 2 (2014): 269–93.

D'Angelo, Lorenzo, and Robert J. Pijpers. "Mining Temporalities: An Overview." *Extractive Industries and Society* 5, no. 2: 215–22.

Danquah, J. B., ed. *Cases in Akan Law*. London: G. Routledge & Sons, 1928.

———. *The Akan Doctrine of God: A Fragment of Gold Coast Ethics and Religion*. London: Lutterworth Press, 1944.

Darian-Smith, Eve. "Ethnographies of Law." In *The Blackwell Companion to Law and Society*, edited by Austin Sarat, 545–68. Malden, MA: Blackwell, 2004.

Das, Veena. *Life and Words: Violence and the Descent into the Ordinary*. Berkeley: University of California Press, 2006.

Davidson, Basil. *Black Star: A View of the Life and Times of Kwame Nkrumah*. Oxford, UK: James Currey, 2007 [1973].

D'Avignon, Robyn. "Primitive Techniques: From 'Customary' to 'Artisanal' Mining in French West Africa." *Journal of African History* 59, no. 2 (2018): 179–97.

Davis, Elizabeth. *Bad Souls: Madness and Responsibility in Modern Greece*. Durham, NC: Duke University Press, 2012.

De Boeck, Filip. "Beyond the Grave: History, Memory, and Death in Postcolonial Congo/Zaire." In *Memory and the Postcolony: African Anthropology and the Critique of Power*, edited by Richard Werbner. New York: Zed Books, 1998.

——. "Domesticating Diamonds and Dollars: Expenditure, Identity, and Sharing in Southwestern Zaire." *Development and Change* 29 (1998): 777–810.

——. "Borderland Breccia: The Mutant Hero in the Historical Imagination of a Central-African Diamond Frontier." *Journal of Colonialism and Colonial History* 1, no. 2 (2000): 1–44.

De Heusch, Luc. *The Drunken King; or, The Origin of the State*. Translated by R. Willis. Bloomington: Indiana University Press, 1982.

——. *Sacrifice in Africa: A Structuralist Approach*. Manchester, UK: Manchester University Press, 1986.

Deibert, Michael. "A Glittering Demon: Mining, Poverty and Politics in the Democratic Republic of Congo." *CorpWatch*, June 26, 2008, available at: https://corpwatch.org/article/glittering-demon-mining-poverty-and-politics-democratic-republic-congo.

Deleuze, Gilles, and Felix Guattari. *A Thousand Plateaus: Capitalism and Schizophrenia*. Translated by Brian Massumi. Minneapolis: University of Minnesota Press, 1987 [1980].

Deren, Maya. *Divine Horsemen: The Living Gods of Haiti*. Kingston, NY: McPherson, 1983.

Derrida, Jacques. "Force of Law: The 'Mystical Foundation of Authority.'" Translated by M. Quaintance. In *Acts of Religion*, edited by G. Anidjar. London: Routledge, 2002 [1994].

Desan, Christine. *Making Money: Coin, Currency, and the Coming of Capitalism*. Oxford: Oxford University Press, 2015.

Descola, Philippe. *Beyond Nature and Culture: Proceedings of the British Academy, Vol. 139*. Oxford: Oxford University Press, 2006.

Dickson, Kwamina B. *A Historical Geography of Ghana*. London: Cambridge University Press, 1969.

Dirks, Nicholas B. "Introduction." In *Colonialism and Culture*, edited by Nicholas B. Dirks, 1–26. Ann Arbor: University of Michigan Press, 1992.

Domfeh, Kofi Adu. "Ghana EITI to Explore Impact of Mining on Local Economy—Obuasi under Spotlight." MAC: Mines and Communities, July 23, 2014. Available at: http://www.minesandcommunities.org/article.php?a=12716.

Douglas, Mary. *Purity and Danger: An Analysis of Concepts of Pollution and Taboo*. London: Routledge, 2002 [1966].

Dumett, Raymond E. *El Dorado in West Africa: The Gold-Mining Frontier, African Labor, and Colonial Capitalism in the Gold Coast, 1875–1900*. Athens: Ohio University Press, 1998.

Duranti, Alessandro. "Husserl, Intersubjectivity and Anthropology." *Anthropological Theory* 10, no. 1 (2010): 16–35.

Durkheim, Emile. *The Elementary Forms of the Religious Life: A Study in Religious Sociology*. Translated by Joseph Ward Swain. Glencoe, IL: Free Press, 1947 [1912].

——. *The Division of Labor in Society*. Translated by W. D. Halls. New York: Free Press, 1984 [1893].

Eboyi-Anza, F. K. *The Akan Concept of Man (Nzema Case Study)*. Accra, Ghana: New Times Corporation, 1997.

Edelman, Marc. "Bringing the Moral Economy of the Peasant Back in . . . to the Study of 21st-Century Transnational Peasant Movements." *American Anthropologist* 107, no. 3 (2005): 331–45.

Eliade, Mircea. *Myths, Dreams, and Mysteries*. Translated by Philip Mairet. New York: Harper & Brothers, 1960.

————. *The Forge and the Crucible: The Origins and Structures of Alchemy*. Translated by Stephen Corrin. Chicago: University of Chicago Press, 1978.

Ellimah, Richard. *A Study of the Tax Structure and the Impact of Large-Scale Mining on Local Communities in Obuasi, Ghana*. Unpublished thesis, on file with author.

Elyachar, Julia. *Markets of Dispossession: NGOs, Economic Development, and the State in Cairo*. Durham, NC: Duke University Press, 2005.

Emel, J., M. T. Huber, and M. H. Makene. "Extracting Sovereignty: Capital, Territory, and Gold Mining in Tanzania." *Political Geography* 30: 70–79.

Eng, David L., and David Kazanjian. "Introduction: Mourning Remains." In *Loss*, edited by David L. Eng and David Kazanjian, 1–28. Berkeley: University of California Press, 2003.

Engelke, Matthew. *A Problem of Presence: Beyond Scripture in an African Church*. Berkeley: University of California Press, 2007.

Englund, Harri. "Witchcraft, Modernity and the Person: The Morality of Accumulation in Central Malawi." *Critique of Anthropology* 16, no. 3 (1996): 257–79.

————, ed. *Christianity and Public Culture in Africa*. Athens: Ohio University Press, 2011.

Ephirim-Donkor, Anthony. "Akom: The Ultimate Mediumship Experience among the Akan." *Journal of the American Academy of Religion* 76 (2008): 54–81.

————. *African Spirituality: On Becoming Ancestors*. Lanham, MD: University Press of America, 2011.

Eriksen, Thomas Hylland. *Boomtown: Runaway Globalisation on the Queensland Coast*. London: Pluto Press, 2018.

Ernst & Young. "Business Risks Facing Mining and Metals 2012–2013." Available at: http://www.ey.com/GL/en/Industries/Mining---Metals/Business-risks-facing-mining-and-metals-2012---2013.

Esposito, Roberto. *Bios: Biopolitics and Philosophy*. Translated by Timothy Campbell. Minneapolis: University of Minnesota Press, 2008.

Evans-Pritchard, E. E. *Witchcraft, Oracles, and Magic among the Azande*. Oxford, UK: Clarendon Press, 1968 [1937].

————. "The Meaning of Sacrifice among the Nuer." *Journal of the Royal Anthropological Institute of Great Britain and Ireland* 84 (1954): 21–33.

Eze, Emmanuel Chukwudi, ed. *African Philosophy: An Anthology*. Cambridge, MA: Blackwell Publishers, 1997.

Fanon, Frantz. *Black Skin, White Masks*. Translated by Charles Lam Markmann. New York: Grove Press, 1952.

————. *Wretched of the Earth*. Translated by Constance Farrington. New York: Grove Press, 1963.

Fassin, Didier. "Policing Borders, Producing Boundaries: The Governmentality of Immigration in Dark Times." *Annual Review of Anthropology* 40 (2011): 213–26.

Faudree, Paja. *Singing for the Dead: The Politics of Indigenous Revival in Mexico*. Durham, NC: Duke University Press, 2013.

Feeley-Harnik, Gillian. "Divine Kingship and the Meaning of History among the Sakalava (Madagascar)." *Man* 13 (1978): 402–17.

——. "The Political Economy of Death: Communication and Change in Malagasy Colonial History." *American Ethnologist* 11, no. 1 (1984): 1–19.

——. "Issues of Divine Kingship." *Annual Review of Anthropology* 14 (1985): 273–313.

Ferguson, James. *The Anti-Politics Machine.* Chicago: University of Chicago Press, 1994.

——. *Expectations of Modernity: Myths and Meanings of Urban Life on the Zambian Copperbelt.* Berkeley: University of California Press, 1999.

——. "Seeing Like an Oil Company: Space, Security, and Global Capital in Neoliberal Africa." *American Anthropologist* 107, no. 3 (2005): 377–82.

——. *Global Shadows: Africa in the Neoliberal World Order.* Durham, NC: Duke University Press, 2006.

——. "Declarations of Dependence: Labor, Personhood, and Welfare in Southern Africa." *Journal of the Royal Anthropological Institute* 19 (2013): 223–42.

Ferguson, James, and Akhil Gupta. "Spatializing States: Toward an Ethnography of Neoliberal Governmentality." *American Ethnologist* 29, no. 4 (2002): 981–1002.

Ferme, Mariane. *The Underneath of Things: Violence, History and the Everyday in Sierra Leone.* Berkeley: University of California Press, 2001.

——. "Flexible Sovereignty? Paramount Chiefs, Deterritorialization and Political Mediations in Sierra Leone." *Cambridge Anthropology* 23, no. 2 (2003): 21–35.

——. "Deterritorialized Citizenship and the Resonances of the Sierra Leonean State." In *Anthropology in the Margins of the State,* edited by Veena Das and Deborah Poole. Santa Fe, NM: School of American Research Press, 2004.

Ferry, Elizabeth. "Fetishism and Hauism in Central Mexico: Using Marx and Mauss to Understand Commodity Production in a Cooperative Setting." In *Anthropological Perspectives on Economic Development and Integration,* edited by Norbert Dannhaeuser and Cynthia Werner, 261–81. Bingley, UK: Emerald Group Publishing, 2003.

——. "Geologies of Power: Value Transformations of Mineral Specimens from Guanajuato, Mexico." *American Ethnologist* 32, no. 3 (2005): 420–36.

——. *Minerals, Collecting, and Value across the US-Mexico Border.* Bloomington: Indiana University Press, 2013.

——. "On Not Being a Sign: Gold's Semiotic Claims." *Signs and Society* 4, no. 1 (2016): 57–79.

——. "Gold Prices as Material-Social Actors: The Case of the London Gold Fix." *Extractive Industries and Society* 3 (2016): 82–85.

——. "Royal Roads and Entangled Webs: Mining Metals and Making Value in El Cubo, Guanajuato, Mexico." *Journal of Anthropological Research* 75, no. 1 (2019): 6–20.

Fischer, Michael. *Emergent Forms of Life and the Anthropological Voice.* Durham, NC: Duke University Press, 2003.

Fitch, Robert, and Mary Oppenheimer. *Ghana: End of an Illusion.* New York: Monthly Review Press, 1968.

Fitzgerald, F. Scott. *This Side of Paradise.* New York: Penguin, 2006 [1920].

Flikke, Rune. "Healing in Polluted Places: Mountains, Air, and Weather in Zulu Zionist Ritual Practice." *Journal for the Study of Religion, Nature, and Culture* 12, no. 1 (2018): 76–95.

Fortes, Meyer. *The Web of Kinship among the Tallensi: The Second Part of an Analysis of the Social Structure of a Trans-Volta Tribe.* London: Oxford University Press, 1949.

————. *Oedipus and Job in West African Religion*. Cambridge: Cambridge University Press, 1959.

————. *Kinship and the Social Order: The Legacy of Lewis Henry Morgan*. Chicago: Aldine Publishing, 1969.

————. *Time and Social Structure and Other Essays*. New York: Humanities Press, 1970.

Fortes, Meyer, and E. E. Evans-Pritchard. "Introduction." In *African Political Systems*, edited by Meyer Fortes and E. E. Evans-Pritchard. Oxford: Oxford University Press, 1970 [1940].

Fortun, Kim. *Advocacy after Bhopal: Environmentalism, Disasters, New Global Orders*. Chicago: University of Chicago Press, 2001.

Foucault, Michel. *Madness and Civilization: A History of Insanity in the Age of Reason*. New York: Pantheon, 1965 [1962].

————. *Discipline and Punish: The Birth of the Prison*. Translated by Alan Sheridan. New York: Pantheon Books, 1977.

————. *Power/Knowledge: Selected Interviews and Other Writings, 1972–1977*. Edited by C. Gordon. New York: Pantheon Books, 1980.

————. "Governmentality (1977)." In *The Foucault Effect: Studies in Governmentality*. Translated by R. Braidotti, 87–104. Chicago: University of Chicago Press, 1991.

————. *"Society Must Be Defended": Lectures at the Collège de France, 1975–1976*. Translated by David Macey. New York: Picador, 2003.

————. *Security, Territory, Population: Lectures at the Collège de France, 1977–1978*. Translated by Graham Burchell. New York: Palgrave Macmillan, 2007.

————. *The Birth of Biopolitics: Lectures at the Collège de France, 1981–1982*. Translated by Graham Burchell. New York: Palgrave Macmillan, 2008.

Franz, Marie-Louis von. *Alchemy: An Introduction to the Symbolism and the Psychology*. Toronto, ON: Inner City Books, 1980.

Frazer, James George. *The Golden Bough*. Oxford: Oxford University Press, 2009 [1890].

Freiku, Sebastian R. "Ghana: Miners Want Probe over Discrimination." *Ghanaian Chronicle*. March 8, 2001. Available at: http://allafrica.com/stories/200103080276.html.

Freud, Sigmund. *On Dreams*. Translated by M. D. Eder. London: William Heinemann, 2001 [1914].

————. *Introductory Lectures on Psycho-Analysis*. Translated and edited by James Strachey. New York: W. W. Norton, 1920.

Freund, Bill. *Capital and Labour in the Nigerian Tin Mines*. Atlantic Highlands, NJ: Humanities Press, 1981.

Fromm, Erich. "Politics and Psychoanalysis." In *Critical Theory and Society: A Reader*, edited by Stephen Eric Bronner and Douglas MacKay Kellner, 213–18. London: Routledge, 1989.

Fry, Peter. *Spirits of Protest: Spirit Mediums and the Articulation of Consensus among the Zezuru of Southern Rhodesia*. Cambridge: Cambridge University Press, 1976.

Frynas, J. G. "Political Instability and Business: Focus on Shell in Nigeria." *Third World Quarterly* 19, no. 3 (1998): 457–78.

Fung, Archon, and Erik Olin Wright. "Thinking about Empowered Participatory Governance." In *Deepening Democracy: Institutional Innovations in Empowered Participatory Governance*, edited by Archon Fung and Erik Olin Wright, 3–42. London: Verso, 2003.

The Ghanaian Chronicle. "Obuasi Mine Faces Closure; Over 1,000 Workers to Be Laid-Off." January 18, 2014. Available at: http://www.ghanaweb.com/GhanaHomePage/News Archive/artikel.php?ID=298173.

Garcia, Angela. "The Promise: On the Morality of the Marginal and the Illicit." *Ethos* 42, no. 1 (2014): 51–64.

Garrard, Timothy F. *Akan Weights and the Gold Trade*. New York: Longman, 1980.

Geertz, Clifford. "Local Knowledge: Fact and Law in Comparative Perspective." In *Local Knowledge: Further Essays in Interpretive Anthropology*. New York: Basic Books, 2000 [1983].

———. "What Is a State If It Is Not Sovereign? Reflections on Politics in Complicated Places." *Current Anthropology* 45, no. 5 (2004): 577–93.

Gellner, Ernest. *Nations and Nationalism*. Ithaca, NY: Cornell University Press, 2009 [1983].

George, Susan. *Shadow Sovereigns: How Global Corporations Are Seizing Power*. New York: Polity, 2015.

Geschiere, Peter. *The Modernity of Witchcraft: Politics and the Occult in Postcolonial Africa*. Charlottesville: University of Virginia Press, 1997.

———. "Globalization and the Power of Indeterminate Meaning: Witchcraft and Spirit Cults in Africa and East Asia." In *Globalization and Identity: Dialectics of Flow and Closure*, edited by Birgit Meyer and Peter Geschiere, 211–38. Oxford: Oxford University Press, 1999.

———. "Witchcraft and the Limits of the Law: Cameroon and South Africa." In *Law and Disorder in the Postcolony*, edited by Jean Comaroff and John L. Comaroff, 219–46. Chicago: University of Chicago Press, 2006.

———. *The Perils of Belonging: Autochthony, Citizenship, and Exclusion in Africa and Europe*. Chicago: University of Chicago Press, 2009.

———. *Witchcraft, Intimacy, and Trust: Africa in Comparison*. Chicago: University of Chicago Press, 2013.

Ghana Business News. "AGC Says Obuasi Strike Costing 2,500 Ounces of Gold Daily." May 20, 1999. Available at: http://www.ghanaweb.com/GhanaHomePage/economy/artikel .php?ID=6864.

———. "AGC Says Ghana Losing 700,000 Dollars a Day in Obuasi Strike." May 21, 1999. Available at: http://www.ghanaweb.com/GhanaHomePage/NewsArchive/artikel.php ?ID=6860.

Ghana Chamber of Mines. "Performance of the Industry in 2008." Available at: http://www .ghanachamberofmines.org/site/publications/.

———. "Performance of the Industry in 2009." Available at: http://www.ghanachamber ofmines.org/site/publications/.

———. "Performance of the Mining Industry in 2017—GcoM Report." January 6, 2018. Available at http://ghanachamberofmines.org/wp-content/uploads/2016/11/Performance-of -the-Industry-2017.pdf.

Ghana News Agency. "Ashanti Gold Miners Strike for Higher Pay." May 16, 1999. Available at: http://ghanaweb.net/GhanaHomePage//economy/artikel.php?ID=6532.

Ghana Radio 1. "Government Destroys 77 Galamsey Pits." March 2013. Available at: http:// www.ghradio1.com/view_news.php?id=383.

Ghanaian Chronicle. "NDC Sacks Obuasi Independent Candidate." November 30, 2004. Available at: http://www.modernghana.com/news/67595/1/ndc-sacks-obuasi-independent-candidate.html.

Gilroy, Paul. *After Empire: Melancholia or Convivial Culture.* London: Routledge, 2004.

Ginsburg, Tom, and Tamir Moustafa, eds. *Rule by Law: The Politics of Courts in Authoritarian Regimes.* New York: Cambridge University Press, 2008.

Girard, René. *Violence and the Sacred.* Translated by Patrick Gregory. Baltimore: Johns Hopkins University Press, 1977.

———. *Sacrifice.* Translated by Matthew Pattillo and David Dawson. East Lansing: Michigan State University Press, 2011 [2003].

Gloppen, Siri, Roberto Gargarella, and Elin Skaar, eds. *Democratization and the Judiciary: The Accountability Function of Courts in New Democracies.* London: Frank Cass, 2004.

Gluckman, Max. "The Village Headman in British Central Africa: Introduction." *Africa* 19, no. 2 (1949): 89–94.

———. *Custom and Conflict in Africa.* Oxford, UK: Blackwell, 1955.

———. "Preface." In *Schism and Continuity in an African Society: A Study of Ndembu Village Life,* by Victor Turner. Manchester, UK: Manchester University Press, 1957.

———. *An Analysis of a Social Situation in Modern Zululand.* Rhodes-Livingstone Papers, No. 28. New York: Humanities Press, 1958.

Godoy, Ricardo. "Mining: Anthropological Perspectives." *Annual Review of Anthropology* 14 (1985): 199–217.

Goldstone, Brian. "A Prayer's Chance." *Harper's,* May 2017. Available at: https://harpers.org/archive/2017/05/a-prayers-chance/7/.

Golub, Alex. *Making the Ipili Feasible: Imagining Local and Global Actors at the Porgera Gold Mine, Enga Province, Papua New Guinea.* Doctoral thesis, University of Chicago. On file at Mansueto Library, 2006.

———. *Leviathans at the Gold Mine: Creating Indigenous and Corporate Actors in Papua New Guinea.* Durham, NC: Duke University Press, 2014.

Good, Byron J. "Medical Anthropology and the Problem of Belief." In *A Reader in Medical Anthropology: Theoretical Trajectories, Emergent Realities,* edited by Byron J. Good, Michael M.J. Fischer, Sarah S. Willen, and Mary-Jo DelVecchio Good, 64–76. Malden, MA: Wiley-Blackwell, 2010.

Goodale, Mark. *Dilemmas of Modernity: Bolivian Encounters with Law and Liberalism.* Stanford, CA: Stanford University Press, 2009.

Goodale, Mark, and Sally Engle Merry, eds. *The Practice of Human Rights: Tracking Law Between the Global and the Local.* New York: Cambridge University Press, 2007.

Goodie, J.-A. *The Invention of the Environment as a Legal Subject.* Doctoral dissertation, Murdoch University, 2006.

Goody, Jack. "Anomie in Ashanti." *Africa* 27 (1957): 356–63.

———. "Ethnohistory and the Akan of Ghana." *Africa* 29, no. 1 (1959): 67–81.

———. *Death, Property, and the Ancestors: A Study of the Mortuary Customs of the LoDagaa of West Africa.* Stanford, CA: Stanford University Press, 1962.

———, ed. *Changing Social Structure in Ghana: Essays in the Comparative Sociology of a New State and Old Tradition.* London: International African Institute, 1975.

Gordon, David F. "On Promoting Democracy in Africa: The International Dimension." In *Democracy in Africa: The Hard Road Ahead*, edited by Marina Ottaway, 153–64. Boulder, CO L. Rienner, 1997.

Gordon, David M. *Invisible Agents: Spirits in a Central African History*. Athens: Ohio University Press, 2012.

Government of Ghana. "Minerals and Mining Act of 2006."

Graeber, David. *Toward an Anthropological Theory of Value: The False Coin of Our Own Dreams*. New York: Palgrave, 2001.

———. "Fetishism as Social Creativity: Or, Fetishes Are Gods in the Process of Construction." *Anthropological Theory* 5, no. 4 (2005): 407–38.

Grant, Richard. *Globalizing City: The Urban and Economic Transformation of Accra, Ghana*. Syracuse, NY: Syracuse University Press, 2009.

Gratton, Peter. *The State of Sovereignty: Lessons from the Political Fictions of Modernity*. Albany: State University of New York Press, 2012.

Greene, Sandra. *Sacred Sites and the Colonial Encounter: A History of Meaning and Memory in Ghana*. Bloomington: Indiana Univ. Press, 2002.

Greenhouse, Carol. "Hegemony and Hidden Transcripts: The Discursive Arts of Neoliberal Legitimation." *American Anthropologist* 107, no. 3 (2005): 356–68.

———. "Introduction." In *Ethnographies of Neoliberalism*, edited by Carol Greenhouse, 1–12. Philadelphia: University of Pennsylvania Press, 2012.

Greenough, Paul, and Anna Lowenhaupt Tsing, eds. *Nature in the Global South: Environmental Projects in South and Southeast Asia*. Durham, NC: Duke University Press, 2003.

Grier, Beverly. "Pawns, Porters, and Petty Traders: Women in the Transition to Cash Crop Agriculture in Colonial Ghana." *Signs* 17, no. 2 (1992): 304–28.

Grove, Richard. *Green Imperialism: Colonial Expansion, Tropical Island Edens and the Origins of Environmentalism, 1600–1800*. Cambridge: Cambridge University Press, 1995.

Guyer, Jane. "Prophecy and the Near Future: Thoughts on Macroeconomic, Evangelical, and Punctuated Time." *American Ethnologist* 34, no. 3 (2007): 409–21.

Gyekye, Kwame. *An Essay on African Philosophical Thought: The Akan Conceptual Scheme*. Philadelphia: Temple University Press, 1995.

Hale, Robert. "Coercion and Distribution in a Supposedly Non-Coercive State." *Political Science Quarterly* 38 (1923): 470–78.

Hallen, Barry, and J. Olubi Sodipo. *Knowledge, Belief, and Witchcraft: Analytic Experiments in African Philosophy*. Stanford, CA: Stanford University Press, 1997 [1986].

Hammoudi, Abdellah. *The Victim and Its Masks: An Essay on Sacrifice and Masquerade in the Maghreb*. Chicago: University of Chicago Press, 1993.

Hanks, William F. *Referential Practice: Language and Lived Space among the Maya*. Chicago: University of Chicago Press, 1990.

———. *Converting Words: Maya in the Age of the Cross*. Berkeley: University of California Press, 2010.

———. "Counterparts: Co-presence and Ritual Intersubjectivity." *Language & Communication* 33 (2013): 263–77.

Hansen, Thomas Blom. *Melancholia of Freedom: Social Life in an Indian Township in South Africa*. Princeton, NJ: Princeton University Press, 2012.

Hansen, Thomas Blom, and Finn Stepputat, eds. *Sovereign Bodies: Citizens, Migrants, and States in the Postcolonial World.* Princeton, NJ: Princeton University Press, 2005.

———. "Sovereignty Revisited." *Annual Review of Anthropology* 35 (2006): 295–315.

Harcourt, Bernard. *Illusion of Free Markets.* Cambridge, MA: Harvard University Press, 2011.

Hardin, Rebecca. "Concessionary Politics: Property, Patronage, and Political Rivalry in Central African Forest Management." *Current Anthropology* 52, no. 3 (2011): S113–S125.

———. "Contradictions of Corporate Conservation." In "Corporate Social Responsibility," edited by Catherine Dolan and Dinah Rajak, special issue, *Focaal: Journal of European Anthropology* 60 (2011).

Hardt, Michael, and Antonio Negri. *Empire.* Cambridge, MA: Harvard University Press, 2000.

———. *Multitude: War and Democracy in the Age of Empire.* New York: Penguin, 2004.

Hart, Keith. "Informal Income Opportunities and Urban Employment in Ghana." *Journal of Modern African Studies* 11, no. 1 (1973): 61–89.

———. "Market and State after the Cold War: The Informal Economy Reconsidered." In *Contesting Markets: Analyses of Ideology, Discourse and Practice,* edited by R. Dilley. Edinburgh, UK: Edinburgh University Press, 1992.

Harvey, David. *A Brief History of Neoliberalism.* New York: Oxford University Press, 2005.

Hegel, Georg Wilhelm Friedrich. *The Phenomenology of Spirit.* Translated and edited by Terry Pinkard (New York: Cambridge University Press, 2017 [1807]).

Herbst, Jeffrey. *The Politics of Reform in Ghana, 1982–1991.* Berkeley: University of California Press, 1993.

Herzfeld, Michael. *The Body Impolitic: Artisans and Artifice in the Global Hierarchy of Value.* Chicago: University of Chicago Press, 2004.

Hickey, Samuel, and Giles Mohan, eds. *Participation: From Tyranny to Transformation? Exploring New Approaches to Participation in Development.* London: Zed Books, 2004.

Higginson, John. *A Working Class in the Making: Belgian Colonial Labor Policy, Private Enterprise, and the African Mineworker, 1907–1951.* Madison: University of Wisconsin Press, 1989.

Hill, Polly. *The Migrant Cocoa-Farmers of Southern Ghana: A Study in Rural Capitalism.* London: Cambridge University Press, 1963.

———. *Studies in Rural Capitalism in West Africa.* Cambridge: Cambridge University Press, 1970.

Hilson, Gavin. "A Contextual Review of the Ghanaian Small-Scale Mining Industry." *Mining, Minerals and Sustainable Development, No. 76.* London: International Institute for Environment and Development, 2001.

———, ed. *The Socioeconomic Impacts of Artisanal and Small-Scale Mining in Developing Countries.* Rotterdam, Netherlands: A. A. Balkema, 2003.

———, ed. *Small-Scale Mining, Rural Subsistence and Poverty in West Africa.* Warwickshire, UK: Practical Action Publishing, 2006.

Hirsch, Susan F., and M. Lazarus-Black. "Performance and Paradox: Exploring Role in Hegemony and Resistance." In *Contested States: Law, Hegemony and Resistance,* edited by M. Lazarus-Black and Susan F. Hirsch, 1–13. New York: Routledge, 1994.

Hobbes, Thomas. *Leviathan; or, The Matter, Forme, and Power of a Commonwealth Ecclesiastical and Civil*. New York: Simon & Schuster, 1964 [1651].

Hobsbawm, Eric. "Introduction: Inventing Traditions." In *The Invention of Tradition*, edited by Eric Hobsbawm and Terence Ranger, 1–14. New York: Cambridge University Press, 1983.

———. *Nations and Nationalism Since 1780: Programme, Myth, Reality*. Cambridge: Cambridge University Press, 1992.

———. *The Age of Extremes: The Short Twentieth Century, 1914–1991*. New York: Pantheon Books, 1994.

Hobsbawm, Eric, and Terence Ranger, eds. *The Invention of Tradition*. New York: Cambridge University Press, 1983.

Hocart, A. M. *Kingship*. Oxford: Oxford University Press, 1927.

Hochschild, Adam. *King Leopold's Ghost: A Story of Greed, Terror, and Heroism in Colonial Africa*. Boston, MA: Houghton Mifflin, 1999.

Hoffman, Danny. "Corpus: Mining the Border." *Cultural Anthropology*, 2012. Available at: https://culanth.org/fieldsights/corpus-mining-the-border.

———. "Yellow Woman: Suspicion and Cooperation on Liberia's Gold Mines." *American Anthropologist* 121, no. 1 (2019): 138–48.

Honneth, Axel. *The Struggle for Recognition: The Moral Grammar of Social Conflicts*. Cambridge, MA: MIT Press, 1995.

Hopkins, Anthony. *An Economic History of West Africa*. London: Longman, 1973.

———. "Asante and the Victorians: Transition and Partition on the Gold Coast." In *Imperialism, Decolonization, and Africa: Studies Presented to John Hargreaves*, edited by Roy Bridges, 25–64. New York: St. Martin's Press, 2000.

Horkheimer, Max, and Theodor W. Adorno. *Dialectic of Enlightenment*. Translated by Edmund Jephcott. Stanford, CA: Stanford University Press, 2002 [1944].

Hubert, Henri, and Marcel Mauss. *Sacrifice: Its Nature and Functions*. Chicago: University of Chicago Press, 1991 [1898].

Human Rights Watch. "The Curse of Gold." June 1, 2005 report, available at: www.hrw.org.

Hussain, Nasser. *The Jurisprudence of Emergency: Colonialism and the Rule of Law*. Ann Arbor: University of Michigan Press, 2003.

Ilgen, Thomas L. "Reconfigured Sovereignty in the Age of Globalization." In *Reconfigured Sovereignty: Multi-Layered Governance in the Global Age*, edited by Thomas L. Ilgen, 6–35. Farnham, UK: Ashgate, 2003.

Ishii, Miho. "Acting with Things: Self-Poiesis, Actuality, and Contingency in the Formation of Divine Worlds." *HAU: Journal of Ethnographic Theory* 2, no. 2 (2012): 371–88.

Jackson, Michael. *Minima Ethnographica: Intersubjectivity and the Anthropological Project*. Chicago: University of Chicago Press, 1998.

James, William. *The Varieties of Religious Experience: A Study in Human Nature*. New York: Penguin, 1982 [1902–1910].

James, Wilmot G. *Our Precious Metal: African Labour in South Africa's Gold Industry, 1970–1990*. Bloomington: Indiana University Press, 1992.

Johnson, Paul Christopher. "Spirits and Things in the Making of the Afro-Atlantic World." In *Spirited Things: The Work of "Possession" in Afro-Atlantic Religions*, edited by Paul Christopher Johnson, 1–22. Chicago: University of Chicago Press, 2014.

Johnson, Trevor. "Ghana's Ashanti Goldfields Going for a Song." World Socialist Web Site, October 30, 1999. Available at: http://www.wsws.org/en/articles/1999/10/gold-030.html.

Jones-Quartey, K. A. B. *History, Politics and Early Press in Ghana: The Fictions and the Facts.* Accra, Ghana: Jones-Quartey, 1975.

Joy Online. "Casual AGC Workers Demonstrate." *Ghana Web*, September 17, 2001. Available at: https://www.ghanaweb.com/GhanaHomePage/NewsArchive/Casual-AGC-Workers -Demonstrate-18148#.

Jung, Carl. *Alchemical Studies.* Princeton, NJ: Princeton University Press, 1967.

Kahn, Jeffrey. *Islands of Sovereignty: Haitian Migration and the Borders of Empire.* Chicago: University of Chicago Press, 2018.

Kalmo, Hent, and Quentin Skinner. "Introduction: A Concept in Fragments." In *Sovereignty in Fragments: The Past, Present and Future of a Contested Concept,* edited by Hent Kalmo and Quentin Skinner, 1–25. New York: Cambridge University Press, 2010.

Kalu, Ogbu. *African Pentecostalism: An Introduction.* Oxford: Oxford University Press, 2008.

Kantorowicz, Ernst. *The King's Two Bodies: A Study in Medieval Political Theology.* Princeton, NJ: Princeton University Press, 1957.

Kapferer, Bruce. *The Feast of the Sorcerer: Practices of Consciousness and Power.* Chicago: University of Chicago Press, 1997.

Kauanui, J. Kēhaulani. "Sovereignty: An Introduction." *Cultural Anthropology* 32, no. 3 (2017): 323–29.

Keane, Webb. *Christian Moderns: Freedom and Fetish in the Mission Encounter.* Berkeley: University of California Press, 2006.

Kennedy, David. *The Dark Sides of Virtue: Reassessing International Humanitarianism.* Princeton, NJ: Princeton University Press, 2005.

Kennedy, Duncan. *A Critique of Adjudication [fin de siècle].* Cambridge, MA: Harvard University Press, 1997.

———. "The Critique of Rights in Critical Legal Studies." In *Left Legalism, Left Critique,* edited by Janet Halley and Wendy Brown, 178–228. Durham, NC: Duke University Press, 2002.

———. "Three Globalizations of Law and Legal Thought: 1850–2000." In *The New Law and Economic Development,* edited by David M. Trubek and Alvaro Santos, 19–73. New York: Cambridge University Press, 2006.

Kentridge, William, and Rosalind C. Morris. *Accounts and Drawings from Underground: The East Rand Proprietary Mines Cash Book, 1906.* Chicago: Seagull, University of Chicago Press, 2015.

Kesse, G. O. *Mineral and Rock Resources of Ghana.* Rotterdam, Netherlands: A. A. Balkema, 1985.

Kimble, David. *A Political History of Ghana: The Rise of Gold Coast Nationalism, 1850–1928.* Oxford: Oxford University Press, 1963.

Kirsch, Stuart. *Reverse Anthropology: Indigenous Analysis of Social and Environmental Relations in New Guinea.* Stanford, CA: Stanford University Press, 2006.

———. "Indigenous Movements and the Risks of Counterglobalization: Tracking the Campaign against Papua New Guinea's Ok Tedi Mine." *American Ethnologist* 34, no. 2 (2007): 303–21.

————. "Social Relations and the Green Critique of Capitalism in Melanesia." *American Anthropologist* 11, no. 3 (2008): 288–98.

————. *Mining Capitalism: The Relationship between Corporations and Their Critics*. Berkeley: University of California Press, 2014.

Klein, Norman A. "Toward a New Understanding of Akan Origins." *Africa* 66, no. 2 (1996): 248–73.

Kohn, Eduardo. *How Forests Think: Toward an Anthropology Beyond the Human*. Berkeley: University of California Press, 2013.

Konadu, Kwasi, ed. *The Akan People: A Documentary History*. Princeton, NJ: Markus Wiener, 2013.

Konings, Piet. *The State and Rural Class Formation in Ghana: A Comparative Analysis*. London: Routledge and Kegan Paul, 1986.

Koskenniemi, Martti. *The Gentle Civilizer of Nations: The Rise and Fall of International Law, 1870–1960*. New York: Cambridge University Press, 2002.

————. "Conclusion: Vocabularies of Sovereignty—Powers of a Paradox." In *Sovereignty in Fragments: The Past, Present and Future of a Contested Concept*, edited by Hent Kalmo and Quentin Skinner, 222–42. New York: Cambridge University Press, 2010.

Kostal, R.W. *A Jurisprudence of Power: Victorian Empire and the Rule of Law*. New York: Oxford University Press, 2005.

Krasner, Stephen D. *Sovereignty: Organized Hypocrisy*. Princeton, NJ: Princeton University Press, 1999.

————. "Rethinking the Sovereign State Model." *Review of International Studies* 27, no. 5 (2001): 17–42.

————. *Power, the State, and Sovereignty: Essays on International Relations*. London: Routledge, 2009.

Kristeva, Julia. *The Powers of Horror: An Essay on Abjection*. New York: Columbia University Press, 1982.

Lambek, Michael. "Spirits and Spouses: Possession as a System of Communication among the Malagasy Speakers of Mayotte." *American Ethnologist* 7, no. 2 (1980): 318–31.

————. *Human Spirits: A Cultural Account of Trance in Mayotte*. New York: Cambridge University Press, 1981.

————. "Sacrifice and the Problem of Beginning: Mediations from Sakalava Mythopraxis." *Journal of the Royal Anthropological Institute* 13, no. 1 (2007): 19–38.

Lan, David. *Guns and Rain: Guerillas and Spirit Mediums in Zimbabwe*. Berkeley: University of California Press, 1985.

Lanzano, Cristiano. "Gold Digging and the Politics of Time: Changing Timescapes of Artisanal Mining in West Africa." *Extractive Industries and Society* 5, no. 2 (2018): 253–59.

Laretta, Enrique Rodriguez. *"Gold Is Illusion": The Garimpeiros of Tapajos Valley in the Brazilian Amazonia*. Stockholm, Sweden: Studies in Social Anthropology, 2002.

Larkin, Brian. *Signal and Noise: Media, Infrastructure, and Urban Culture in Nigeria*. Durham, NC: Duke University Press, 2008.

Law, Robin, ed. *From Slave Trade to "Legitimate" Commerce: The Commercial Transition in Nineteenth-Century West Africa*. Cambridge: Cambridge University Press, 1995.

Lawrance, Benjamin N., Emily Lynn Osborn, and Richard L. Roberts. "Introduction: African Intermediaries and the 'Bargain' of Collaboration." In *Intermediaries, Interpreters, and Clerks: African Employees in the Making of Colonial Africa*, edited by Benjamin N. Lawrance, Emily Lynn Osborn, and Richard L. Roberts, 3–36. Madison: University of Wisconsin Press, 2006.

Lazarus-Black, Mindie, and Susan Hirsch, eds. *Contested States: Law, Hegemony and Resistance*. New York: Routledge, 1994.

Lederman, Rena. "Sorcery and Social Change in Mendi." *Social Analysis* 8 (1981): 15–26.

Lee, Ching Kwan. *Against the Law: Labor Protests in China's Rustbelt and Sunbelt*. Berkeley: University of California Press, 2007.

Lentz, Carola. "The Chief, the Mine-Captain and the Politician: Legitimating Power in Northern Ghana." *Africa* 68 (1998): 46–67.

———. "Decentralization, the State, and Conflicts over Local Boundaries in North-Western Ghana." In *Twilight Institutions: Public Authority and Local Politics in Africa*, edited by Christian Lund. Hoboken, NJ: Wiley-Blackwell, 2007.

———. "Is Land Inalienable?: Historical and Current Debates on Land Transfers in Northern Ghana." *Africa* 80, no. 1 (2010): 56–80.

Lentz, Carola, and Veit Erlmann. "A Working Class in Formation: Economic Crisis and Strategies for Survival among Dagara Mine Workers in Ghana." *Cahiers d'Études Africaines* 113 (1989): 69–111.

Lévi-Strauss, Claude. *Structural Anthropology*. Translated by Claire Jacobsen and Brooke Grundfest Schoepf. Garden City, NY: Anchor Books, 1967.

Li, Fabiana. *Unearthing Conflict: Corporate Mining, Activism, and Expertise in Peru*. Durham, NC: Duke University Press, 2015.

Li, Tania. *The Will to Improve*. Durham, NC: Duke University Press, 2007.

———. *Land's End: Capitalist Relations on an Indigenous Frontier*. Durham, NC: Duke University Press, 2014.

Lienhardt, Godfrey. *Divinity and Experience: The Religion of the Dinka*. Oxford: Oxford University Press, 1961.

Liste, Philip. "Geographical Knowledge at Work: Human Rights Litigation and Transnational Territoriality." *European Journal of International Relations* 22, no. 1 (2016): 217–39.

———. "Colliding Geographies: Space at Work in Global Governance." *Journal of International Relations and Development* 19, no. 2 (2016): 199–221.

Lobel, Orly. "The Paradox of Extralegal Activism: Critical Legal Consciousness and Transformative Politics." *Harvard Law Review* 120 (2007): 937–88.

Lukács, Georg. *History and Class Consciousness*. Translated by R. Livingstone. Cambridge, MA: MIT Press, 1971 [1923].

Lund, Christian, ed. *Twilight Institutions: Public Authority and Local Politics in Africa*. Hoboken, NJ: Wiley-Blackwell, 2007.

———. "Recategorizing 'Public' and 'Private' Property in Ghana." *Development and Change* 40, no. 1 (2009): 131–48.

———. *Local Politics and the Dynamics of Property in Africa*. Cambridge: Cambridge University Press, 2010.

Lunig, Sabine. "Liberalisation of the Gold Mining Sector in Burkina Faso." *Review of African Political Economy* 117 (2008): 25–39.

———. "Corporate Social Responsibility (CSR) for Exploration: Consultants, Companies and Communities in Processes of Engagements." *Resources Policy* 36 (2012): 205–11.

———. "Gold, Cosmology, and Change in Burkina Faso." In *Lives in Motion, Indeed: Interdisciplinary Perspectives on Social Change in Honour of Danielle de Lame*, edited by Cristiana Panella, 323–40. Tervuren, Belgium: Royal Musuem for Central Africa, 2012.

———. "The Future of Artisanal Miners from a Large-Scale Perspective: From Valued Pathfinders to Disposable Illegals?" *Futures* 62 (2014): 67–74.

———. "Mining Temporalities: Future Perspectives." *Extractive Industries and Society* 5, no. 2 (2018): 281–86.

Luning, Sabine, and Robert Jan Pijpers. "Governing Access to Gold in Ghana: In-depth Geopolitics on Mining Concessions." *Africa* 87, no. 4 (2017): 758–79.

———. "Shifting Alliances in Accessing the Underground." *Africa* 88, no. 4 (2018): 876–80.

Luongo, Katherine. *Witchcraft and Colonial Rule in Kenya, 1900–1955*. New York: Cambridge University Press, 2011.

MacGaffey, Wyatt. *Custom and Government in the Lower Congo*. Berkeley: University of California Press, 1970.

———. "Fetishism Revisited: Kongo Nkisi in Sociological Perspective." *Africa* 47, no. 2 (1977): 172–84.

———. "African Objects and the Idea of the Fetish." *Res* 25 (1994): 123–31.

———. *Kongo Political Culture: The Conceptual Challenge of the Particular*. Bloomington: Indiana University Press, 2000.

———. "Changing Representations in Central African History." *Journal of African History* 46 (2005): 189–207.

Malette, S. "Foucault for the Next Century: Eco-Governmentality." In *A Foucault for the Twenty-First Century*, edited by S. Binkley and J. Capetillo, 222–39. Newcastle upon Tyne, UK: Cambridge Scholars Press, 2009.

Mamdani, Mahmood. *Citizen and Subject: Contemporary Africa and the Legacy of Late Colonialism*. Princeton, NJ: Princeton University Press, 1996.

Mann, Kristin, and Richard Roberts, eds. *Law in Colonial Africa*. London: James Currey, 1991.

Manson, Andrew, and Bernard Mbenga. "'The Richest Tribe in Africa': Platinum-Mining and the Bafokeng in South Africa's North West Province, 1965–1999." *Journal of Southern African Studies* 29, no. 1 (2003): 25–47.

Marcus, George. "Ethnography in/of the World System: The Emergence of Multi-sited Ethnography." *Annual Review of Anthropology* 24 (1995): 95–117.

Markell, Patchen. *Bound by Recognition*. Princeton, NJ: Princeton University Press, 2003.

Marks, Shula, and Richard Rathbone, eds. *Industrialization and Social Change in South Africa: African Class Formation, Culture and Consciousness, 1870–1930*. New York: Longman, 1982.

Marshall, Ruth. *Political Spiritualities: The Pentecostal Revolution in Nigeria*. Chicago: University of Chicago Press, 2009.

Martin, D. Bruce. "Sacred Identity and the Sacrificial Spirit: Mimesis and Radical Ecology." In *Critical Ecologies: The Frankfurt School and Contemporary Environmental Crises*, edited by Andrew Biro, 111–38. Toronto, ON: University of Toronto Press, 2011.

Martin, David. *Pentecostalism: The World Their Parish*. Wiley-Blackwell, 2001.

Marx, Karl. *Capital, Vols. I–III*. New York: New World Paperbacks, 1967 [1867].

Masquelier, Adeline. *Prayer Has Spoiled Everything: Possession, Power, and Identity in an Islamic Town of Niger*. Durham, NC: Duke University Press, 2001.

———. *Fada: Boredom and Belonging in Niger*. Chicago: University of Chicago Press, 2009.

Maurer, Bill. *Recharting the Caribbean: Land, Law, and Citizenship in the British Virgin Islands*. Ann Arbor: University of Michigan Press, 1997.

Maurer, Bill, and Gabriele Schwab, eds. *Accelerating Possession: Global Futures of Property and Personhood*. New York: Columbia University Press, 2006.

Mauss, Marcel. *A General Theory of Magic*. Translated by Robert Brain. New York: Routledge, 2001 [1950].

———. *The Gift: Forms and Functions of Exchange in Archaic Societies*. Translated by I. Cunnison. New York: Norton, 1965 [1925].

Mazzarella, William. *The Mana of Mass Society*. Chicago: University of Chicago Press, 2017.

Mbembe, Achille. "At the Edge of the World: Boundaries, Territoriality, and Sovereignty in Africa." *Public Culture* 12, no. 1 (2000): 259–84.

———. *On the Postcolony*. Berkeley: University of California Press, 2001.

———. "Necropolitics." *Public Culture* 15, no. 1 (2003): 11–40.

———. *Sortir de la Grande Nuit: Essai sur l'Afrique Décolonisée*. Paris, France: Découverte, 2010.

McCaskie, Thomas C. "Anti-Witchcraft Cults in Asante: An Essay in the Social History of an African People." *History in Africa* 8 (1981): 125–54.

———. "Accumulation, Wealth, and Belief in Asante History. I. To the Close of the Nineteenth Century." *Africa* 53 (1983): 23–43.

———. "People and Animals: Constru(ct)ing the Asante Experience." *Africa* 62, no. 2 (1992): 221–47.

———. *State and Society in Pre-colonial Asante*. Cambridge: Cambridge University Press, 1995.

———. *Asante Identities: History and Modernity in an African Village, 1850–1950*. Bloomington: Indiana University Press, 2000.

———. "*Akwantemfi*—'In Mid Journey': An Asante Shrine Today and Its Clients." *Journal of Religion in Africa* 38 (2008): 57–80.

McGovern, Mike. *Making War in Côte d'Ivoire*. Chicago: University of Chicago Press, 2011.

McLeod, Malcom. "On the Spread of Anti-Witchcraft Cults in Modern Asante." In *Changing Social Structure in Ghana: Essays in the Comparative Sociology of an New State and an Old Tradition*, edited by Jack Goody, 107–18. London: International African Institute, 1975.

McMillan, L. Jane. "Colonial Traditions, Co-optations, and *Mi'kmaq* Legal Consciousness." *Law and Social Inquiry* 36, no. 1 (2011): 171–200.

McPhee, Allan. *The Economic Revolution in British West Africa*. London: Frank Cass, 1971 [1926].

Meillassoux, Claude. "The Social Organization of the Peasantry: The Economic Basis of Kinship." *Journal of Peasant Studies* 1, no. 1 (1973): 81–90.

Memmi, Albert. *The Colonizer and the Colonized.* Boston: Beacon Press, 1995 [1965].

Mendonsa, Eugene L. *The Politics of Divination: A Processual View of Reactions to Illness and Deviance among the Sisala of Northern Ghana.* Berkeley: University of California Press, 1982.

Merleau-Ponty, Maurice. *Phenomenology of Perception.* Translated by Colin Smith. London: Routledge, 1962.

Merry, Sally Engle. "Anthropology and the Study of Alternative Dispute Resolution." *Journal of Legal Education* 34 (1984): 277–84.

———. "Law and Colonialism." *Law and Society Review* 25, no. 4 (1991): 889–922.

———. "Anthropology, Law, and Transnational Processes." *Annual Review of Anthropology* 21 (1992): 357–79.

———. *Colonizing Hawai'i: The Cultural Power of Law.* Princeton, NJ: Princeton University Press, 2000.

———. "Colonial and Postcolonial Law." In *The Blackwell Companion to Law and Society,* edited by Austin Sarat, 569–88. Malden, MA: Blackwell, 2004.

Meyer, Birgit. "The Power of Money: Politics, Occult Force, and Pentecostalism in Ghana." *African Studies Review* 41, no. 3 (1998): 15–37.

———. "Commodities and the Power of Prayer: Pentecostalist Attitudes Towards Consumption in Contemporary Ghana." In *Globalization and Identity: Dialectics of Flow and Closure,* edited by Birgit Meyer and Peter Geschiere, 151–76. Oxford: Oxford University Press, 1999.

———. *Translating the Devil: Religion and Modernity among the Ewe of Ghana.* Trenton, NJ: Africa World Press, 1999.

Meyer, Birgit, and Peter Pels. *Magic and Modernity: Interfaces of Revelation and Concealment.* Stanford, CA: Stanford University Press, 2003.

Meyerowitz, Eva L. R. "Concepts of the Soul among the Akan of the Gold Coast." *Africa* 21, no. 1 (1951): 24–31.

———. "A Note on the Origins of Ghana." *African Affairs* 51, no. 205 (1952): 319–23.

———. *The Sacred State of the Akan.* London: Faber and Faber, 1953.

———. "The Akan and Ghana." *Man* (1957): 83–88.

———. *The Divine Kingship in Ghana and Ancient Egypt.* London: Faber and Faber, 1960.

Miescher, Stephan F. "Building the City of the Future: Visions and Experiences of Modernity in Ghana's Akosombo Township." *Journal of African History* 53, no. 3 (2012): 367–90.

Mikell, Gwendolyn. *Cocoa and Chaos in Ghana.* St. Paul, MN: Paragon House, 1989.

Minow, Martha. *Between Vengeance and Forgiveness: Facing History after Genocide and Mass Violence.* Boston: Beacon Press, 1998.

Mintz, Sidney. *Sweetness and Power: The Place of Sugar in Modern History.* New York: Penguin, 1986.

Mitchell, J. Clyde. *The Kalela Dance: Aspects of Social Relationship among Urban Africans in Northern Rhodesia.* Manchester, UK: Manchester University Press, 1956.

Mitchell, Timothy. *Colonising Egypt.* Cambridge: Cambridge University Press, 1988.

Mnookin, Robert H., and Lewis Kornhauser. "Bargaining in the Shadow of the Law: The Case of Divorce." *Yale Law Journal* 88, no. 5 (1979): 950–97.

Montesquieu, Charles de Secondat. *The Spirit of the Laws*. Translated and edited by A.M. Cohler, B.C. Miller, and H.S. Stone. Cambridge: Cambridge University Press, 1989 [1748].

Moodie, T. Dunbar. "Ethnic Violence on the South African Gold Mines." In *States of Violence*, edited by Fernando Coronil and Julie Skurski. Ann Arbor: University of Michigan Press, 2006.

Moodie, T. Dunbar, and Vivienne Ndatshe. *Going for Gold: Men, Mines, and Migration*. Berkeley: University of California Press, 1994.

Moore, Donald. "Clear Waters and Muddied Histories: Environmental History and the Politics of Community in Zimbabwe's Eastern Highlands." *Journal of Southern African Studies* 24 (1988): 377–403.

———. "The Crucible of Cultural Politics: Reworking 'Development' in Zimbabwe's Eastern Highlands." *American Ethnologist* 26, no. 3 (1999): 654–89.

———. *Suffering for Territory: Race, Place, and Power in Zimbabwe*. Durham, NC: Duke University Press, 2005.

Moore, J.W. "Capitalism as World-Ecology: Braudel and Marx on Environmental History." *Organization and Environment* 16, no. 4 (2003): 431–58.

Moore, Sally Falk. "Law and Social Change: The Semi-Autonomous Social Field as an Appropriate Object of Study." *Law and Society Review* 7, no. 4 (1973): 719–46.

———. *Law as Process*. London: Routledge & Kegan Paul, 1978.

———. *Social Facts and Fabrications: "Customary" Law on Kilimanjaro*. Cambridge: Cambridge University Press, 1986.

———. "History and the Redefinition of Custom on Kilimanjaro." In *History and Power in the Study of Law: New Directions in Legal Anthropology*, 277–301. Ithaca, NY: Cornell University Press, 1989.

———. "Comparisons: Possible and Impossible." *Annual Review of Anthropology* 34 (2005): 1–11.

Moors, Annelise. "Wearing Gold, Owning Gold: The Multiple Meanings of Gold Jewelry." *Etnofoor* 25, no. 1 (2013): 79–110.

Morris, Meghan. "Speculative Fields: Property in the Shadow of Post-Conflict Colombia." *Cultural Anthropology*, forthcoming.

———. *Property in the Shadow of Post-Conflict Colombia*. Book manuscript on file with author.

Morris, Rosalind C. *In the Place of Origins: Modernity and Its Mediums in Northern Thailand*. Durham, NC: Duke University Press, 2000.

———. "Returning the Body without Haunting: Mourning 'Nai Phi' and the End of Revolution in Thailand." In *Loss*, edited by David L. Eng and David Kazanjian, 29–58. Berkeley: University of California Press, 2003.

———. "The Mute and the Unspeakable: Political Subjectivity, Violent Crime, and the 'Sexual Thing' in a South African Mining Community." In *Law and Disorder in the Postcolony*, edited by Jean Comaroff and John Comaroff, 57–101. Chicago: University of Chicago Press, 2006.

———. "The Miner's Ear." *Transition* 98 (2008): 96–115.

———. "Mediation, the Political Task: Between Language and Violence in Contemporary South Africa." *Current Anthropology* 58, no. 17 (2017): 123–34.

———. "Shadows in the Cave: Deindustrialization and the Afterlives of Gold in South Africa." Talk delivered in the Department of Anthropology at Princeton University, paper on file with author, 2017.

———. "Shadow and Impress: Ethnography, Film, and the Task of Writing History in the Space of South Africa's Deindustrialization." *History & Theory* 57, no. 4 (2018): 102–25.

———. *Unstable Ground: The Lives, Deaths, and Afterlives of Gold in South Africa*. Manuscript on file with author.

Morris, Rosalind, and Daniel Leonard. *The Returns of Fetishism: Charles de Brosses's The Worship of Fetish Gods and Its Legacies*. Chicago: University of Chicago Press, 2017.

Mudimbe, Valentin Y. *The Invention of Africa: Gnosis, Philosophy, and the Order of Knowledge*. Bloomington: Indiana University Press, 1988.

Muehlebach, Andrea. *The Moral Neoliberal: Welfare and Citizenship in Italy*. Chicago: University of Chicago Press, 2012.

Munger, Frank. "Rights in the Shadow of Class: Poverty, Welfare, and the Law." In *The Blackwell Companion to Law and Society*, edited by Austin Sarat, 330–53. Malden, MA: Blackwell, 2004.

Munn, Nancy. *The Fame of Gawa: A Symbolic Study of Value Transformation in a Massim (Papua New Guinea) Society*. Cambridge: Cambridge University Press, 1986.

Nader, Laura. "The Anthropological Study of Law." *American Anthropologist* 67, no. 6 (1965): 3–32.

Nash, June. *We Eat the Mines and the Mines Eat Us: Dependency and Exploitation in Bolivian Tin Mines*. New York: Columbia University Press, 1993 [1979].

National Coalition on Mining (NCOM), Ghana. "NCOM Condemns AngloGold-Ashanti (AGA) for Allegedly Burying Alive 40 Small-Sale Miners at Blackis Pit Near Obuasi." *TWN Africa*, September 14, 2009. Available at: http://apps.twnafrica.org/blog/index.cfm?c=ncom&p=2.

———. "NCOM Statement on the Galamsey Problem." *TWN Africa*, April 21, 2013. Available at: http://www.twnafrica.org/ncomstatement.html.

National Resource Watch. *Report on Ghana*, February 2012. Available at: https://oxfamibis.dk/en/explore-oxfam-ibis/

Negri, Antonio. "Sovereignty between Government, Exception, and Governance." In *Sovereignty in Fragments: The Past, Present and Future of a Contested Concept*, edited by Hent Kalmo and Quentin Skinner, 205–21. New York: Cambridge University Press, 2010.

Newell, Sasha. "Estranged Belongings: A Moral Economy of Theft in Abidjan, Côte d'Ivoire." *Anthropological Theory* 6, no. 2 (2006): 179–203.

Nketia, J. H. *Funeral Dirges of the Akan*. Ghana: Achimota, 1955.

Nkrumah, Kwame. *Dark Days in Ghana*. London: Zed Books, 1968.

Nordstrom, Carolyn. "Shadows and Sovereigns." *Theory, Culture, and Society* 17, no. 4 (2000): 35–54.

———. *Shadows of War: Violence, Power, and International Profiteering in the Twenty-First Century*. Berkeley: University of California Press, 2004.

———. *Global Outlaws: Crime, Money, and Power in the Contemporary World*. Berkeley: University of California Press, 2007.

Northern Miner. "Obuasi Strike Could Dent Ashanti." May 31, 1999. Available at: http://www.northernminer.com/news/obuasi-strike-could-dent-ashanti/1000102371/.

Nugent, David. "Property Relations, Production Relations, and Inequality: Anthropology, Political Economy, and the Blackfeet." *American Ethnologist* 20, no. 2 (1993): 336–62.

Nugent, Paul. "States and Social Contracts in Africa." *New Left Review* 63 (2010): 35–68.

Obarrio, Juan. *The Spirit of the Laws in Mozambique.* Chicago: University of Chicago Press, 2014.

Obeyesekere, Gananath. *Medusa's Hair: An Essay on Personal Symbols and Religious Experience.* Chicago: University of Chicago Press, 1981.

Obuasi CSOs Platform. "Obuasi CSOs Platform Condemn Abrogation of Contract between Mining and Building Contractors (MBC) and AngloGold Ashanti (AGA)." *Modern Ghana,* April 22, 2014. Available at: http://www.modernghana.com/news/536744/1/obuasi-csos-platform-condemn-abrogation-of.html.

Odotei, Irene K., and Albert K. Awedoba, eds. *Chieftancy in Ghana: Culture, Governance and Development.* Accra, Ghana: Sub-Saharan Publishers, 2006.

Oduyoye, Modupe. "Man's Self and Its Spiritual Double." In *Traditional Religion in West Africa,* edited by E. A. Ade Adegbola, 150–69. Ibadan, Nigeria: Daystar Press, 1983.

Ofori-Atta, Angela. "Prayer Camps and Biomedical Care in Ghana: A Response to Brian Goldstone." *Critical Investigations into Humanitarianism in Africa.* June 30, 2017. Available at: http://www.cihablog.com/prayer-camps-biomedical-care-ghana-response-brian-goldstone/.

Ofosu-Mensah, Emmanuel Ababio. "Traditional Gold Mining in Adanse." *Nordic Journal of African Studies* 19 (2010): 124–47.

———. "Mining as a Factor of Social Conflict in Ghana." *Global Journal of History and Culture* 1, no. 1 (2011): 7–21.

———. "Labour Migration during the Colonial Period to the Obuasi Mines in Ghana." *International Research Journal of Library Information and Archival Studies* 1, no. 1 (2011): 6–22.

———. "Gold Mining and the Socio-economic Development of Obuasi in Adanse." *African Journal of History and Culture* 3, no. 4 (2011): 54–64.

———. *Gold Mining in Adanse: Pre-colonial and Modern.* Saarbrücken, Germany: Lambert Academic Publishing, 2014.

Ogunnaike, Oludamini. "African Philosophy Reconsidered: Africa, Religion, Race, and Philosophy." *Journal of Africana Religions* 5, no. 2 (2017): 181–216.

Okali, Christine. *Cocoa and Kinship in Ghana: The Matrilineal Akan of Ghana.* London: Kegan Paul International, 1983.

Olaniyan, Tejumola, and Ato Quayson, eds. *African Literature: An Anthology of Criticism and Theory.* Malden, MA: Blackwell, 2007.

Olupona, Jacob Kehinde, ed. *African Traditional Religion in Contemporary Society.* New York: Paragon Press, 1990.

———. "Religion, Law, and Order: State Regulation of Religious Affairs in Nigeria." *Social Compass: International Review of Sociology of Religion* 37, no. 1 (1990): 127–35.

———, ed. *African Spirituality: Forms, Meanings, and Expressions.* New York: Crossroads Press, 2000.

———. "Yoruba Goddesses and Sovereignty in Southwestern Nigeria." In *Goddesses Who Rule*, edited by Elisabeth Bernard and Beverly Moon, 19–132. Oxford: Oxford University Press, 2000.

———. "Introduction." In *Beyond Primitivism: Indigenous Religious Traditions and Modernity*, edited by Jacob K. Olupona, 1–19. London: Routledge, 2004.

———. "Religion and Ecology in African Culture and Society." In *The Oxford Handbook of Religion and Ecology*, edited by Roger S. Gottlieb. Oxford: Oxford University Press, 2006.

———. "Thinking Globally about African Religion." In *The Oxford Handbook of Global Religions*, edited by Mark Juergensmeyer. Oxford: Oxford University Press, 2006.

———. *The City of 201 Gods: Ile-Ife (Nigeria) in Time, Space and the Imagination*. Berkeley: University of California Press, 2011.

O'Neill, Kevin Lewis. *City of God: Christian Citizenship in Postwar Guatemala*. Berkeley: University of California Press, 2010.

———. *Secure the Soul: Christian Piety and Gang Prevention in Guatemala*. Berkeley: University of California Press, 2015.

Ong, Aiwa. *Spirits of Resistance and Capitalist Discipline: Factory Women in Malaysia*. Albany: State University of New York Press, 1987.

———. *Neoliberalism as Exception: Mutations in Citizenship and Sovereignty*. Durham, NC: Duke University Press, 2006.

Onselen, Charles van. *Chibaro: African Mine Labour in Southern Rhodesia, 1900–1933*. London: Pluto Press, 1976.

Opoku, Kofi A. *West African Traditional Religion*. Accra, Ghana: FEP Int., 1978.

Opokuwaa, Nana Akua Kyerewaa. *The Quest for Spiritual Transformation: Introduction to Traditional Akan Religion, Rituals, and Practices*. Lincoln, NE: iUniverse, 2005.

Ottaway, Marina. "From Political Opening to Democratization?" In *Democracy in Africa: The Hard Road Ahead*, edited by Marina Ottaway, 1–14. Boulder, CO: L. Rienner, 1997.

Oushakine, Serguei. *The Patriotism of Despair: Nation, War, and Loss in Russia*. Ithaca, NY: Cornell University Press, 2009.

Palmié, Stephan. *Wizards and Scientists: Explorations in Afro-Cuban Modernity and Tradition*. Durham, NC: Duke University Press, 2002.

Pandolfo, Stefania. *Knot of the Soul: Madness, Psychoanalysis, Islam*. Chicago: University of Chicago Press, 2018.

Parish, Jane. "The Dynamics of Witchcraft and Indigenous Shrines among the Akan." *Africa* 69, no. 3 (1999): 426–48.

———. "Black Market, Free Market: Anti-Witchcraft Shrines and Fetishes among the Akan." In *Magical Interpretations, Material Realities: Modernity, Witchcraft and the Occult in Postcolonial Africa*, edited by Henrietta L. Moore and Todd Sanders, 118–35. London: Routledge, 2001.

———. "Beyond Occult Economies: Akan Spirits, New York Idols, and Detroit Automobiles." *HAU: Journal of Ethnographic Theory* 5, no. 2 (2015): 101–20.

Parker, John. "Witchcraft, Anti-Witchcraft and Trans-Regional Ritual Innovation in Early Colonial Ghana: Sakrabundi and Aberewa, 1889–1910." *Journal of African History* 45, no. 3 (2004): 393–420.

Parpart, Jane L. *Labor and Capital on the African Copperbelt*. Philadelphia: Temple University Press, 1983.

———. *Gender, Ideology, and Power: Marriage in the Colonial Copperbelt Towns of Zambia*. Johannesburg, South Africa: University of the Witwatersrand, African Studies Institute, 1991.

Parrinder, Geoffrey. *West African Religion: A Study of the Belief and Practices of Akan, Ewe, Yoruba, Ibo and Kindred Peoples*. London: Epworth Press, 1969.

Pearce, R. D. *The Turning Point in Africa: British Colonial Policy 1938–1948*. London: Frank Cass, 1982.

Pels, Peter. "The Spirit of Matter: On Fetish, Rarity, Fact, and Fancy." In *Border Fetishisms: Material Objects in Unstable Spaces*, edited by Patricia Spyer, 91–122. New York: Routledge, 1998.

———. "Spirits of Modernity: Alfred Wallace, Edward Tylor, and the Visual Politics of Fact." In *Magic and Modernity: Interfaces of Revelation and Concealment*, edited by Birgit Meyer and Peter Pels, 241–71. Stanford, CA: Stanford University Press, 2003.

Peluso, Nancy Lee, and Michael Watts. "Violent Environments." In *Violent Environments*, edited by Nancy Lee Peluso and Michael Watts, 3–38. Ithaca, NY: Cornell University Press, 2001.

Perelman, Jeremy, and Lucie White. "Stones of Hope: Experience and Theory in African Economic and Social Rights Activism." In *Stones of Hope: How African Activists Reclaim Human Rights to Challenge Global Poverty*, edited by Lucie E. White and Jeremy Perelman, 149–71. Stanford, CA: Stanford University Press, 2010.

Pierre, Jemima. *The Predicament of Blackness: Postcolonial Ghana and the Politics of Race*. Chicago: University of Chicago Press, 2012.

Pietz, William. "The Problem of the Fetish I." *RES: Journal of Anthropology and Aesthetics* 9 (1985): 5–17.

———. "The Problem of the Fetish II: The Origin of the Fetish." *RES: Journal of Anthropology and Aesthetics* 13 (1987): 23–45.

———. "The Problem of the Fetish IIIa: Bosman's Guinea and the Enlightenment Theory of Fetishism." *RES: Journal of Anthropology and Aesthetics* 16 (1988): 105–23.

———. "Fetishism and Materialism: The Limits of Theory in Marx." In *Fetishism as Cultural Discourse*, edited by Emily Apter and William Pietz (Ithaca, NY: Cornell University Press, 1993).

———. "The Spirit of Civilization: Blood Sacrifice and Monetary Debt." *RES: Journal of Anthropology and Aesthetics* 28 (1995): 23–38.

———. "Death and the Deodand: Accursed Objects and the Money Value of Human Life." In *(Un)Fixing Representation*, edited by Judith Farquhar, Tomoko Masuzawa, and Carol Mavor. Minneapolis: University of Minnesota Press, 1995.

Pijpers, Robert Jan, and Thomas Hylland Eriksen, eds. *Mining Encounters: Extractive Industries in an Overheated World*. London: Pluto Press, 2019.

Piot, Charles. *Nostalgia for the Future: West Africa After the Cold War*. Chicago: University of Chicago Press, 2010.

Plato. *The Republic*. New York: Penguin, 2007 [380 BC].

Postone, Moishe. *Time, Labor, and Social Domination: A Reinterpretation of Marxist Critical Theory*. New York: Cambridge University Press, 1993.

Povinelli, Elizabeth. *Labor's Lot: The Power, History, and Culture of Aboriginal Action*. Chicago: University of Chicago Press, 1993.

———. *Economies of Abandonment: Social Belonging and Endurance in Late Liberalism*. Durham, NC: Duke University Press, 2011.

———. *Geontologies: A Requiem to Late Liberalism*. Durham, NC: Duke University Press, 2016.

Powdermaker, Hortense. *Copper Town: Changing Africa; the Human Situation on the Rhodesian Copperbelt*. New York: Harper & Row, 1962.

Prempeh, Agyeman. *'The History of Ashanti Kings and the Whole Country Itself' and Other Writings*, edited by Emmanuel Akyeampong, A. Adu Boahen, N. Lawler, T. C. McCaskie, and Ivor Wilks. Oxford: Oxford University Press, 2008 [1907].

Puett, Michael. "Ritual and the Subjunctive." In *Ritual and Its Consequences: An Essay on the Limits of Sincerity*, edited by A. Seligman, R. Weller, and B. Simon. Oxford: Oxford University Press, 2008.

———. "Economies of Ghosts, Gods, and Goods: The History and Anthropology of Chinese Temple Networks." In *Radical Egalitarianism: Local Realities, Global Relations*, edited by M. M. J. Fischer, F. Aulino, M. Goheen, and S. J. Tambiah, 91–100. New York: Fordham University Press, 2013.

Quayson, Ato. *Oxford Street, Accra: City Life and the Itineraries of Transnationalism*. Durham, NC: Duke University Press, 2014.

Radcliffe-Brown, A. R. "Preface." In *African Political Systems*, edited by Meyer Fortes and E. E. Evans-Pritchard. London: Oxford University Press, 1970 [1940].

Rajah, Jothie. *Authoritarian Rule of Law: Legislation, Discourse and Legitimacy in Singapore*. Cambridge: Cambridge University Press, 2012.

Rajak, Dinah. *In Good Company: An Anatomy of Corporate Social Responsibility*. Stanford, CA: Stanford University Press, 2011.

Ralph, Laurence. "The Memory of Gold: Happy Slaves and the Problem of Security." *Transition* 105 (2011): 88–105.

———. *Renegade Dreams: Living through Injury in Gangland Chicago*. Chicago: University of Chicago Press, 2014.

Ralph, Michael. *Forensics of Capital*. Chicago: University of Chicago Press, 2015.

Ralph, Michael, and Lauren Coyle. "Resource Curse?" *Transition* 107 (2012): 151–59.

Ramsey, Kate. *The Spirits and the Law: Vodou and Power in Haiti*. Chicago: University of Chicago Press, 2011.

Ranger, Terence. "Invention of Tradition in Colonial Africa." In *The Invention of Tradition*, edited by Eric Hobsbawm and Terence Ranger, 211–62. Cambridge: Cambridge University Press, 1983.

Rathbone, Richard. *Nkrumah and the Chiefs: The Politics of Chieftaincy in Ghana, 1951–1960*. Athens: Ohio University Press, 2000.

———. "From Kingdom to Nation: Changing African Constructions of Identity." In *Chieftaincy in Ghana: Culture, Governance and Development*, edited by Irene K. Odotei and Albert K. Awedoba, 43–54. Accra, Ghana: Sub-Saharan Publishers, 2006.

Rattray, R. Sutherland. *Ashanti Proverbs*. Translated by R. Sutherland Rattray. Oxford, UK: Clarendon Press, 1916.

———. *Ashanti.* Oxford, UK: Clarendon Press, 1923.

———. *Religion and Art in Ashanti.* Oxford, UK: Clarendon Press, 1927.

———. *Ashanti Law and Constitution.* Oxford, UK: Clarendon Press, 1929.

———. *Akan-Ashanti Folk-Tales.* Oxford, UK: Clarendon Press, 1930.

———. *The Golden Stool of Ashanti: A Sacred Shrine Regarded as a Symbol of the Nation's Soul, and Never Lost or Surrendered, Its True History, a Romance of African Colonial Administration.* London: Illustrated London News, 1935.

Ray, Donald I. "Divided Sovereign: Traditional Authority and the State in Ghana." *Journal of Legal Pluralism and Unofficial Law* 28 (1996): 181–202.

Reindorf, Carl C. *History of the Gold Coast and Asante, Based on Tradition and Historical Facts.* Accra, Ghana: Ghana Universities Press, 2007 [1895].

Reno, William. *Warlord Politics and African States.* Boulder, CO: Lynne Rienner, 1998.

———. "How Sovereignty Matters: International Markets and the Political Economy of Local Politics in Weak States." In *Intervention and Transnationalism in Africa: Global-Local Networks of Power,* edited by Thomas M. Callaghy, Ronald Kassimir, and Robert Latham. New York: Cambridge University Press, 2001.

Richard, François. "Thinking through 'Vernacular Cosmopolitanisms': Historical Archaeology in Senegal and the Material Contours of the African Atlantic." *International Journal of Historical Archaeology* 71, no. 1 (2013): 40–71.

Richland, Justin. "Hopi Tradition as Jurisdiction: On the Potentializing Limits of Hopi Sovereignty." *Law and Social Inquiry* 36, no. 1 (2011): 201–34.

Riles, Annelise. *Collateral Knowledge: Legal Reasoning in the Global Financial Markets.* Chicago: University of Chicago Press, 2011.

Robotham, Donald Keith. *Moneystone: Consciousness and Kinship amongst Miners in Ghana.* Doctoral thesis, Department of Anthropology, University of Chicago, 1987. On file at Mansueto Library.

———. *Militants or Proletarians? The Economic Culture of Underground Gold Miners in Southern Ghana, 1906–1976.* Cambridge, UK: African Studies Centre, 1989.

———. *Culture, Society, and Economy: Bringing Production Back In.* Washington, DC: Sage, 2005.

Rodney, Walter. "Gold and Slaves on the Gold Coast." *Transactions of the Historical Society of Ghana* 10 (1969): 13–28.

———. *How Europe Underdeveloped Africa.* Washington, DC: Howard University Press, 1974.

Rodriguez-Garavito, Cesar. "Ethnicity.gov: Global Governance, Indigenous Peoples, and the Right to Prior Consultation in Social Minefields." *Indiana Journal of Global Legal Studies* 18, no. 1 (2011): 263–305.

Roitman, Janet. *Fiscal Disobedience: An Anthropology of Economic Regulation in Central Africa.* Princeton, NJ: Princeton University Press, 2005.

———. "The Ethics of Illegality in the Chad Basin." In *Law and Disorder in the Postcolony,* edited by Jean Comaroff and John L. Comaroff, 247–72. Chicago: University of Chicago Press, 2006.

Rolston, Jessica Smith. *Mining Coal and Undermining Gender: Rhythms of Work and Family in the American West.* New Brunswick, NJ: Rutgers University Press, 2014.

Roob, Alexander. *Alchemy and Mysticism.* Los Angeles: Taschen, 2019.

Rose, Carol M. *Property and Persuasion: Essays on the History, Theory, and Rhetoric of Ownership*. Boulder, CO: Westview, 1994.

Rose, Gillian. *Love's Work*. New York: Penguin, 2011 [1995].

———. *Mourning Becomes the Law: Philosophy and Representation*. Cambridge: Cambridge University Press, 1996.

Rose, Nikolas. *Powers of Freedom: Reframing Political Thought*. Cambridge, UK: Cambridge University Press, 1999.

Rosen, Lawrence. *Law as Culture: An Invitation*. Princeton, NJ: Princeton University Press, 2006.

Rossi, Ino. *The Unconscious in Culture*. New York: Dutton, 1974.

Rouse, Carolyn. "Don't Let the Lion Tell the Giraffe's Story: Law, Violence, and Ontological Insecurities in Ghana." In *Bioinsecurity and Vulnerability*, edited by Nancy N. Chen and Lesley A. Sharp, 121–42. Santa Fe, NM: School for Advanced Research Press, 2014.

———. *Development Hubris: Adventures Trying to Save the World*. Manuscript on file with author.

Rousseau, Jean-Jacques. "On the Social Contract." In *The Basic Political Writings*. Translated and edited by Donald A. Cress, 153–252. New York: Hackett, 1987.

Rowlands, Michael, and Jean-Pierre Warnier. "Sorcery, Power, and the Modern State in Cameroon." *Man* 23, no. 1 (1988): 118–32.

Rutherford, Danilyn. *Laughing at Leviathan: Sovereignty and Audience in West Papua*. Chicago: University of Chicago Press, 2012.

Sahlins, Marshall. "Cosmologies of Capitalism: The Trans-Pacific Sector of the 'World-System.'" In *Culture/Power/History: A Reader in Contemporary Social Theory*, edited by Nicholas B. Dirks, Geoff Eley, and Sherry B. Ortner, 412–56. Princeton, NJ: Princeton University Press, 1994.

———. "The Sadness of Sweetness: The Native Anthropology of Western Cosmology." *Current Anthropology* 37, no. 3 (1996): 395–428.

Santner, Eric. *The Royal Remains: The People's Two Bodies and the Endgames of Sovereignty*. Chicago: University of Chicago Press, 2011.

Sarat, Austin. "Vitality Amidst Fragmentation: On the Emergence of Postrealist Law and Society Scholarship." In *The Blackwell Companion to Law and Society*, edited by Austin Sarat, 1–11. Malden, MA: Blackwell, 2004.

Sarpong, Peter Kwasi. *The Sacred Stools of the Akan*. Accra, Ghana: Ghana Publishing Corporation, 1971.

———. *Libation*. Accra, Ghana: Anansesem Publications, 1996.

Sassen, Saskia. *Territory, Authority, Rights: From Medieval to Global Assemblages*. Princeton, NJ: Princeton University Press, 2006.

Savigny, Friedrich Karl von. *Jural Relations; or, The Roman Law of Persons as Subjects of Jural Relations, Being a Translation of the Second Book of Savigny's System of Modern Roman Law*. Westport, CT: Hyperion Press, 1979 [1884].

Scarry, Elaine. *The Body in Pain: The Making and Unmaking of the World*. New York: Oxford University Press, 1985.

Schmitt, Carl. *Political Theology: Four Chapters on the Concept of Sovereignty*. Translated by George Schwab. Chicago: University of Chicago Press, 2005 [1922].

———. *Legality and Legitimacy.* Translated by J. Seitzer. Durham, NC: Duke University Press, 2004 [1932].

———. *The Concept of the Political.* Translated by George Schwab. Chicago: University of Chicago Press, 1995 [1932].

———. *Political Theology II: The Myth of the Closure of Any Political Theology.* Translated by M. Hoelzl and G. Ward. Chicago: University of Chicago Press, 2008 [1970].

Schrijver, Nico. *Sovereignty over Natural Resources: Balancing Rights and Duties.* New York: Cambridge University Press, 1997.

Scott, James C. *Seeing Like a State: How Certain Schemes to Improve the Human Condition Have Failed.* New Haven, CT: Yale University Press, 1998.

Sewell, William. *Logics of History: Social Theory and Social Transformation.* Chicago: University of Chicago Press, 2009.

Shaw, Rosalind. *Memories of the Slave Trade: Ritual and the Historical Imagination in Sierra Leone.* Chicago: University of Chicago Press, 2002.

Shipley, Jesse Weaver. "Comedians, Pastors, and the Miraculous Agency of Charisma in Ghana." *Cultural Anthropology* 24, no. 3 (2009): 523–52.

———. *Living the Hiplife: Celebrity and Entrepreneurship in Ghanaian Popular Music.* Durham, NC: Duke University Press, 2013.

———. *Trickster Theatre: The Poetics of Freedom in Urban Africa.* Bloomington: Indiana University Press, 2015.

Siegel, James. *Naming the Witch.* Stanford, CA: Stanford University Press, 2006.

Silbey, Susan S. "After Legal Consciousness." *Annual Review of Law and Social Science* 1 (2005): 323–68.

Silver, Jim. "The Failure of European Mining Companies in the Nineteenth-Century Gold Coast." *Journal of African History* 22 (1981): 511–29.

Simone, AbdouMaliq. *Improvised Lives: Rhythms of Endurance in an Urban South.* Hoboken, NJ: John Wiley & Sons, 2018.

Simpasa, Anthony, Degol Hailu, Sebastian Levine, and Roberto Julio Tibana. "Capturing Mineral Revenues in Zambia: Past Trends and Future Prospects." United Nations Development Programme. Discussion paper, August 2013, available at: http://www.un.org/en/land-natural-resources-conflict/pdfs/capturing-mineral-revenues-zambia.pdf.

Singh, Bhrigupati. "The Headless Horseman of Central India: Sovereignty at Varying Thresholds of Life." *Cultural Anthropology* 27, no. 2 (2012): 383–407.

Sivaramakrishnan, K. "Colonialism and Forestry in India: Imagining the Past in Present Politics." *Comparative Studies in Society and History* 37 (1995): 3–40.

Skinner, Quentin. "The Sovereign State: A Genealogy." In *Sovereignty in Fragments: The Past, Present and Future of a Contested Concept*, edited by Hent Kalmo and Quentin Skinner, 26–46. New York: Cambridge University Press, 2010.

Skurski, Julie, and Fernando Coronil. "Introduction: States of Violence and the Violence of States." In *States of Violence*, edited by Fernando Coronil and Julie Skurski, 1–32. Ann Arbor: University of Michigan Press, 2006.

Slaughter, Anne-Marie. "Disaggregated Sovereignty: Towards the Public Accountability of Global Government Networks." *Government and Opposition* 39 (2004): 159–90.

Smith, Daniel Jordan. *A Culture of Corruption: Everyday Deception and Popular Discontent in Nigeria.* Princeton, NJ: Princeton University Press, 2007.

Smith, James H. *Bewitching Development: Witchcraft and the Reinvention of Development in Neoliberal Kenya.* Chicago: University of Chicago Press, 2008.

———. "Tantalus in the Digital Age: Coltan Ore, Temporal Dispossession, and 'Movement' in the Eastern Democratic Republic of the Congo." *American Ethnologist* 38, no. 1 (2011): 17–35.

———. "May It Never End: Price Wars, Networks and Temporality in the '3Ts' Mining Trade of the Eastern DR Congo." *HAU: Journal of Ethnographic Theory* 5, no. 1 (2015): 1–35.

———. "Colonizing Banro: Kingship, Temporality, and Mining of Futures in the Goldfields of South Kivu, DRC." In *The Politics of Custom: Chiefship, Capital, and the State,* edited by John L. Comaroff and Jean Comaroff, 279–304. Chicago: University of Chicago Press, 2018.

Smith, James H., and Ngeti Mwadime. *Email from Ngeti: An Ethnography of Sorcery, Redemption, and Friendship in Global Africa.* Berkeley: University of California Press, 2014.

Smith, James H., and Rosalind I. J. Hackett, eds. *Displacing the State: Religion and Conflict in Neoliberal Africa.* Notre Dame, IN: University of Notre Dame Press, 2011.

Smith, Jessica M., and Frederico Helfgott. "Flexibility or Exploitation? Corporate Social Responsibility and the Perils of Universalization." *Anthropology Today* 26, no. 3 (2010): 20–23.

Snyder, Francis G. *Capitalism and Legal Change: An African Transformation.* New York: Academic Press, 1981.

———. "Colonialism and Legal Form: The Creation of 'Customary Law' in Senegal." In *Crime, Justice, and Underdevelopment,* edited by Colin Sumner. London: Heinemann, 1982.

———. "Economic Globalisation and the Law in the 21st Century." In *The Blackwell Companion to Law and Society,* edited by Austin Sarat, 624–40. Malden, MA: Blackwell, 2004.

Soothill, Jane E. *Gender, Social Change, and Spiritual Power: Charismatic Christianity in Ghana.* Leiden, Netherlands: Brill, 2007.

Spear, Thomas. "Neo-traditionalism and the Limits of Invention." *Journal of African History* 44 (2003): 3–27.

Spivak, Gayatri Chakravorty. *A Critique of Postcolonial Reason: Toward a History of the Vanishing Present.* Cambridge, MA: Harvard University Press, 1999.

Spyer, Patricia, ed. *Border Fetishisms: Material Objects in Unstable Spaces.* New York: Routledge, 1998.

Stanger, Darci. "Galamsey: Environmental Impact of Illegal Gold Mining in Ghana." *Georgetown Environmental Law Review.* February 13, 2015. Available at: https://gelr.org/2015/02/13/galamsey-environmental-impact-of-illegal-gold-mining-in-ghana/.

Starr, June, and Jane F. Collier, eds. *History and Power in the Study of Law: New Directions in Legal Anthropology.* Ithaca, NY: Cornell University Press, 1989.

Stewart, Charles. "Dreams of Treasure: Temporality, Historicization, and the Unconscious." *Anthropological Theory* 3 (2003): 481–500.

Stoler, Ann. "Between Metropole and Colony: Rethinking a Research Agenda." In *Tensions of Empire: Colonial Cultures in a Bourgeois World,* edited by Frederick Cooper and Ann Laura Stoler, 1–56. Berkeley: University of California Press, 1997.

———. "Intimidations of Empire: Predicaments of the Tactile and the Unseen." In *Haunted by Empire: Geographies of Intimacy in North American History*, edited by Ann Stoler, 1–22. Durham, NC: Duke University Press, 2006.

Stoller, Paul. *Fusion of the World: An Ethnography of Possession Among the Songhay of Niger.* Chicago: University of Chicago Press, 1989.

Stone, Katherine. *Private Justice: The Law of Alternative Dispute Resolution.* New York: Foundation Press, 2000.

Sturm, Circe. "Reflections on the Anthropology of Sovereignty and Settler Colonialism: Lessons from Native North America." *Cultural Anthropology* 32, no. 3 (2017): 340–48.

Subramanian, Ajantha. *Shorelines: Space and Rights in South India.* Stanford, CA: Stanford University Press, 2009.

Sweet, James. *Domingos Álvares, African Healing, and the Intellectual History of the Atlantic World.* Chapel Hill: University of North Carolina Press, 2011.

Szablowski, David. *Transnational Law and Local Struggles: Mining, Communities, and the World Bank.* Oxford, UK: Hart Publishing, 2007.

Talton, Ben. *Politics of Social Change in Ghana: The Konkomba Struggle for Political Equality.* New York: Palgrave Macmillan, 2010.

Talton, Ben, and Quincy Mills, eds. *Black Subjects in Africa and Its Diasporas: Race and Gender in Research and Writing.* New York: Palgrave Macmillan, 2011.

Tambiah, Stanley. *Magic, Science, Religion, and the Scope of Rationality.* Cambridge: Cambridge University Press, 1990.

Tashjian, Victoria B., and Jean Allman. *"I Will Not Eat Stone": A Women's History of Colonial Asante.* Portsmouth, NH: Heinemann, 2000.

Taussig, Michael. *The Devil and Commodity Fetishism in South America.* Chapel Hill: University of North Carolina Press, 1980.

———. *Shamanism, Colonialism, and the Wild Man: A Study in Terror and Healing.* Chicago: University of Chicago Press, 1987.

———. *The Magic of the State.* New York: Routledge, 1997.

———. *Law in a Lawless Land: Diary of a Limpieza in Colombia.* Chicago: University of Chicago Press, 2003.

Taylor, Charles. *Modern Social Imaginaries.* Durham, NC: Duke University Press, 2004.

Thomas, Deborah A. *Exceptional Violence: Embodied Citizenship in Transnational Jamaica.* Durham, NC: Duke University Press, 2011.

———. "The Problem with Violence: Exceptionality and Sovereignty in the New World." *Journal of Transnational American Studies* 5 (2013), no. 1.

———. "Time and the Otherwise: Plantations, Garrisons, and Being Human in the Caribbean." *Anthropological Theory* 16, nos. 2–3 (2016): 177–200.

Thomas, Deborah A., and M. Kamari Clarke. "Globalization and Race: Structures of Inequality, New Sovereignties, and Citizenship in a Neoliberal Era." *Annual Review of Anthropology* 42 (2013): 305–25.

Thomas, Roger. "Forced Labour in British West Africa: The Case of the Northern Territories of the Gold Coast, 1906–1927." *Journal of African History* 14 (1973): 79–103.

Thompson, E. P. *The Making of the English Working Class.* New York: Vintage Books, 1963.

———. *Customs in Common: Studies in Traditional Popular Culture*. New York: New Press, 1993.

Thompson, Robert Farris. *Flash of the Spirit: African and Afro-American Art and Philosophy*. New York: Random House, 1983.

Thornton, John K. "Cannibals, Witches, and Slave Traders in the Atlantic World." *William and Mary Quarterly* 60, no. 2 (2003): 273–94.

Tilley, Helen. *Africa As a Living Laboratory: Empire, Development, and the Problem of Scientific Knowledge, 1860–1960*. Chicago: University of Chicago Press, 2010.

Trouillot, Michel-Rolph. "The Anthropology of the State in the Age of Globalization: Close Encounters of the Deceptive Kind." *Current Anthropology* 42 (2001): 125–38.

Trubek, David M., and Alvaro Santos, eds. *The New Law and Economic Development: A Critical Appraisal*. New York: Cambridge University Press, 2006.

Tsing, Anna. *In the Realm of the Diamond Queen: Marginality in an Out-of-the-Way Place*. Princeton, NJ: Princeton University Press, 1993.

———. "The Global Situation." *Cultural Anthropology* 15, no. 3 (2000): 327–60.

———. *Friction: An Ethnography of Global Connection*. Princeton, NJ: Princeton University Press, 2005.

Turner, Terence S. "Anthropology and the Politics of Indigenous Peoples' Struggles." *Cambridge Journal of Anthropology* 5, no. 1 (1979): 1–43.

———. "Social Body and Embodied Subject: The Production of Bodies, Actors and Society Among the Kayapo." *Cultural Anthropology* 10, no. 2 (1995): 143–70.

———. "An Indigenous People's Struggle for Socially Equitable and Ecologically Sustainable Production: The Kayapo Revolt against Extractivism." *Journal of Latin American and Caribbean Anthropology* 1, no. 1 (1995): 98–121.

———. *The Fire of the Jaguar*. Chicago: University of Chicago Press, 2017.

Turner, Victor. *Schism and Continuity in an African Society: A Study of Ndembu Village Life*. Manchester, UK: Manchester University Press, 1957.

———. "Witchcraft and Sorcery: Taxonomy Versus Dynamics." *Africa* 34, no. 4 (1964): 314–25.

———. *The Forest of Symbols: Aspects of Ndembu Ritual*. Ithaca, NY: Cornell University Press, 1967.

———. "Symbolic Studies." *Annual Review of Anthropology* 4 (1975): 145–61.

———. "Images of Anti-Temporality: An Essay in the Anthropology of Experience." *Harvard Theological Review* 75, no. 2 (1982): 243–65.

Turrell, Robert V. *Capital and Labour on the Kimberley Diamond Fields, 1871–1890*. Cambridge: Cambridge University Press, 1987.

Twining, William L. *Globalisation and Legal Theory*. London: Butterworths, 2000.

Ubink, Janine. "Struggles for Land in Peri-urban Kumasi and Their Effect on Popular Perceptions of Chiefs and Chieftaincy." In *Contesting Land and Custom in Ghana*, edited by Janine M. Ubink and Kojo S. Amanor, 155–82. Leiden, Netherlands: Leiden University Press, 2008.

Ullucci, Daniel C. *The Christian Rejection of Animal Sacrifice*. Oxford: Oxford University Press, 2012.

United Nations Commission on Sustainable Development (UNCSD), Ghana Office. "A Report on Ghana's Mining Sector for the 18th Session of the UN Commission on Sustainable Development." 2010.

Valeri, Valerio. *Kingship and Sacrifice: Ritual and Society in Ancient Hawaii.* Translated by Paula Wissing. Chicago: University of Chicago Press, 1985.

Van de Walle, Nicholas. "Economic Reform and the Consolidation of Democracy in Africa." In *Democracy in Africa: The Hard Road Ahead*, edited by Marina Ottaway, 15–42. Boulder, CO: L. Rienner, 1997.

Van der Geest, Sjaak. "Money and Respect: The Changing Value of Old Age in Rural Ghana." *Africa* 67, no. 4 (1997): 534–59.

Vansina, Jan. *Oral Tradition as History.* Madison: University of Wisconsin Press, 1986.

Van Velsen, J. "Procedural Informality, Reconciliation, and False Comparisons." In *Ideas and Procedures in African Customary Law*, edited by Max Gluckman, 137–52. London: Oxford University Press, 1969.

———. *The Politics of Kinship: A Study in Social Manipulation among the Lakeside Tonga of Malawi.* Manchester, UK: Manchester University Press, 1971.

Verdery, Katherine. *The Political Lives of Dead Bodies: Reburial and Postsocialist Change.* New York: Columbia University Press, 1999.

Verdery, Katherine, and Caroline Humphrey, eds. *Property in Question: Value Transformation in the Global Economy.* New York: Berg, 2004.

Vilar, Pierre. *A History of Gold and Money, 1450–1920.* Translated by Judith White. New York: Verso, 2011.

Von Laue, Theodore H. "Anthropology and Power: R. S. Rattray among the Ashanti." *African Affairs* 75 (1976): 33–54.

Wacam. "Man Shot at AngloGold Ashanti Obuasi Mine Dies." Ghana Web, August 15, 2011. Available at: https://www.ghanaweb.com/GhanaHomePage/NewsArchive/Man-shot -at-AngloGold-Ashanti-Obuasi-Mine-dies-216399#.

Walker, Neil, ed. *Sovereignty in Transition.* Oxford, UK: Hart, 2003.

Wallerstein, Immanuel. *The Road to Independence: Ghana and the Ivory Coast.* Berlin, Germany: Mouton, 1964.

Walsh, Andrew. "'Hot Money' and Daring Consumption in a Northern Malagasy Sapphire-Mining Town." *American Ethnologist* 30, no. 2 (2003): 290–305.

Ward, Barbara F. "Some Observations on Religious Cults in Asante." *Africa* 26 (1956): 7–61.

Warner, Michael. *Publics and Counterpublics.* Cambridge, MA: Zone Books, 2001.

Waswo, Richard. "The Formation of Natural Law to Justify Colonialism, 1539–1689." *New Literary History* 27, no. 4 (1996): 743–59.

Watts, Michael J. *Silent Violence.* Berkeley: University of California Press, 1983.

———. "Petro-Violence: Community, Extraction, and Political Ecology of a Mythic Commodity." In *Violent Environments*, edited by Nancy Lee Peluso and Michael Watts, 189–212. Ithaca, NY: Cornell University Press, 2001.

———. "Violent Environments: Petroleum Conflict and the Political Ecology of Rule in the Niger Delta, Nigeria." In *Liberation Ecologies: Environment, Development, Social Movements*, edited by Richard Peet and Michael Watts. London: Routledge, 2004.

———. "Resource Curse? Governmentality, Oil and Power in the Niger Delta, Nigeria." *Geopolitics* 9, no. 1 (2004): 50–80.

———. "Ecologies of Rule: African Environments and the Climate of Neoliberalism." In *The Deepening Crisis: Governance Challenges after Neoliberalism*, edited by Craig

Calhoun and Georgi Derluguian, 67–92. New York: New York University Press, 2011.

Watts, Michael, and Richard Peet. "Towards a Theory of Liberation Ecology." In *Liberation Ecologies: Environment, Development, and Social Movements*, edited by Richard Peet and Michael Watts, 260–69. London: Routledge, 1996.

Weber, Max. *Economy and Society: An Outline of Interpretive Sociology, 2 Volumes.* Translated by Ephraim Fischoff. Edited by Guenther Roth and Claus Wittich. Berkeley: University of California Press, 1978 [1922].

———. *The Vocation Lectures.* Translated by Rodney Livingstone. Edited by David Owen and Tracy Strong. Indianapolis: Hackett Books, 2004 [1919].

———. *The Protestant Ethic and the Spirit of Capitalism.* Translated by Stephen Kalberg. New York: Oxford University Press, 2011 [1905].

Weber, Samuel. "Taking Exception to Decision: Walter Benjamin and Carl Schmitt." *Diacritics* 22 (1992): 5–18.

Weiss, Brad. *The Making and Unmaking of the Haya Lived World: Consumption, Commoditization, and Everyday Practice.* Durham, NC: Duke University Press, 1996.

———. *Sacred Trees, Bitter Harvests: Globalizing Coffee in Northwest Tanzania.* Portsmouth, NH: Heinemann, 2003.

Weitzner, Viviane. "Between Panic and Hope: Indigenous Peoples, Gold, Violence(s) and FPIC in Colombia, Through the Lens of Time." *Journal of Legal Pluralism and Unofficial Law* 51 (2019): 3–28.

Welker, Marina. "'Corporate Security Begins in the Community': Mining, the Corporate Social Responsibility Industry, and Environmental Advocacy in Indonesia." *Cultural Anthropology* 24, no. 1 (2009): 142–79.

———. "The Green Revolution's Ghost: Unruly Subjects of Participatory Development in Rural Indonesia." *American Ethnologist* 39, no. 2 (2012): 389–406.

———. *Enacting the Corporation: An American Mining Firm in Postauthoritarian Indonesia.* Berkeley: University of California Press, 2014.

Werthmann, Katja. "The President of the Gold Diggers: Sources of Power in a Gold Mine in Burkina Faso." *Ethnos* 68, no. 1 (2003): 95–111.

West, Harry G. "'Who Rules Us Now?': Identity Tokens, Sorcery, and Other Metaphors in the 1994 Mozambican Elections." In *Transparency and Conspiracy: Ethnographies of Suspicion in the New World Order*, edited by Harry G. West and Todd Sanders, 92–124. Durham, NC: Duke University Press, 2003.

———. *Kupilikula: Governance and the Invisible Realm in Mozambique.* Chicago: University of Chicago Press, 2005.

West, Harry G., and Todd Sanders, eds. *Transparency and Conspiracy: Ethnographies of Suspicion in the New World Order.* Durham, NC: Duke University Press, 2003.

Whitaker, Kati. "Ghana Witch Camps: Widows' Lives in Exile." *BBC News.* September 1, 2012. Available at: http://www.bbc.com/news/magazine-19437130.

White, Hylton. "In the Shadow of Time." *Journal of the Royal Anthropological Institute* 19 (2013): 256–67.

White, Luise. *Speaking with Vampires: Rumor and History in Colonial Africa.* Berkeley: University of California Press, 2000.

White, Luise, Stephan Miescher, and David William Cohen. "Introduction." In *African Words, African Voices: Critical Practices in Oral History*, edited by Luise White, Stephan Miescher, and David William Cohen. Bloomington: Indiana University Press, 2001.

Whiteman, Gail, and Katy Mamen. "Community Consultation in Mining." *Cultural Survival Quarterly* 25 (2001): 30–35.

Whitfield, Lindsay. "Trustees of Development from Conditionality to Governance: Poverty Reduction Strategy Papers in Ghana." *Journal of Modern African Studies* 43, no. 4 (2005): 641–64.

Widner, Jennifer A. *Building the Rule of Law: Francis Nyalali and the Road to Judicial Independence in Africa.* New York: W. W. Norton, 2001.

Wilks, Ivor. *Asante in the Nineteenth Century: The Structure and Evolution of a Political Order.* Cambridge: Cambridge University Press, 1975.

———. *Forests of Gold: Essays on the Akan and the Kingdom of Asante.* Athens: Ohio University Press, 1993.

———. "'Unity and Progress': Asante Politics Revisited." In *Akan Worlds: Identity and Power in West Africa*, edited by Pierluigi Valsecchi and Fabio Viti, 43–68. Paris: L'Harmattan, 1999.

Williams, John P. "Legal Reform in Mining: Past, Present, and Future." In *International and Comparative Mineral Law and Policy: Trends and Prospects*, edited by Elizabeth Bastida, Thomas Walde, and Janeth Warden-Fernández. The Hague, Netherlands: Kluwer Law International, 2005.

Williams, Raymond. "Tragic Resignation and Sacrifice." *Critical Quarterly* 5, no. 1 (1963): 5–19.

———. *Marxism and Literature.* New York: Oxford University Press, 1977.

Williamson, S. G. *Akan Religion and Christian Faith.* Accra, Ghana: Ghana Universities Press, 1974.

Wilson, Monica. "Witch Beliefs and Social Structure." *American Journal of Sociology* 56, no. 4 (1951): 307–13.

Wilson, Peter J. "Status Ambiguity and Spirit Possession." *Man* 2 (1967): 366–78.

Winchell, Mareike. "Economies of Obligation: Patronage as Relational Wealth in Bolivian Gold Mining." *HAU: Journal of Ethnographic Theory* 7, no. 3 (2017): 159–83.

Wittgenstein, Ludwig. *Culture and Value.* Edited by G. H. von Wright. Translated by Peter Winch. Chicago: University of Chicago Press, 1980.

Wolf, Eric. *Europe and the People without History.* Berkeley: University of California Press, 1982.

Worger, William. *South Africa's City of Diamonds: Mine Workers and Monopoly Capitalism in Kimberley, 1867–1895.* New Haven, CT: Yale University Press, 1987.

World Bank. "Ghana: Mining Sector Rehabilitation Project (Credit 1921-GH) and Mining Sector Development and Environment Project (Credit 2743-GH)." Project Performance Assessment Report, Operation Evaluations Department, July 1, 2003.

———. "Ghana Receives a Total of US$295 Million for Three Projects." News Release, Washington, DC, March 31, 2011.

———. "Increasing Local Procurement by the Mining Industry in West Africa." Road-test version. Report No. 66585-AFR. January 2012.

———. "World Bank Group in Extractive Industries: 2012 Annual Review." January 1, 2012. Available at: http://documents.worldbank.org/curated/en/165421468326682912/World -Bank-group-in-extractive-industries-2012-annual-review.

XYZ News. "National Security Rescues 'Buried' Illegal Miners." March 22, 2013. Available at: http://vibeghana.com/2013/03/22/national-security-rescues-burried-illegal-miners/.

Young, Crawford. *The African Colonial State in Comparative Perspective.* New Haven, CT: Yale University Press, 1994.

———. *The Postcolonial State in Africa: Fifty Years of Independence, 1960–2010.* Madison, WI: University of Wisconsin Press, 2012.

Zack-Williams, Alfred B. *Tributors, Supporters, and Merchant Capital: Mining and Under-development in Sierra Leone.* Brookfield, VT: Avebury, 1995.

Zempleni, Andras. "From Symptom to Sacrifice: The Story of Khady Fall." Translated by Karen Merville. In *Case Studies in Spirit Possession.* Edited by Vincent Crapanzano and Vivian Garrison, 87–139. New York: John Wiley & Sons, 1977.

Zuesse, Evan M. *Ritual Cosmos: The Sanctification of Life in African Religions.* Athens: Ohio University Press, 1979.

INDEX

Founded in 1893,
UNIVERSITY OF CALIFORNIA PRESS
publishes bold, progressive books and journals
on topics in the arts, humanities, social sciences,
and natural sciences—with a focus on social
justice issues—that inspire thought and action
among readers worldwide.

The UC PRESS FOUNDATION
raises funds to uphold the press's vital role
as an independent, nonprofit publisher, and
receives philanthropic support from a wide
range of individuals and institutions—and from
committed readers like you. To learn more, visit
ucpress.edu/supportus.